Better Homes and Gardens®

ENCYCLOPEDIA
of
COOKING

Volume 8

Gelatin wonders include this Fruited Nectar Salad (see page 1033 for recipe.) Mandarin oranges, green grapes, and apple pieces intermingle in the apricot- and lemon-flavored gelatin.

On the cover: For a dish to please the hunter, serve Pheasant with Apples. Drizzle the creamy wine sauce over the golden pheasant, then garnish the platter with Sautéed Apples.

BETTER HOMES AND GARDENS BOOKS
NEW YORK • DES MOINES

FRUMENTY (*froo 'muhn tē*)—A wheat porridge, usually sweetened and quite often flavored with various spices and raisins.

FRY—To cook in hot fat or oil, in particular, sautéeing, panfrying or frying, and deep-fat frying. Sautéeing generally refers to browning food quickly in a small amount of fat, while panfrying refers to a longer cooking in slightly more fat. A deep-fat fried food has been cooked by immersing it in a large amount of hot fat.

Chicken-Fried Burgers

1½ pounds ground beef
¼ cup finely chopped onion
½ teaspoon salt
⅛ teaspoon pepper
. . .
1 beaten egg
1 2⅜-ounce package seasoned
coating mix for chicken
Shortening

Combine beef, onion, salt, and pepper; mix well. Shape into 6 patties. Dip patties in beaten egg, then in coating mix. Slowly brown on both sides in small amount of hot shortening for a total of 15 minutes. Makes 6 servings.

FRYPAN—1. A shallow, flat-bottomed, usually long-handled utensil used on top of the range for frying, sautéeing, or panbroiling. 2. A tabletop electrical appliance with the same shape and use.

FUDGE—A soft, creamy candy made of sugar, milk or cream, butter, and flavoring. Nuts or chopped fruits such as candied cherries are quite often added to the fudge.

Types of fudge: Fudge can be divided into three basic types according to its predominant flavor—chocolate fudge, white or blond fudge, and penuche.

Chocolate is undoubtedly the favorite type of fudge. Unsweetened chocolate squares, unsweetened cocoa powder, or chocolate pieces are usually used to give the chocolate flavor. Chopped nuts are a popular ingredient in this type of fudge.

How to rescue fudge failures

Too stiff—overbeaten
Knead until fudge softens enough to press into buttered pan.

Too thin—undercooked or underbeaten
Add ¼ cup milk. Recook to given temperature; cool and beat to proper consistency.

White or blond fudge is the basic vanilla fudge. Both nuts and candied fruit are popular additions to this type of fudge.

Penuche is actually brown sugar fudge. Although the flavor differentiates penuche from other fudges, both candies are prepared in the same way.

How to prepare: Fudge with a smooth creamy texture is achieved by beating the cooked mixture until the crystals are so small that they are imperceptible. Ingredients such as milk, butter, chocolate, marshmallow creme, and corn syrup are used in fudge because they help prevent the formation of undesirable large crystals.

When making fudge, there are two critical temperatures to watch—the temperature to which the sugar and milk mixture is cooked and the temperature to which the fudge mixture is cooled before being beaten. The fudge can withstand slight variations at both of these temperatures, but large deviations will cause problems. The best way to determine the temperature accurately is to use a candy thermometer. However, if no thermometer is available, the cold-water test can be used.

As soon as the fudge reaches the soft-ball stage (234° to 240°), remove from the heat and cool it, without stirring, to 110° (bottom of pan should feel comfortably warm to your hand). At this stage, the fudge is beaten vigorously until it *starts* to stiffen and lose its gloss. It's then spread in a buttered pan.

How to store: To keep the fudge smooth and creamy for several weeks, wrap the pieces individually. Then store the pieces in an airtight container in a cool, dry place. For longer periods of storage, freeze the

Steps to perfect fudge

1. Completely butter sides of heavy pan. This prevents grains of sugar from clinging and forming unwanted sugar crystals.

2. Stir till syrup boils and sugar dissolves. One undissolved sugar grain can start a chain reaction and make the fudge grainy.

3. After syrup reaches 220°, double check the thermometer by dropping some syrup in cold water. At 234°, a soft ball forms.

4. Let candy cool *undisturbed* to 110°, then add flavoring and start beating vigorously and constantly. Get help, if needed.

5. Just as fudge starts to stiffen and lose its gloss, stir in nuts and quickly pour into pan. Don't scrape saucepan sides.

6. Using knife, score fudge while warm. Top each piece with a nut half, if desired. When candy is cool, cut along score marks.

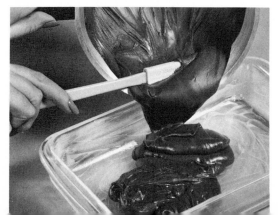

fudge. A convenient freezing container is a disposable foil pan. Pour the beaten fudge directly into this pan, cool, and wrap tightly before freezing. (See *Candy, Penuche* for additional information.)

Old-Time Fudge

  2 cups sugar
  ¾ cup milk
  2 1-ounce squares unsweetened
    chocolate
  1 teaspoon light corn syrup
  2 tablespoons butter or margarine
  1 teaspoon vanilla
  ½ cup broken nuts (optional)

Butter sides of heavy 2-quart saucepan. In it combine first 4 ingredients and dash salt. Cook and stir over medium heat till sugar dissolves and mixture boils. Cook sugar mixture to the soft-ball stage (234°), stirring only if necessary.

Immediately remove pan from heat; add butter or margarine without stirring. Cool to lukewarm (110°). Add vanilla. Beat vigorously till fudge becomes very thick and starts to lose its gloss. Quickly stir in nuts, if desired. Immediately spread in buttered, shallow pan. Score while warm; cut when cool and firm.

Blue Ribbon Fudge

  2 cups sugar
  1 6-ounce can evaporated milk
  2 1-ounce squares unsweetened
    chocolate
  1 teaspoon light corn syrup
  2 tablespoons butter or margarine
  1 teaspoon vanilla
  ½ cup chopped walnuts

Butter sides of a heavy 2-quart saucepan. In it combine first 4 ingredients and dash salt. Cook and stir over medium heat till chocolate melts and sugar dissolves. Cook to soft-ball stage (234°). Immediately remove from heat.

Add butter or margarine *without stirring*. Cool to lukewarm (110°). Add vanilla and beat vigorously till fudge stiffens and loses its gloss. Quickly stir in nuts. Push from pan (don't scrape sides) into buttered, shallow pan. Score while warm; cut when the fudge is cool and firm.

Opera Fudge

A creamy white version —

  2 cups sugar
  ½ cup milk
  ½ cup light cream
  1 tablespoon light corn syrup
  ½ teaspoon salt
      •   •   •
  1 tablespoon butter or margarine
  1 teaspoon vanilla
  ¼ cup chopped candied cherries

Butter sides of a heavy 2-quart saucepan. In it combine sugar, milk, light cream, light corn syrup, and salt. Cook over medium heat, stirring constantly, till sugar dissolves and mixture boils. Cook to soft-ball stage (234°). Immediately remove from heat; cool to lukewarm (110°) *without stirring*.

Add butter or margarine and vanilla. Beat vigorously till fudge stiffens and loses its gloss. Quickly stir in chopped candied cherries. Spread in buttered 9x5x3-inch pan. Score while warm; cut when cool and firm.

Double-Layer Fudge

  4½ cups sugar
  1 1-pint jar marshmallow creme
  2 6-ounce cans evaporated milk
    (1⅓ cups)
  ½ cup butter or margarine
    Dash salt
      •   •   •
  1 6-ounce package semisweet
    chocolate pieces (1 cup)
  1 5½-ounce package peanut butter
    pieces (about 1 cup)

In a 3-quart saucepan combine sugar, marshmallow creme, evaporated milk, butter or margarine, and salt. Cook over medium heat, stirring constantly, till mixture boils. Boil gently, stirring frequently, for 5 minutes. Divide mixture in half. To *half* (about 3 cups), stir in semisweet chocolate pieces till melted and blended. Pour into buttered 13x9x2-inch pan. To remaining half of mixture, add the peanut butter pieces, beating till smooth.* Pour over chocolate layer. Cool; cut into 1-inch squares.

*You may have to beat mixture with rotary beater at this point till all peanut butter pieces are melted and mixture is smooth.

Remarkable Fudge

> 4 cups sugar
> 1 14½-ounce can evaporated milk
>   (1⅔ cups)
> 1 cup butter or margarine
>   . . .
> 1 12-ounce package semisweet
>   chocolate pieces (2 cups)
> 1 1-pint jar marshmallow creme
> 1 teaspoon vanilla
> 1 cup broken walnuts

Butter sides of heavy 3-quart saucepan. Add sugar, evaporated milk, and butter or margarine. Cook over medium heat to soft-ball stage (234°), stirring frequently. Remove from heat.

Add chocolate pieces, marshmallow creme, vanilla, and walnuts. Beat till chocolate melts. Pour into buttered 13x9x2-inch pan. Score while warm; cut into pieces when cool and firm.

Rocky Road

A quick and easy fudgelike candy —

> 4 4½-ounce milk chocolate bars
> 3 cups miniature marshmallows
> ¾ cup coarsely broken walnuts

Partially melt chocolate bars over hot water; remove from heat. Beat till smooth. Stir in miniature marshmallows and walnuts. Spread in buttered 8x8x2-inch pan. Chill. Cut when firm.

FUDGE SAUCE—A rich, chocolate sauce usually served over ice cream, cake, or other desserts. (See also *Sauce.*)

Quick Fudge Sundaes

> 1 6-ounce package semisweet
>   chocolate pieces (1 cup)
> 1 6-ounce can evaporated milk
> ½ 1-pint jar marshmallow creme
> Vanilla ice cream

In saucepan combine chocolate pieces and evaporated milk. Heat slowly, stirring to blend. Beat in marshmallow creme till blended. Serve warm or cool over ice cream. Makes 2 cups.

Crunchy, toasted almonds garnish these cups of Almond Fudge Delight. The fluffy, rum-fudge topping is ready in a jiffy.

Almond Fudge Delight

A fluffy, rum-flavored fix-up using purchased fudge topping —

> ½ cup whipping cream
> 1 tablespoon sugar
> ¼ teaspoon rum flavoring
> 1 cup milk chocolate fudge
>   topping
>   . . .
> Vanilla ice cream
> Sliced almonds, toasted

In small mixer bowl whip whipping cream with sugar and rum flavoring; fold in milk chocolate fudge topping. Serve over ice cream. Top with toasted almonds. Makes about 2 cups.

FUMET *(fyoo' mit)*—A concentrated broth or stock used to flavor sauces or other dishes. Fumet is made by simmering fish, meat, or poultry in a seasoned liquid, usually water and/or wine, and then boiling down the broth to concentrate the flavor.

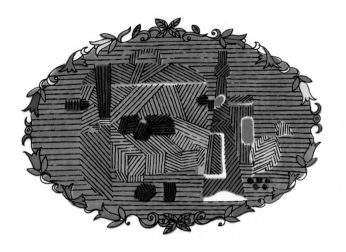

G

GALANTINE *(gal′ uhn tēn′, gal′ uhn tēn′)*—An elaborate aspic containing cooked chicken or other poultry or meat.

GALETTE *(guh let′)*—A flat wafer made of flaky pastry. In France, galettes are traditionally served on Twelfth Night.

GAME—A wild bird or animal, including bear, deer, pheasant, quail, and rabbit, hunted for food. From the time of primitive man through the time of the American pioneer, game was man's primary source of meat. Today, however, the vast majority of man's meat supply comes from domestic animals and game hunting is for sport.

Hunting most types of game is regulated by the state and/or federal government and is legal only during specified "open" seasons. Actually, by the time the cost of license, transportation, equipment, and other overhead costs are added to the cost of the meat, game is quite often the most expensive meat brought into the kitchen. However, hunters will tell you that the enjoyment of this sport is by far the greatest appeal of game hunting.

Cooperation between the hunter and the cook is necessary to maintain the high quality of game meat. If the game is not properly handled in the field, it will not be at its best when served. Immediately after the game is shot, it should be bled, eviscerated, and cooled in the shade; also all scent or oil glands should be removed, if necessary. Unless the hunt is a long one, it will not be necessary to pluck or skin the game before returning to camp.

As with all meat, game is certain to spoil if it is left unrefrigerated. The sooner it can be skinned and iced or refrigerated, the better. Especially in large game, an objectionable flavor is most often attributable to spoiled meat.

Although it is often recommended that game, especially large animals, be left whole and hung for several days at a temperature just above freezing, it is a matter of personal preference whether you wish to age the flavor of the meat in this way. However, if the meat is to be frozen, freeze it as you do domestic birds or animals with similar characteristics.

Game can be divided into game birds, small game, and large game. Game birds include ducks, geese, pheasants, quail, grouse, doves, partridges, and turkeys. Rabbits, squirrels, raccoons, opossums, woodchucks, and muskrats are all small game. Large game animals include bear, deer, elk, moose, bison, and antelope.

How to prepare game birds: Since game birds fly more than domestic birds, their muscle development differs and this affects the tenderness of the meat. In gen-

eral, dry heat cookery methods (broiling, roasting, and baking) are appropriate for small or young birds, while older birds should be cooked using moist heat (braising, simmering, and steaming).

The variety of food eaten by game birds makes their flavor different from the flavor of their domestic relatives. There are special tricks to make game birds "good eating." Some of the water fowl, such as the various wild ducks, have a fishy or muddy taste because of their eating habits. You can get rid of much of this by rubbing the cleaned bird with a lemon half or soaking it in water with lemon juice or vinegar. Small game birds need larding or frequent basting with butter to keep them moist during roasting.

How to prepare small game: Small game makes up a large proportion of the game killed. In fact, more rabbits are killed each year than any other game animal. Epidemics of tularemia sometimes affect the rabbit population. Since this disease is readily transmitted to man, check with local officials to make sure the area is tularemia-free. Since the liver of a rabbit with tularemia becomes discolored with white spots, this is an organic way to check for the presence of the disease.

The cooking of small game is much like cooking domestic animals of similar size. Keep in mind the general rule of using dry heat for young animals and moist heat for the older animals. Older game may need parboiling before it is cooked.

How to prepare large game: Large game resembles beef in that it can be cut up similarly. Although tenderness varies greatly from animal to animal, in general, tender cuts come from behind the shoulders, while the legs and shoulders are less tender portions of the animal.

Since large game provides meat for

many meals, it is usually necessary to freeze most of the meat. Meat from large game should be frozen just like beef. Just remember that freezing can only maintain, not improve, the quality of the meat.

Fat carries much of the wild flavor, so if you object to this flavor, trim away as much fat as you can without making the cooked meat dry. For all large game, you can broil chops and roast loins (marinating helps ensure tenderness). For best cooking results, pot roast, stew, or grind the less tender cuts of meat.

Venison, any game from the deer family (deer, elk, moose, reindeer), probably makes up the largest proportion of meat in the large game class. This meat is regarded by many as the choicest wild meat available. In general, cook venison similar to beef and lard it with bacon or salt pork.

Elegant Duckling with Sauce

1 4-pound ready-to-cook duckling
¾ cup chopped onion
½ cup chopped carrot
½ cup chopped celery
2 tablespoons cooking oil
1¼ cups chicken broth
¾ cup grenadine syrup
1 tablespoon butter or margarine
1 tablespoon sugar
1 tablespoon lemon juice
1 tablespoon lime juice
1 teaspoon cornstarch
¼ cup Grand Marnier

Trim wings of duckling and remove giblets and neck; set aside. Prick duckling; truss. Roast on rack at 375° for 1½ hours; then at 425° till golden brown and tender, about 15 minutes.

Meanwhile, to make sauce, brown giblets, neck, wing tips, and vegetables in hot oil. Add broth; cover and simmer 1 hour. Strain. Add ½ *cup* of the grenadine syrup; simmer till sauce is reduced to half. In saucepan melt the butter; blend in sugar and cook it till brown. Add lemon juice, lime juice, and remaining grenadine syrup. Stir in broth mixture.

Remove duckling from pan; keep hot. Skim off fat; then add remaining meat juices to sauce. Blend cornstarch with Grand Marnier; add to sauce. Cook and stir for 2 to 3 minutes more. Serve sauce with the roast duckling. Makes 2 servings.

A hunter's special

←Simmered in wine, then drizzled with a creamy wine sauce, this Pheasant with Apples is a dish that will please all.

Roasting Chart For Game Birds

General Instructions: Salt inside of ready-to-cook bird. Stuff as desired. Truss bird; place, breast side up, on rack in shallow roasting pan. Except for wild duck, brush with salad oil, melted butter or margarine, or lay bacon slices over breast. Roast, uncovered, till tender. Times may vary with age of bird; young birds are best for roasting. Baste occasionally with drippings. When necessary, place foil loosely over bird to prevent excess browning.

Game Birds	Ready-To-Cook Weight	Oven Temp.	Roasting Time	Amount per Serving	Special Instructions
Wild Duck	1-2 lbs.	400°	60-90 min.	1-1½ lbs.	Stuff loosely with quartered onions and apples; discard stuffing before serving. Do not brush with oil.
Wild Goose	2-4 lbs. 4-6 lbs.	400°	1½-3 hrs. 3-4 hrs.	1-1½ lbs.	Stuff loosely with quartered onions and apples; discard stuffing before serving. Baste frequently with drippings.
Partridge	½-1 lb.	450°	30-45 min.	½-1 lb.	Place bacon slices over breast.
Pheasant	1-3 lbs.	350°	1-2½ hrs.	1-1½ lbs.	Place bacon slices over breast.
Quail	4-6 oz.	400°	30-45 min.	½-1 lb.	Place bacon slices over breast.
Squab	12-14 oz.	400°	40-50 min.	12-14 oz.	Place bacon slices over breast.

Broiled Venison Steaks

4 ½-inch venison steaks from
    leg, rib, or loin chops of
    young animal
2 tablespoons salad oil

. . .

¼ cup butter or margarine, melted
1 tablespoon onion juice

Brush steaks with salad oil; let stand 15 minutes. Broil 3 inches from heat 7 to 10 minutes; turn. Broil on other side 7 to 10 minutes. Combine butter or margarine, onion juice, and dash salt; brush on broiled steaks. Makes 4 servings.

Squab with Apricot Sauce

4 12- to 14-ounce ready-to-cook
    squab, halved lengthwise
¼ cup butter or margarine
½ cup chicken broth
½ cup apricot nectar
2 teaspoons cornstarch

Season squab with salt. In skillet brown squab, skin side down, in butter. Turn and simmer, covered, till tender, about 35 minutes. Remove to platter. Combine remaining ingredients. Add to pan drippings. Simmer and stir till thickened and bubbly. Pour over birds. Serves 4.

Pheasant with Apples

    ¼ cup all-purpose flour
    1 teaspoon salt
    ¼ teaspoon pepper
    2 1½- to 3-pound ready-to-cook
        pheasants, cut up

        . . .

    6 tablespoons butter or margarine
    ¾ cup sauterne

        . . .

    ¾ cup light cream
    3 egg yolks
        Sautéed Apples

Combine flour, salt, and pepper in a plastic bag. Add 2 or 3 pieces at a time; shake to coat. Brown pheasant lightly in butter or margarine. Add sauterne; simmer, covered, till tender, about 35 to 55 minutes. Remove pheasant to warm platter.

Beat cream with egg yolks. Slowly stir into pan drippings; cook over medium heat, stirring constantly, just until sauce is smooth and thickened. *Do not boil.* Place pheasants on platter. Pour wine sauce over. Garnish platter with Sautéed Apples. Makes 4 to 6 servings.

Sautéed Apples: Add 2 cooking apples, cored and sliced into wedges, to 3 tablespoons butter or margarine in medium skillet. Sprinkle with 1 teaspoon sugar; cook, turning frequently, till the apples are lightly browned.

Smothered Quail

    4 4- to 6-ounce ready-to-cook
        quail, halved lengthwise
    ¼ cup butter or margarine
        Salt
        Pepper
    ½ cup chopped onion
    ½ cup light cream

        . . .

    1 teaspoon cornstarch
    2 tablespoons cold water

In skillet brown halved quail in butter or margarine; season with salt and pepper. Top with chopped onion; pour light cream over. Cover and simmer till birds are tender, about 30 minutes. Remove quail to a warm platter. Combine cornstarch and cold water; add to pan drippings. Simmer, stirring constantly, till mixture is thickened and bubbly. Pour gravy over quail. Makes 4 servings.

Wine-Sauced Birds

    4 pigeons, quail, *or* other small
        game birds
    1 lemon, halved
        Parsley
        About ¼ cup butter or margarine
    1 cup tomato juice

        . . .

    1 cup dry wine
    2 tablespoons butter or margarine
    4 slices toast, buttered

Rub thoroughly cleaned and plucked birds inside and out with lemon. Season with salt and pepper. Place some parsley in the cavity. Brown birds well in the ¼ cup butter or margarine. Add tomato juice; cover and cook slowly till tender, about 30 to 45 minutes, basting the birds two or three times.

Remove birds from skillet. Add wine and the 2 tablespoons butter or margarine to pan drippings; bring to boiling. Place each bird on a slice of buttered toast. Spoon some of the wine sauce over each bird. Makes 4 servings.

Wild Duck in Wine

    2 1- to 2-pound ready-to-cook
        wild ducks, split in quarters
    2 tablespoons butter or margarine
    2 tablespoons all-purpose flour
    1 cup chicken broth
    1 3-ounce can broiled, sliced,
        mushrooms, undrained
    ¼ cup red Burgundy
    2 tablespoons chopped onion
    1 small bay leaf
    ½ teaspoon salt
        Snipped parsley

Simmer duck in small amount of salted water for 20 to 30 minutes; drain. Brown duck in butter or margarine in skillet; transfer duck to 2-quart casserole. Blend flour into pan drippings; cook and stir until mixture is bubbly. Blend in chicken broth, mushrooms, Burgundy, onion, bay leaf, salt, and dash pepper; bring mixture to a boil and simmer 5 minutes, stirring occasionally.

Pour sauce over ducks. Cover and bake at 350° till tender, about 1¼ to 1½ hours.

Remove duck to platter; sprinkle with parsley. Remove bay leaf from sauce and skim off excess fat. Pass sauce with duck. Makes 4 servings.

GAME SHEARS—Another name for poultry shears. These sturdy, curved shears are used to cut bones of feathered game.

GARBANZO—Edible seed related to the bean. In America, the most common garbanzo is white, but these small seeds can also be red or black. They are also called chick-peas.

Garbanzos contain proteins, carbohydrates, minerals, and B vitamins. A half cup, uncooked and dried, has 360 calories.

This vegetable is widely cultivated in certain areas of Asia, Africa, and Latin America. Many of these same areas lack sufficient sources of animal protein, so garbanzos often supply a large portion of the protein needed in the diet.

California grows most of the garbanzos sold in American markets. They are available in the dry form or canned.

Garbanzos are used in soups, stews, many foreign dishes, and as a cooked vegetable. They are also toasted and ground for use as a coffee substitute.

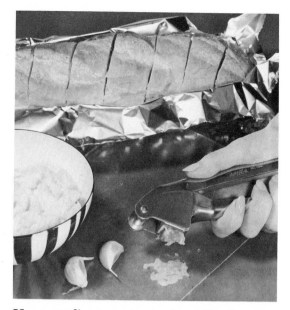

Use a garlic press to crush garlic the easy way. Place peeled garlic clove in press, then clamp the handles together.

Pepperoni Salad

 6 cups torn lettuce
 2 tomatoes, cut in wedges
 4 ounces mozzarella cheese, cubed (1 cup)
 1 cup drained garbanzos
 ½ cup thinly sliced pepperoni
 ¼ cup sliced green onion
 ½ cup Italian-style salad dressing

In large salad bowl combine all ingredients *except* dressing. Pour salad dressing over. Toss lettuce mixture lightly with dressing. Sprinkle with salt and freshly ground black pepper to taste. Serves 8 or 9.

Garbanzos add unusual texture to many dishes.

GARLIC—A strongly scented, pungent herb related to the onion. The root, which divides into bulblets called cloves, is the edible portion of the herb.

In the United States garlic is used primarily in small quantities as a seasoning. However, through the centuries, this native of central Asia has had various uses associated with religion, superstition, and the treatment of disease.

The religious uses of garlic date back to the ancient Egyptians who used it as an offering to their gods. In later years, during the development of the Mohammedan religion, it was believed that garlic sprang up in the place where Satan's left foot touched as he fled the Garden of Eden.

Garlic has also played a part in the superstitions of many cultures: the early Chinese prized it as a food that would in-

A magnificent salad

Garbanzos, pepperoni, mozzarella cheese,→ and Italian-style dressing give Pepperoni Salad a different flair.

Before adding garlic cloves to soups or stews, spear them with wooden picks. This makes a handle for removing the garlic.

crease their intelligence; ancient Roman soldiers ate garlic because they believed it would make them more courageous; and many ancient people thought garlic's strong aroma would protect them from serpents and scorpions. Even today, people in many parts of the world wear bunches of garlic around their necks and hang it in their homes because they believe that it will ward off evil spirits and disease.

For centuries, garlic has been used as a medicine. Around 400 B.C., Hippocrates used it for medicinal purposes, and several hundred years later, Greek physicians were still using it to treat a variety of diseases. Its medicinal use, however, is not limited to ancient times. During World War I, the British used garlic juice as an antiseptic. In some parts of the world, garlic is still used as a treatment for the common cold and bronchial disorders.

How to select and store: Garlic is sold fresh, dehydrated, and as an oil or liquid. Fresh garlic bulbs are sold singly or in groups. Dehydrated or dried garlic is packaged as large sliced, sliced, large chopped, chopped, minced, ground, granulated, powdered, and blended with salt. Base your selection on personal preference, intended use, and frequency of use.

The pungent aroma of garlic permeates everything it comes in contact with, so be sure to store all forms of garlic in airtight containers. Keep fresh and dehydrated garlic dry and preferably in a cool storage place. Food seasoned with garlic should be covered tightly before refrigerating.

How to use: Since the garlic bulb is a compound unit consisting of several smaller cloves, you can separate the cloves without releasing the garlic aroma or flavor. This flavor is so intense that one clove usually is sufficient for seasoning.

If you wish, you can heighten the flavor by slashing the fresh garlic clove several times before adding it to liquids. Spear each clove with a wooden pick to hold it together. Then at serving time, it's a snap to find and to remove the garlic. When minced garlic is called for, mince it the easy way by squeezing it over a wide mouthed jar or a bowl with a garlic press.

Dehydrated garlic is becoming increasingly popular in the home. If it is used in a dish with quite a bit of liquid, dehydrated garlic will rehydrate as the dish cooks. Otherwise, it should be rehydrated in a

Garnish desserts with chocolate curls. Use a vegetable peeler to shave curls from room temperature, sweet chocolate.

A bouquet of Vegetable Flowers makes a distinctive centerpiece. Cut the vegetables with cookie and hors d'oeuvre cutters.

small amount of water or other liquid before using. Dehydrated garlic is concentrated, so use it sparingly. As a general guide, ⅛ teaspoon garlic powder is equivalent to 1 clove of fresh garlic.

Garlic salt, garlic oil, and liquid garlic are convenient seasonings. Garlic salt can be used to season dishes where both garlic and salt are to be used. When using garlic oil or liquid garlic, read label directions for the right amount to use.

The distinctive flavor of garlic is famous in many European specialties, particularly French and Italian dishes. Garlic is particularly good with tossed salad. For just a hint of garlic, rub the salad bowl with a cut clove. As you toss the salad, the garlic flavor penetrates the greens. Another way of adding garlic is to drop a slit garlic clove into the salad oil or wine vinegar. Remove the garlic after one or two days, then use the garlic-flavored oil or vinegar as part of a salad dressing.

Also try adding a pinch of garlic to cooked vegetables such as corn, limas, and eggplant. Meat dishes, spaghetti and pizza sauce, fish and seafood dishes, dressings, and gravies all perk up with a hint of garlic. Thick slices of French bread spread liberally with garlic butter are a particular treat with spaghetti. No matter how you use it, do acquaint your family with this flavorful herb. (See also *Herb.*)

Garlic French Dressing

In screw-top jar combine ½ cup salad oil, 2 tablespoons vinegar, 2 tablespoons lemon juice, 1 teaspoon sugar, ½ teaspoon salt, ½ teaspoon paprika, ½ teaspoon dry mustard, ¼ teaspoon garlic powder, and dash cayenne. Cover; shake well.

Toasty Garlic Bread

Melt ⅓ cup butter in 11x7x1½-inch baking pan. Add 1 or 2 cloves garlic, minced. Add six 1-inch thick slices French bread, turning quickly to butter both sides. Let stand 10 minutes. Heat at 350° till toasty, about 20 minutes.

Deviled Lamburgers

Combine 1 tablespoon prepared mustard; ½ teaspoon garlic salt; ¼ teaspoon dried thyme leaves, crushed; and dash pepper. Add 1 pound ground lamb and mix well. Shape into 4 patties. In skillet brown patties in 1 tablespoon hot shortening; drain. Top *each* with 1 onion slice. Add 2 tablespoons water; cover and simmer for 10 minutes. Top *each* burger with 1 green pepper ring and 1 lemon slice; cook, covered, till done, about 10 to 15 minutes. Makes 4 servings.

GARNISH—1. A decorative item, usually edible, that enhances the eye appeal of foods. 2. To enhance the eye appeal of foods. This is done by attractively arranging the food or by adding a decorative touch. The garnish should add a complementary or contrasting flavor and color.

One of the easiest ways to garnish is to arrange the accompaniment foods pleasingly. Fluffy dumplings heaped around a

Elegant looking Turnip Lilies and Tomato Roses actually are easy to make with only a little time and practice. These vegetable garnishes are particularly suitable for vegetable salads or main dishes. Next time substitute rutabagas for the turnips or make small rosettes from cherry tomatoes.

Quickly spruce up any meal with Cheese Apples, Apple Rings, or Frosted Grapes (See *Grape* for recipe). *Apple Rings:* Peel apples, if desired. Cut out core. Slice to desired thickness. Brush with ascorbic acid color keeper or lemon juice-water.

chicken-vegetable stew, golden brown corn fritters circling a platter of fried chicken, peas and carrots served in a hollowed-out tomato, or buttered corn served in a green pepper cup are all ways of serving food differently and pleasingly.

Main dishes are probably the part of the meal most commonly garnished. Pineapple slices centered with a maraschino cherry complement the flavor of baked ham. Sprigs of fresh mint accent any lamb dish, and lemon slices or wedges are almost a must as a garnish for fish. Cold meats and fish, such as poached salmon, may lend themselves to a vegetable garnish embedded in an aspic glaze. A twist of orange, lemon, or lime is appropriate for any seafood dish. Tomato wedges, green pepper or onion rings, mushrooms, and the old stand-by, parsley, make attractive garnishes for any meat.

Even a casserole becomes a special dish when you top it with grated cheese, cheese or pastry cutouts, green pepper slices or rings, croutons, lemon slices or wedges, dumplings, tiny biscuits, chow mein noodles, or bread or cracker crumbs. If the casserole contains shrimp or small pieces of meat, reserve a few for a garnish.

The contrasting color or texture of a garnish can transform a plain soup into a distinctive one. To avoid losing the garnish in the soup, be sure to wait until the last minute to add the garnish. Top clear soups with lemon slices, snipped parsley or chives, chopped green pepper, avocado slices, a pat of butter, or a dollop of sour cream. Croutons, sliced frankfurters, parsley, sliced or sieved hard-cooked eggs, toasted almonds, shredded cheese, and sour cream all add a pretty and delicious touch to creamed soups.

To keep in character with the temperature of the soup, try a dollop of sour cream, lemon or cucumber slices, paprika, or snipped parsely or chives as a garnish for cold soups. Hot soups need a heartier garnish, such as a cracker topped with a fluff of whipped cheese, sliced frankfurters, crumbled bacon, crushed corn chips, popcorn, or toasted bread cubes.

When garnishing salads, it is better to stick to vegetable garnishes for vegetable salads and fruit garnishes for fruit salads.

With just a little practice, you can turn bright red radishes into Radish Daisies, Roses, or Accordions. *Radish Accordions:* Cut long radishes crosswise, *cutting to, but not through,* in 8 narrow slices. Chill in ice water so slices will fan out, accordion-style. Use as a relish or plate trim.

Melon Bowls make attractive and unusual serving containers for fruit or meat salads or ice cold punches. A small cantaloupe bowl holds an individual serving while a large watermelon can be used as a punch bowl at a summer luncheon or buffet.

Ripe or pimiento-stuffed green olive slices, avocado crescents, cherry tomatoes, and radish slices add a decorative touch to vegetable salads. Appropriate garnishes for fruit salads include pomegranate seeds, kiwi slices, and frosted grapes. Serving the salad on a bed of crisp greens is another way of garnishing it.

Although the family seldom needs added incentive to get them to eat dessert, an appropriate garnish will add just the right finishing touch. Whipped cream or one of the whipped toppings is especially compatible with many desserts, and it also lends itself to several methods of application. It can be spread in a layer on cream pies, spooned into dollops atop puddings and cakes, and piped into a decorative border by using a pastry tube.

Fresh fruit or berries, vanilla wafer or chocolate cookie crumbs, crushed peppermint candies, gumdrops, and chocolate curls can all be used as cream pie garnishes. For two-crust pies, use pastry cutouts or a lattice for the top crust. Hard-sauce balls or cutouts complement some fruit pies, and cheese cutouts are particularly popular with apple pie.

Although any type of cake decoration is a garnish, preparing elaborate cake decorations has become a separate art. (See also *Cake Decorating.*) The use of simple cake garnishes, however, is easily mastered. One of the easiest cake trims is achieved by placing a lacy, paper doily on the cake top and sifting and pressing confectioners' sugar through the doily. When you remove the doily, the lacy design is left.

Frosted cakes can be quickly garnished by sprinkling them with coconut, chopped nuts, grated orange or lemon peel, or grated chocolate. Gumdrops, marshmallows, chocolate kisses, small cookie decorations, peppermint candies, and other small candies also make attractive trims.

You have probably all envied the chef who garnished the crusty, brown roast with tomato or radish roses, the succulent ham with orange chrysanthemums or fruit baskets, or the roasted pork loin with bright red apple rings. Although many of these garnishes involve special handiwork, you can add them to the foods you serve by just following these directions.

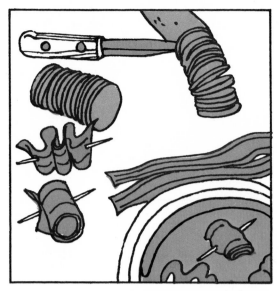

Carrot Curls or Zigzags: Rest peeled carrot on cutting surface. Using vegetable peeler, slice thin lengthwise strips cutting away from you. For curls, roll up strips; secure with wooden pick. For zigzags, thread on wooden pick accordion-style. Crisp in ice water; remove picks. Also try Carrot Corkscrews.

A perky bow adorns the handle of the finished Fruit Basket. Each whole grapefruit or orange makes two individual salad containers. Combine the fruit removed from the peel with other fruit and a dressing and then spoon into the baskets.

Radish Roses

Cut root tip off radish. Using a grapefruit knife or point of paring knife, cut 4 or 5 thin petals around radish, leaving a little red between the petals. (If desired, leave on some green leaves at stem for trim.) Chill in ice water till petals open like a flower. Use as a relish, garnish, or plate trim.

Radish Daisies

Starting at root tip, score 6 petals on radish with point of knife. Following markings and beginning at tip, cut thin petals following shape of radish *almost* to base (stem end). Chill in ice water till petals open like a flower. Use radish daisy as an appetizer, relish, garnish, or plate trim.

Tomato Roses

Turn tomato stem end down. With sharp knife, cut 5 or 6 petals, cutting through skin but not into seed pocket. Gently separate petals slightly. Season with salt and pepper to taste. For added color, sprinkle center with sieved hard-cooked egg yolks. Use to garnish buffet platters or tossed salads. Tiny cherry tomato rosettes, cut in similar manner, are particularly suitable to garnish individual tossed or molded vegetable salad servings.

Carrot Corkscrews

Insert point of short-bladed paring knife into peeled whole carrot, *cutting to, but not through,* center at slight angle; rotate carrot slowly, cutting a continuous spiral. Make deeper cut into carrot, if necessary to make corkscrew flexible. Chill carrot corkscrew in ice water to make it open.

Pickle Garnishes

Pickle Fans: Make thin lengthwise slices *almost* to stem end. Spread fan and press uncut end of pickle so fan will hold its shape.

Stuffed Pickle Slices: Cut thin slice from stem end of large dill pickle. Hollow pickle with apple corer. Stuff with softened cream cheese or any cheese of spreading consistency. Chill pickles thoroughly, then slice crosswise, 1/4 inch thick.

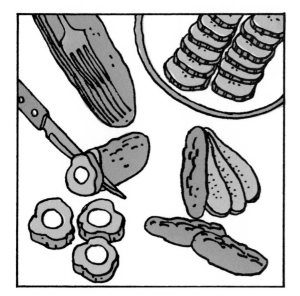

Crisp Pickle Fans or Stuffed Pickle Slices serve as both a garnish and accompaniment for sandwiches. Also try Scored Cucumbers in tossed salads or as a relish.

Vegetable Flowers

Slice peeled large carrot and turnip crosswise, 1/8 inch thick. Cut flowers using cookie and tiny hors d'oeuvre cutters.

To prepare centerpiece pictured, thread green onion tops over wooden skewers. Attach desired flowers to ends of skewers. Use green onion and carrot pieces for centers.

Turnip Lilies

For each lily, cut 2 thin crosswise slices from a peeled turnip. Curve one slice into cone shape. Shape second slice around cone in opposite direction. Insert thin strip of carrot down center of cone. Secure lily with wooden picks. Chill in ice water till crisp. Rutabaga slices are a good substitute for the turnip slices if turnip is not available.

Scored Cucumbers

For fancy cucumber slices, run tines of fork lengthwise down unpeeled cucumber, pressing to break through peel. Repeat around entire cucumber. Slice straight across or on the bias.

Fruit Baskets

Halve large grapefruit *or* orange. With grapefruit or paring knife, cut around each section to loosen fruit; carefully remove fruit, leaving membrane intact. Snip out whole membrane.

Leaving 1 inch uncut in center of opposite sides, cut around each grapefruit *or* orange half with paring knife 3/8 inch below rim to make basket handles. Carefully lift up the 2 resulting cut strips and tie with ribbon.

Refill basket with a fruit salad combination containing the fruit sections. If desired, top salad with tiny scoops of sherbet made with spoon or melon ball cutter. Serve immediately.

Cheese Apples

Moisten shredded natural cheese with mayonnaise or salad dressing *or* cut process cheese with melon ball cutter. Roll in balls. Make an indentation in each end. Insert whole cloves in one end and half a green wooden pick in other end. Roll cheese balls in paprika for rosy color.

Melon Bowls

Zigzag Bowl: Cut small cantaloupe in half zigzag fashion by inserting knife into center of melon at an angle. Pull knife out and make next cut at reverse angle. Repeat around melon. Pull halves apart; remove seeds. If desired, use heavy paper pattern as cutting guide.

Scalloped Bowl: Set watermelon on end. Cut thin slice off bottom to make it sit flat. Cut top third off melon. Using a cup as guide, trace scallops around edge of melon. Carve scalloped edge following pattern. Scoop out fruit.

Orange Chrysanthemum

Score peel of 2 or more oranges into 8 sections, *cutting to, but not through,* base of peel. Gently remove peel from fruit, keeping shell in one piece. Pull fruit sections of 1 orange apart slightly; remove excess membrane. Use remaining fruit for salad.

With scissors, cut sectioned peels into narrow "petals," *cutting to, but not through,* bases. Replace prepared orange in 1 shell. Insert this shell and orange into remaining petaled orange shells.

GAZPACHO—A classic cold vegetable soup of Spanish origin. Although there are many versions of gazpacho, the recipes usually include onion, garlic, green pepper, tomato, and cucumber. Crisp croutons are frequently sprinkled atop each serving of soup. (See also *Spanish Cookery.*)

Spanish Gazpacho

In bowl combine 2 to 2½ cups tomato juice; ½ cup finely chopped celery; ½ cup finely chopped cucumber; ½ cup finely chopped green pepper; ⅓ cup finely chopped green onions; 2 teaspoons snipped parsley; 1 small clove garlic, minced; 2 to 3 tablespoons wine vinegar; 2 tablespoons olive oil; 1 teaspoon salt; ¼ teaspoon freshly ground pepper; and ½ teaspoon Worcestershire sauce. Cover and *chill thoroughly*, at least 4 hours. Serve gazpacho in chilled bowls with crisp, buttered croutons, if desired. Makes 6 to 8 servings.

GEFILTE, GEFÜLLTE FISH (guh fil' tuh)— A popular fish dish from the Jewish cuisine. Boned whitefish, yellow pike, or carp are ground or pounded with green pepper, carrot, onion, celery and seasonings. Using egg and matzo meal as a binder, the fish mixture is then formed into balls or small rolls. After being cooked in a fish stock, the balls and stock are chilled. The fish stock forms a jelly that often accompanies the cold fish. Although traditionalists prepare gefilte fish from scratch, time-saving canned gefilte fish is available in some of today's supermarkets.

In Jewish families, gefilte fish are served as the Sabbath main dish with lettuce, the jellied fish broth, vegetable relishes, and horseradish accompaniment. However, they are equally suitable and adaptable to hors d'oeuvres, to salads, or, when thinly sliced, to gourmet salad sandwich fillings. (See also *Jewish Cookery.*)

Spanish Gazpacho can be a colorful and appealing meal opener or a refreshing and light main dish on a hot summer day. Garnish each serving with a cucumber slice, if desired.

Beet-Jellied Gefilte Fish

    1 16-ounce can beets, sliced *or*
       julienne-cut
    1 envelope unflavored gelatin
    ¼ cup cold water
    1 3-ounce package lemon-flavored
       gelatin
    3 tablespoons sugar
    ¼ cup lemon juice
    3 tablespoons prepared horseradish
    ½ teaspoon seasoned salt
    1 16-ounce jar gefilte fish, drained
       and sliced, *or* gefilte fish balls,
       drained
    Cucumber Dressing

Drain beets, reserving liquid. Add water to liquid to make 2½ cups. Finely chop beets; refrigerate. Soften unflavored gelatin in ¼ cup cold water. Heat *1 cup* beet liquid to boiling. Remove from heat; add softened gelatin, lemon gelatin, and sugar, stirring till dissolved. Add remaining beet liquid, lemon juice, horseradish, and salt. Chill till partially set.

Stir in chopped beets. Pour into 6½-cup mold and arrange gefilte fish evenly throughout the jellied mixture. Chill till firm. Serve with Cucumber Dressing. Makes 8 servings.

Cucumber Dressing: Combine 1 cup dairy sour cream; ½ cup chopped, peeled, seeded cucumber; 1 tablespoon prepared horseradish; 1 teaspoon grated onion; ½ teaspoon salt, and dash freshly ground pepper. Chill dressing thoroughly.

Distribute the fish pieces evenly in the Beet-Jellied Gefilte Fish mold by arranging them in the partially set gelatin.

GELATIN—A protein derived from collagen, the chief part of the bones, skins, and white connective tissue of animals. The word gelatin is a derivative of the Latin word *gelata* which describes its ability to form a gel in a liquid.

Today, gelatin is readily available at grocery stores; but not long ago, homemakers who needed gelatin had to extract it themselves by slowly boiling veal knuckles and bones, then clarifying the broth. The involved method by which gelatin was obtained caused most homemakers to use gelatin sparingly for cooking.

Although the first commercial gelatin was made in France in 1682, it was not until after the French Revolution that gelatin use increased. At this time, the French government attempted to improve the nutrition of poverty-stricken classes by requiring all public eating institutions to add gelatin to soups and broths. Since these were distasteful mixtures, the people ate them out of necessity rather than desire.

A gap of over 200 years separated the first commercial attempts and modern versions of gelatin preparation. In 1890, Charles Knox developed a process in America whereby processed gelatin could be converted to granular form.

Nutritional value: Since unflavored gelatin is pure protein, it is often used in special diets. However, in the normal diet it supplements protein from other sources. When mixed with fruit juice, unflavored gelatin is a particularly beneficial way to satisfy hunger urges without adding many calories and to prevent brittle fingernails. One envelope of unflavored gelatin contains only 28 calories.

How gelatin is produced: Two types of gelatin, acid and alkaline, are made. Acid-type gelatin is generally used as the gelling ingredient in the commercial flavored gelatin mixes, and is mostly derived from the collagen extracted from animal skins. The alkaline type, on the other hand, is the basic source of unflavored gelatin and is principally derived from the collagen extracted from the long bones of cattle.

The production of both types of gelatin is basically the same. Mineral salts are

first extracted from the raw materials by a series of dilute acid baths. Further refinement of the collagen proceeds with long soaking in limewater. The treated collagen is then dissolved in hot water, concentrated, filtered for purity and clarity, cooled, and dried into glassy, brittle sheets of pure gelatin. The sheets of gelatin are broken up by high-speed mills into tiny, sparkling granules that are suitable for household cooking uses.

As each bath of granules is produced, it is given laboratory tests to prove its cleanliness and to make sure that the gelatin will produce a sparklingly clear and unvarying gel that sets quickly, yet does not melt too fast.

Gelatin products: The simplest gelatin product, unflavored or plain, is pure protein and contains no additives. One envelope of unflavored gelatin (equivalent to one tablespoon) is generally combined with two cups of liquid to produce a firm, yet tender gel when chilled.

To dissolve unflavored gelatin in liquid, use one of four methods. When sugar is not a recipe ingredient, sprinkle the gelatin over a small amount of cold liquid (½ cup liquid per 1 envelope gelatin) and dissolve it over low heat, stirring constantly. Or prepare the gelatin mixture in an electric blender by first softening the gelatin in cold liquid in the blender container. Dissolve it by adding boiling liquid to the blender container, covering, and processing at low speed. To add unflavored gelatin to mixtures which have been prepared separately (such as custards or cooked fruit mixtures), soften gelatin in cold liquid in a small cup, using ¼ cup liquid to 1 envelope gelatin. Add softened gelatin to hot mixture and stir until dissolved. If added to a cold mixture, first dissolve the softened gelatin in ¼ cup liquid by stirring over boiling water.

Gelatin glamour

←Red Raspberry Fluff is whipped light and airy in a blender. Sugar-rimmed glasses, raspberries, and mint are the dress-ups.

The popular fruit-flavored gelatin mixes contain only about 15 percent gelatin. The remaining portion is composed of sugar, flavorings, colorings, and acids. One 3-ounce package of flavored gelatin is usually dissolved in 1 cup boiling liquid then 1 cup cold liquid is stirred in. When partially set, a maximum of 2 cups drained fruit can be folded in.

Other gelatin products vary in composition and preparation method. Dietetic gelatin mixes contain artificial sweeteners rather than sugar. Other specialty mixes contain assorted ingredients, depending on the final characteristics desired. For best results, prepare these mixes following manufacturers' directions.

How to use: In food preparation, gelatin can be used for any one of three reasons: to form a gel, to develop a foam, or to emulsify a food. With one of the gelatin products as a base, a variety of pleasing foods can be prepared including appetizers, jellied soups, salads, main dishes, and desserts; foamy and fluffy candies; or creamy candies and frozen salads, sherbets, ice creams, or desserts.

When a layered effect is desired, carefully pour partially set gelatin over gelatin that is firm but still sticky to the touch.

Although several foods possess gel-forming properties, gelatin is one of the few that produces reversible gels. The dissolved gelatin, naturally soft at room temperature, becomes firm when refrigerated. If allowed to warm to room temperature the gel again softens.

Spring Salad Ring

A green and white beauty —

Dissolve two 3-ounce packages lime-flavored gelatin in 1¾ cups boiling water; add ¼ cup lemon juice. Measure ¾ *cup* gelatin and add ¼ cup water; pour into 6½-cup ring mold. Chill till *almost* firm. Peel 1 large cucumber; halve and scrape out seeds. Grate cucumber; drain. Measure ½ cup grated cucumber.

Blend one 8-ounce package cream cheese, softened, and ¼ cup mayonnaise. Stir in grated cucumber; one 13½-ounce can crushed pineapple, undrained; 2 tablespoons minced onion; and ½ teaspoon grated lemon peel. Mix well. Stir in remaining gelatin mixture. Chill till partially set. Pour over gelatin in mold. Chill till firm. Makes 8 servings.

Fruits, meats, or vegetables carefully arranged in a molded salad or dessert give the dish an added appeal and charm.

Gelatin terms to know

Almost firm: Chilled gelatin mixture appears set, but is sticky to the touch.

Dissolved: There are no visible gelatin granules in liquid.

Firm: Chilled gelatin mixture is completely set and ready to unmold.

Fluffy, light and fluffy: Air is whipped into gelatin till volume is about double.

Foamy, light and foamy: Air is beaten into gelatin till mixture appears frothy.

Mounds when spooned: Chilled gelatin mounds or forms a slight puddle on surface when dropped from a spoon.

Partially set: Chilled gelatin is very syrupy like the consistency of honey or unbeaten egg whites.

Softened: Gelatin granules are completely moistened with liquid.

In addition to forming a gel, gelatin is used as the basis for foam formation. In beating gelatin mixtures, the protein forms a thin film around tiny air bubbles. The resulting texture is light and fluffy. Whips, marshmallows, and some nougat recipes achieve this desired lightness.

Red Raspberry Fluff

A last-minute dessert —

> **Fresh *or* frozen red raspberries**
> **Sugar**
> **1 3-ounce package red raspberry-**
>   **flavored gelatin**
> **½ cup boiling water**
> **1 cup *drained* crushed ice**
> **Fresh mint sprigs**

Dip sherbet glass rims in juice from a few crushed raspberries, then in sugar. Chill. Place gelatin in blender container. Add ½ cup boiling water. Cover; blend 2 minutes. Keeping blender running, slowly add crushed ice. Blend till container feels cool.

Place a few drained raspberries in each sherbet glass. Pour in gelatin. Trim with additional raspberries and mint. Let stand 5 minutes. Serve immediately. Makes 4 to 6 servings.

Fruited Nectar Salad

Pictured on page 1010 —

Heat one 12-ounce can apricot nectar (1½ cups) to boiling. Add one 3-ounce package lemon-flavored gelatin; stir till dissolved. Add ½ cup water and 1 tablespoon lemon juice. Chill till partially set. Fold in one 11-ounce can mandarin oranges, drained; ½ cup halved seedless green grapes; and ¼ cup chopped unpeeled apple. Turn into 4½-cup mold. Chill till firm. To serve, unmold on plate. Garnish with additional seedless green grapes, sliced unpeeled apple, and lettuce leaves. Serve molded salad with mayonnaise or salad dressing. Makes 4 to 6 servings.

Gelatin is also used in foods as an emulsifier. In marshmallows and candies, gelatin aids the development of a creamy texture by reducing the size of the candy crystals. In like manner, gelatin in frozen desserts and sherbets gives smoothness.

The basic, clear gels are prepared with the addition of part-boiling and part-cold liquid. (When in a hurry, use frozen juice concentrate or ice cubes—8 to 12 per 1 cup liquid —in place of the cold liquid.) Chill till firm, or when partially set, fold in drained fruits, then continue chilling. Because fresh and frozen pineapple contain an enzyme that prevents gelatin from setting, they must first be cooked. Boil the fresh or frozen pineapple pieces for two minutes, then cool. Canned pineapple needs no cooking.

Gelatin's gel- and foam-forming properties are the bases for four classes of gel recipes: whips, snows or sponges, chiffons or gelatin-custard mixtures, and gelatin-whipped cream combinations. Whips are made by beating the basic gelatin till it is double in volume. When the basic gelatin is mixed with unbeaten egg whites and beaten, it is called a snow or sponge. Chiffons and egg-base gelatins are mixtures of gelatin, egg yolk, and beaten egg white.

A wreath of lime gelatin tops a cream cheese layer filled with crunchy cucumber and pineapple. Lavish Spring Salad Ring with lettuce, bunches of green grapes, and lemon wedges.

Whipped cream added to a snow or chiffon is the foundation for Bavarian cremes, charlottes, and mousses.

Strawberry Chiffon Pie

Trim with additional whipped cream —

Crush 1 pint fresh strawberries (about 1 cup); add ½ cup sugar. Let stand 30 minutes at room temperature. In saucepan soften 1 envelope unflavored gelatin (1 tablespoon) in ⅔ cup cold water. Heat and stir over low heat till gelatin is dissolved; cool. Add strawberries, 1 tablespoon lemon juice, and dash salt. Chill, stirring occasionally, till partially set.

Beat 2 egg whites to soft peaks; slowly add ¼ cup sugar, beating to stiff peaks. Fold in berry mixture. Whip ½ cup whipping cream; fold into mixture. Chill till mixture mounds when spooned. Pile into one 9-inch *baked*, cooled pastry shell (see *Pastry*). Chill till firm, 5 hours or overnight.

Basic gelatin techniques

Adding fruits, vegetables, meat, etc.: Chill dissolved gelatin till partially set; fold in food, distributing it evenly. If during chilling gelatin becomes too stiff, set bowl of gelatin in pan of hot water. Stir till gelatin is liquid; rechill till partially set.

Adding carbonated beverages: Cool dissolved gelatin to room temperature. Rest beverage bottle on rim of bowl; pour slowly down side. Gently stir up and down. Chill immediately.

Arranging fruit: Spoon thin layer of dissolved gelatin in bottom of mold. Arrange fruit. Chill till almost firm. Add remaining dissolved gelatin. Chill till firm.

Preparing layered salads: Chill first layer till *almost* firm. Pour second layer over; chill till almost firm. Repeat, as desired.

Unmolding gelatin salads: Loosen gelatin around edge of mold with spatula. Dip mold to rim in warm water for a *few seconds*. Tilt and rotate mold slightly easing gelatin away from sides to let air in. Place platter upside-down over mold. Hold platter and mold together, invert and shake gently to release. Lift off mold. If gelatin does not release, tilt again or redip quickly in warm water.

Strawberry Charlotte Russe

Combine one 3-ounce package strawberry-flavored gelatin and ¼ cup sugar; dissolve in 1¼ cups boiling water. Stir in 1 cup miniature marshmallows; cool. Add ¼ cup sugar to 2 cups fresh strawberries;* crush. Add berries, 2 tablespoons lemon juice, and 2 unbeaten egg whites to gelatin mixture. Chill till partially set.

Beat gelatin till fluffy. Whip ½ cup whipping cream; fold into gelatin mixture. Arrange one 9½-ounce package jelly roll, cut in ½-inch slices, on bottom and sides of oiled 3-quart bowl or mold. *Carefully* spoon gelatin over. Chill overnight. Makes 8 to 10 servings.

*Or, substitute one 10-ounce package frozen strawberries, thawed, for the fresh strawberries. Do not sweeten the frozen berries.

GELÉE *(juh' lā)*—A French word for jelly. Any food listed as *en gelée* means that it has been molded in gelatin or aspic jelly.

GEODUCK, GOOEYDUCK *(goo' ē duhk)*—A large, edible clam that can weigh up to 6½ pounds. Largest of the Pacific clams, it has a generous amount of sweet-tasting meat portions and is primarily available as a restaurant menu specialty.

GERMAN COOKERY—The cooking style of Germany characterized by hearty, substantial main dishes, savory sauces, and rich, delicate baked goods. Its traits have evolved from the peoples' needs due to climatic conditions. A cold, damp atmosphere of northern Germany, for instance, necessitates high energy-sustaining foods, while in the warmer south, lighter foods are sufficient energy providers.

These regional characteristics were reinforced by the political structure of Germany through the years. Up until the last century, Germany as a unified nation did not exist. The area consisted of many small

Noodle-based meatballs

Foam-topped beer and Königsberger Klopse →
go hand-in-hand at a hearty German dinner. (See *Königsberger Klopse* for recipe.)

kingdoms that were dominated by a number of more powerful foreign nations.

The robust nature of German cookery was apparent even with the earliest tribes of the area. When the Romans invaded Europe nearly 2,000 years ago, they found the Germans relying on basic foods such as wild game and fruits, coarse breads, milk, cheeses, and gruels—simple by the more refined Roman standards.

Although the Romans left their imprint, not until early in the Middle Ages did noticeable changes in the German cooking style begin to appear. Under Charlemagne's guidance, herb gardens and grape vineyards were established on the fertile soil. Because of its availability, honey was the most used sweetener, and sugar was a little-known luxury. As a result, herbs, wine, and honey became favorite ingredients in traditional German cooking.

Cooking styles from other nationalities were also adapted to German needs. Sauerkraut, though popularly thought to be Germany's national dish, had its beginnings in China. Although the Romans had acquired the sauerkraut technique from the Orient, it was forgotten until the thirteenth century when Tatar conquerors reintroduced it to Europe. During the 1600s and 1700s, elegant and rich French sauces, breads, and confections began to enhance and complement Germany's hearty foods. In addition, potatoes, now used so many ways, and coffee, the favored mealtime beverage, were introduced in the mid-eighteenth century during the reign of Frederick the Great.

Characteristics of German cookery: In general, meat and potatoes are the mainstays of German cuisine. Nonetheless, the foods eaten are not limited to these but extend to vegetables, sauces, and baked goods.

In regards to meat, pork is most plentiful followed by veal and beef. All three are the bases for over 300 sausages called wurst, for which Germans are noted. Poultry (particularly goose), fish, and game are also vital to the German diet.

With a desire to be thrifty, Germans utilize every possible part of meat. In addition to blood, variety meats such as the head, neck, feet, and liver are used to make sausages. Calves' lungs and hearts are made into a tasty hash. Even goose can be served at several meals when the legs are cooked with cabbage, the breast is cured and smoked, the giblets and blood are used in stew, and the goose neck skin is stuffed with a mixture of liver and pork.

German meat cookery is well known for the *Braten* or roasts, considered by many to be the national dish, but other meat and fish cuts are braised or quick-cooked by broiling or frying. Smoked pork chops known as *Kasseler Rippchen* may be simmered in stock, sautéed as breaded chops, or baked in a wrapping of dough. Schnitzel or cutlets, usually veal, may be stuffed, sauced, or topped with a fried egg. Carp are often live-poached in "bleu" fashion or are simmered in beer with an assortment of flavorful herbs and spices.

Chicken in Casserole

Beef bone marrow is used in the dumplings that float atop the chicken-vegetable stew —

Place one 3-pound whole ready-to-cook broiler-fryer chicken with giblets in Dutch oven. Half cover with cold water; bring to boiling then skim. Salt cooking water lightly. Add 4 carrots, bias-cut in 1½-inch pieces; 2 small turnips, halved; 1 cup cut uncooked green beans; 2 medium leeks *or* green onions, sliced; 2 stalks celery, sliced; 1 clove garlic studded with 1 whole clove (spice); and 1 bay leaf.

Cover and simmer slowly 30 minutes, turning chicken once. Add 1 cup uncooked peas and 4 ounces medium noodles. Cook about 10 minutes. Add Marrow Dumplings to broth; simmer till everything is done, about 10 to 12 minutes.

Transfer whole chicken, vegetables, noodles, and Marrow Dumplings to casserole. Discard bay leaf and garlic studded with clove. Add 1 tablespoon chopped parsley and pepper to taste to broth. Pour broth over chicken; trim with additional parsley. Makes 6 servings.

Marrow Dumplings: Strain 1½ tablespoons fresh marrow from 3-inch length of beef bone through a fine sieve. Combine with ⅔ cup cracker or matzoth crumbs; 1 egg; 1 beaten egg yolk; 1 tablespoon butter or margarine, softened; 1 tablespoon chopped parsley; dash nutmeg; dash baking powder; and salt and pepper to taste. (Add more crumbs if needed to hold mixture together.) Form into small marble-size balls. Add to casserole as directed.

German Peasant Platter

Home-style German cooking at its best —

2 small pork shanks
½ teaspoon salt
¼ teaspoon pepper
¼ teaspoon garlic powder
¼ teaspoon caraway seed
3 cups water
3 Bratwurst links
1 16-ounce can sauerkraut,
    heated and drained

Place pork shanks in roasting pan; sprinkle with salt, pepper, garlic powder, and caraway seed. Pour water around (not over) meat. Roast, uncovered, at 400° till done, 3 to 3½ hours. Prick Bratwurst; broil 3 to 4 minutes on each side until golden. Arrange meats on platter around bed of hot sauerkraut.

A vegetable generally accompanies the meat course. *Kartoffelen* (potatoes) appear at meals more often than not in any one of numerous ways—baked, broiled, mashed, as *Pfannukuchen* (pancakes), *Klösse* (dumplings), in soups, or in hot or cold salads. (Contrasting flavor additions of bacon, horseradish, nuts, sour cream, onion, caraway, and brown-buttered crumbs frequent these potato recipes. White varieties of asparagus and fresh mushrooms—the status vegetables—along with cabbages, dried legumes, and root vegetables, are well liked, too. Red cabbage is likely to be cooked with apples, brown sugar, vinegar, and spices. Thick, lentil soup, a popular dish, is flavored with sausage, onions, and pepper.

Sweet-Sour Red Cabbage

Heat 3 tablespoons cooking oil *or* bacon drippings in large skillet; add 1 large head red cabbage, shredded (6 cups); and 3 medium unpeeled apples, cubed (3 cups). Combine ⅓ cup brown sugar, ⅓ cup water, ⅓ cup vinegar, 1½ teaspoons salt, ¾ teaspoon caraway seed, and dash pepper. Pour vinegar mixture over cabbage.

Cover skillet tightly; cook over low heat, stirring occasionally till cabbage and apple are tender, about 15 to 20 minutes. Serves 8.

Bavarian Potato Dumplings

2 to 3 large potatoes (1 pound)
¾ cup all-purpose flour
1 slightly beaten egg
1½ teaspoons salt
    Dash pepper
¼ teaspoon grated onion
    Croutons
1 cup soft bread crumbs
    (about 2 slices)
2 tablespoons butter or margarine,
    melted

Cook potatoes in boiling, salted water to cover till done, 40 to 50 minutes; drain. Cool. Peel and put through a ricer. In a large mixing bowl combine potatoes, flour, egg, salt, pepper, and onion; mix thoroughly. Use ¼ cup of the mixture for each dumpling; flatten each and fill center with 3 or 4 croutons; work dough around croutons to make round ball.

Drop balls into boiling, salted water to cover (1 teaspoon salt to 1 quart water). Simmer 8 to 10 minutes; lift out. Combine bread crumbs with butter; roll dumplings in crumb mixture. Serve hot. Makes 7 dumplings.

Practically all meat and vegetable dishes are cooked in or served with a sauce. Throughout the dishes, one outstanding flavor appears repeatedly—the sweet-and-sour combination. A delicate flavor balance is usually achieved with sugar and vinegar, but dried fruits often accompany meats as part of the sweet flavoring. In salads, piquant dressings are tempered with sugar. Other sauces thickened with flour, egg yolk, or cream are standard to all European cooking including German cuisine. A brown sauce with sugar is the flavorful background for sauerbraten. Fish and vegetables, like asparagus and cauliflower, can sport a mustard sauce.

The marinade, a sauce offshoot, is another means of flavoring foods. Wine marinades enhance game meats. Herring fillets rolled around mustard, pickle, onion, and caper filling marinate in spicy liquid several days for the famous appetizer or supper dish rollmops. Highly-seasoned sausages, on the other hand, simmer in more subtly flavored liquid such as beer.

An outstanding assortment of breads and baked goods used as meal accompaniments, desserts, or between-meal refreshments rounds out German-style cooking. Germans, in fact, have made baking a fine art. Coarse-textured breads, like early Germans used, are just as important as the richer coffee cakes and exotic pastries.

German breads, like those of France, are solid, coarse loaves that often boast of hard, crunchy crusts. Rye breads—many flavored with caraway—come in various shades and kinds and are equal to, if not more popular than, white versions. Pumpernickel, slow-baked and well-crusted, has a sweet-sour taste and a compact, somewhat dry crumb. *Schwartzbrot* (black or heavy rye bread) is usually made of a rye flour-cornmeal combination. A lighter loaf with crisp crust is called *Bauernbrot*.

Sweet rolls and coffee cakes filled with fruit, jam, or almond paste are elegant. Though rich enough for dessert, these Kuchen are favored foods for coffee.

Dried Fruit Bread

Cook ½ cup dried pears and ¼ cup dried prunes in 2 cups water following package directions; drain, reserving liquid. Chop fruit; set aside. Add water to liquid to make 2 cups. Stir in 1 tablespoon sugar, 2 tablespoons shortening, and 1 teaspoon salt. Cool to lukewarm.

In large mixer bowl combine 2 packages active dry yeast, 2 cups sifted all-purpose flour, ¼ teaspoon ground cinnamon, and ¼ teaspoon ground cloves. Add fruit liquid mixture and beat at low speed of electric mixer for ½ minute. Beat 3 minutes at high speed. By hand, stir in reserved fruits, ½ cup raisins, ½ cup currants, ½ cup chopped nuts, and enough sifted all-purpose flour to make a moderately stiff dough, 3½ to 3¾ cups. Turn out onto floured surface.

Knead till smooth and elastic, about 8 minutes. Place in greased bowl, turning once to grease surface. Let rise till double, about 1 hour. Punch down; divide dough in half. Cover and let rest 10 minutes. Shape into 2 loaves. Place in two greased 8½x4½x 2½-inch loaf pans.

Let rise till almost double, about 30 minutes. Bake at 375° till golden, 35 to 40 minutes, covering loosely with foil the last 10 minutes of baking time. Remove from pans; cool on rack.

Desserts at everyday meals are relatively simple—fruit, plain, in dumplings, or in pancakes, rice pudding, Bavarian cream, or baked custard. A big, puffy, baked pancake sprinkled with lemon juice and sugar, or baked over stewed apples and served with whipped or sour cream is a dessert treat.

For special occasions and for company, on the other hand, adept cooks turn out magnificent tortes. The cake or crumb mixtures that form the base for the tortes are almost hidden by fillings of hazelnuts or almonds; fruits; jam; chocolate, mocha, or brandied whipped cream; or butter cream. Typical is the cherry-chocolate Black Forest torte—beautiful and delicious. Linzer torte, between cake and pie, has a nut crust and a lattice top through which the raspberry jam filling peeks.

Cherry Torte, Black Forest-Style

      1 16-ounce can pitted dark sweet
        cherries
    ⅓ cup kirsch
   1½ tablespoons cornstarch
      1 cup moderately soft butter
   4½ cups sifted confectioners' sugar
      3 egg yolks
      2 8-inch sponge cake layers,
        1-inch thick
        Chocolate shot
      1 1-ounce square semisweet
        chocolate, finely shaved

Drain and halve cherries, reserving ¾ cup syrup. Pour kirsch over; let stand 2 hours. Gradually blend syrup into cornstarch; add cherries. Heat and stir till thickened and bubbly; cook and stir 1 minute. Cool, then chill.

Beat butter and sugar till smooth; beat in yolks till light and fluffy. Place 1 cake layer on plate. Using *1 cup* creamed butter, make ½-inch border (1¼ inches high) around top. Using ½ *cup* creamed butter, make circle in center of cake, 2½ inches in diameter (1¼ inches high).

Spread cherry filling between border and center of creamed butter. Top with second cake layer; press lightly. Cover torte with remaining butter. Sprinkle sides with shot. Top with shaved chocolate; trim with maraschino cherries, if desired. Chill. Let stand at room temperature 20 minutes before serving torte. Makes 6 to 8 servings.

Edelweiss Torte

3/4 cup plus 2 tablespoons butter
  or margarine, chilled
2 tablespoons butter or margarine
1 3/4 cups sifted all-purpose flour
1/2 cup ice water

. . .

  Cream Filling
  Glaze
2 cups whipping cream
1/4 cup sugar

Work chilled butter with back of spoon just till pliable as putty. Roll between waxed paper to 8x6-inch rectangle. Chill 1 hour. Cut the 2 tablespoons butter into flour. Gradually add ice water tossing with fork. On lightly floured surface knead 5 minutes. Cover; let rest 10 minutes. Roll dough to 15x9-inch rectangle.

Peel waxed paper from butter; place on *half* the dough. Fold other half over butter; press edges of dough to seal. Wrap; chill 1 hour. Unwrap; roll to 15x9-inch rectangle. (Roll from center *just to* edges.) Brush off excess flour, then fold dough in thirds. Turn and fold dough in thirds again making 9 layers. Press edges to seal; wrap and chill 1 hour.

Roll, fold, and chill dough 2 or 3 times more. Divide dough in 3 parts, roll each to 10-inch circle. Cover circles with waxed paper; stack and chill 2 to 3 hours. Prick each circle well; bake on *ungreased* baking sheet at 350° for 20 minutes; cool thoroughly.

Prepare Cream Filling and Glaze as directed. Whip cream with sugar. To assemble torte, place 1 layer of puff pastry on a serving plate. Spread with Cream Filling. Spread a second layer of puff pastry with 2 cups whipped cream; gently place on top of Cream Filling. Top with remaining layer of puff pastry, bottom side up. Frost sides of torte with remaining whipped cream. Spread Glaze over top. Chill 45 minutes. If desired, decorate top with frosting design and sides with toasted sliced almonds. Chill 2 hours before serving.

Cream Filling: In saucepan combine 2/3 cup sugar, 2 tablespoons cornstarch, and 1/4 teaspoon salt. Stir in 2 cups milk. Cook and stir till thickened and bubbly. Remove from heat; stir small amount of hot mixture into 3 slightly beaten egg yolks; return to hot mixture. Cook and stir 2 minutes. Stir in 1 tablespoon butter or margarine and 1 teaspoon vanilla; cool.

Glaze: Blend together 1 1/2 cups confectioners' sugar, 2 tablespoons water, 2 drops red food coloring, and 2 drops yellow food coloring.

Traditional Christmas baking can keep German cooks busy for weeks. There must be not only Dresden's stollen and fruit-studded sweet breads shaped into wreaths and crowns, but also light and buttery or dark and spicy cookies. Creamy white Springerle are pressed into molds that have been handed down for generations. Lebkuchen, rich in spice and usually sweetened with honey, is made early so it can mellow. Hard little Pfefferneusse are always made with a touch of black pepper to make them truly live up to their peppernut name. And a German Christmas isn't complete without gingerbread boys, a gingerbread house, and molded marzipan.

GHEE *(gē)*—A clarified butter made from water buffalo milk that is used in the cooking of India and other nearby countries.

GHERKIN *(gûr′ kin)*—1. A variety of cucumber, small and prickly, that is usually pickled. 2. Any cucumber variety that is immature, small, and used for pickling.

The name gherkin seems to have originated from *agurke*, an old Dutch word. Most true gherkins are grown in the southern United States and in their native country, the West Indies. (See *Cucumber, Pickle* for additional information.)

GIBLET—The edible viscera of poultry such as the liver, heart, gizzard, wing tips, and neck. They are cooked separately from the other meat and are used in making stock for gravy. Finely chopped, cooked giblets are often added to the finished gravy for flavor and texture interest. Giblets are also tasteful additions in soups, pâtés, and meat sandwich fillings. (See also *Poultry.*)

Cooked Giblets

Place giblets, *except* liver, in saucepan. Add water just to cover giblets; salt lightly. Add a few celery leaves and onion slices to water, if desired. Cover and simmer 1 to 2 hours for chicken giblets (2 hours for turkey giblets). Add the liver and continue to simmer 5 to 10 minutes for chicken liver (20 to 30 minutes for turkey liver). Cool giblets in broth; remove and chop, if desired. Use broth and giblets for gravy or stuffing.

GIGOT *(jig′ uht)*—A French word for a cooked leg of lamb or mutton.

GILL—A little-used liquid measure equal to one-fourth pint (one-half cup).

GIN—An almost colorless spirit flavored primarily with juniper berries. It is made from rectified (purified by redistillation) spirits made from cereal grains.

The origin of gin is attributed to a seventeenth-century Dutch professor of medicine who was looking for a medicine with specific diuretic properties. He found the medicine—gin—but it soon moved out of the realm of medicine and into the category of alcoholic beverages.

Later in the century, gin was introduced to England when British soldiers returned from the European wars. These soldiers had acquired a taste for Dutch gin, and soon gin was also being distilled in England. Early in the eighteenth century, Queen Anne of England promoted English gin by raising the taxes on imports. Although much of the English gin of this time was of very poor quality, it was so cheap to produce that all classes were soon consuming this spirit in many gin houses.

In the United States, the bathtub gin of the Prohibition era marked the popularity peak of this colorless spirit.

The gins of today are generally divided into two types—Dutch gin and English or American gin. Variations in the manufacturing processes of these two types account for their differing characteristics. Dutch gin is full-bodied and has a malty flavor. By comparison, English or American gin is light-bodied and light-flavored.

Although many people think sloe gin is a type of gin, it is actually a liqueur made from gin and flavored with sloe berries. American gin is the most popular type of gin in this country and is the base for many alcoholic drinks, such as the dry martini, gin sling, gin and tonic, and Tom Collins. (See also *Wines and Spirits.*)

GINGER—The root of a semitropical plant used as a distinctive, pungent seasoning.

Although its place of origin is unknown, ginger was cultivated centuries ago in China and Southeast Asia. In fact, Confu-cius, the ancient Chinese philosopher, made mention of ginger in his book, *Analects.* Early Greeks and Romans obtained ginger from Arab traders, making it one of the first oriental spices to appear in Europe. By the second century, the amount of ginger imports to the city of Alexandria, Egypt, was large enough to be taxed.

During the Middle Ages, this spice was so popular in Switzerland that one of the Swiss spice markets was named "Ginger Alley." Ginger covered with a heavy, sugar syrup very similar to today's preserved ginger was a popular imported confection in Europe during this same period.

When the Spanish viceroy to Mexico assumed his position in 1535, he brought ginger with him. As far as is known, this was the first oriental spice in North America.

Like many other spices, ginger has also been used as a medicine. Early Greek physicians used it as a treatment for toothache, stomach or digestion problems, and poisoning. Later, this spice was consumed in large quantities by Englishmen to ward off the plague. Ginger was also prescribed as an antidote for the sorrows of love.

How ginger is produced: The reedlike ginger plant, grown primarily in India, Nigeria, Jamaica, Sierra Leone, Haiti, and Taiwan, reaches a height of two to four feet. Unlike most other spices, it is the plant root (rhizome) that is used as a seasoning. The irregular shape of this root resembles a hand, so the rhizomes are called "hands." These hands are dug when the plants are about one year old.

Although most of the ginger crop is dried, some is exported fresh. To use fresh or green ginger, peel off the outer skin; then grate, slice, mince, or sliver, as the recipe directs. Fresh ginger is usually stocked in the supermarket specialty section.

The most common form of this spice is dried ginger. After washing, the ginger is dried and bleached in the sun, which accounts for the light buff color of ginger. The dried ginger is then ready for export, primarily to the United Kingdom, the Arab countries, and the United States.

Once the dried ginger reaches this country, it can be sold whole, but it is usually further processed to yield cracked or ground

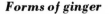
Forms of ginger

Spicy ginger is used as a seasoning—canned, ground, dried, or fresh—and as a confection —candied and preserved.

ginger. Cracked ginger is in small, irregularly shaped pieces, while ground ginger has been ground almost to a powder.

Preserved and crystallized or candied ginger are confections rather than spices. Both of these products are made by immersing fresh ginger in a heavy sugar syrup. Preserved ginger is sold in this syrup, but crystallized ginger is processed one step farther. After the ginger has become fully saturated with the sugar syrup, the part to be crystallized is drained and then generously coated with tiny sugar crystals.

Another important ginger product is ginger oil. This oil, obtained by distillation, is seldom used in cooking but is becoming popular in men's scented colognes.

How to use: The spicy-sweet flavor of ginger is famous in gingerbread, gingersnaps, and ginger ale, but the spice is by no means limited to these traditional uses. Because it continues to release flavor, you'll find whole ginger especially useful for spicing foods that require slow cooking or soaking in a brine such as pickles, chutney, marinated meats, and preserves. Ground ginger has numerous uses in the kitchen. Try a pinch of this spice in bean, onion, and potato soups, baked beans, glazed carrots, squash, sweet potatoes, and beets. Ginger is also compatible with many desserts such as pumpkin pie, puddings, spice cakes, fruit compotes, ice cream sauces, and cookies. And don't forget this spice for seasoning main dishes such as cheese souf-flés, roasted pork, veal, beef, venison, chicken, duck, turkey, and baked fish. Ginger even has a place in fruit salads and fruit salad dressings. (See also *Spice*.)

Rolled Ginger Cookies

1 cup shortening
1 cup sugar
1 egg
1 cup molasses
2 tablespoons vinegar
5 cups sifted all-purpose flour
1½ teaspoons baking soda
2 to 3 teaspoons ground ginger
1 teaspoon ground cinnamon
1 teaspoon ground cloves
½ teaspoon salt
Cinnamon candies (optional)
Confectioners' Icing (see *Confectioners' Sugar*) (optional)

In mixing bowl cream shortening and sugar. Beat in egg, molasses, and vinegar. Sift together flour, baking soda, ginger, cinnamon, cloves, and ½ teaspoon salt; blend in. Chill 3 hours.

Roll dough ⅛ inch thick on lightly floured surface. Cut with round cookie cutter or gingerbread-boy cutter (or draw your own pattern). Place 1 inch apart on greased cookie sheet. Use cinnamon candies for face and buttons on gingerbread boys. Bake at 375° for 5 to 6 minutes. Cool slightly; remove to rack. When thoroughly cool, decorate gingerbread boys with fairly thick Confectioners' Icing. Makes 60 ginger cookies.

Gingered Pineapple

A quick fix-up for canned fruit —

- 1 cup dairy sour cream
- ¼ cup honey
- 2 tablespoons snipped candied ginger
- 1 20½-ounce can pineapple chunks, chilled and drained

Combine sour cream, honey, and candied ginger; chill. To serve, spoon over drained pineapple in individual serving dishes. Makes 6 servings.

Ginger Sundae Sauce

- ⅓ cup light corn syrup
- ¼ cup *finely* chopped candied ginger
- ¼ cup light cream
- ¼ cup butter or margarine
- ½ teaspoon vanilla
  Vanilla ice cream

Combine syrup, candied ginger, *half* the light cream, and dash salt. Simmer 5 minutes. Gradually stir in remaining cream. Heat through but do not boil. Remove from heat; stir in butter and vanilla. Serve over ice cream. Makes ¾ cup.

Impress and delight guests with Ginger-Maple Alaska. The rush of last-minute preparation will be gratifyingly rewarded by compliments as the diners enjoy this delicious dessert.

Ginger Muffins

Serve piping hot —

In mixing bowl cream together ¼ cup shortening and ¼ cup sugar. Beat in 1 egg, then ½ cup molasses. Sift together 1½ cups sifted all-purpose flour, ¾ teaspoon baking soda, ½ teaspoon ground cinnamon, ½ teaspoon ground ginger, ¼ teaspoon salt, and ¼ teaspoon ground cloves; stir into molasses mixture. Gradually add ½ cup hot water, beating till smooth. Fill greased muffin pans ⅔ full. Bake at 375° for 20 to 25 minutes. Makes 12 muffins.

GINGER ALE—A ginger-flavored, carbonated beverage. Although ginger is the predominant flavoring, other spices and citrus oils are frequently added to ginger ale. Pepper of some type is occasionally added to increase the bite of this beverage. Pale ginger ale is nearly colorless, while golden ginger ale has had caramel coloring added.

Ginger ale is commonly drunk alone as a soft drink or used with alcoholic beverages as a mixer. It is also used as a cooking ingredient, particularly to add tang to gelatin salads. (See also *Carbonated Beverage*.)

Strawberry Sparkle Punch

A delicious fruit-flavored beverage —

> 2 cups fresh strawberries, hulled
> 1 3-ounce package strawberry-
>   flavored gelatin
> 1 cup boiling water
> 1 6-ounce can frozen lemonade
>   concentrate
>
> • • •
>
> 3 cups water
> 1 1-quart bottle cranberry juice
>   cocktail, chilled
> 1 28-ounce bottle ginger ale,
>   chilled

Put strawberries in blender container; cover and blend on low speed till fruit is puréed. Dissolve strawberry-flavored gelatin in boiling water. Stir in lemonade concentrate till melted. Add the cold water, cranberry juice cocktail, and the strawberry purée. Pour over ice in large punch bowl. Slowly pour in chilled ginger ale. Makes about 30 servings.

GINGER BEER—A frothy, very slightly alcoholic drink flavored with ginger. The continuation of fermentation after this beverage is bottled accounts for the large number of bubbles in ginger beer.

This beverage was popular and often made at home in colonial America. It is still a popular drink in England where it is traditionally marketed in crocks but now also is available in bottles.

GINGERBREAD—A shortened cake with a predominant ginger flavor.

The date when the first gingerbread was made is obscure, with some sources crediting it to the Greeks about 5,000 years ago and others dating it only as far back as the Middle Ages. It is agreed, nonetheless, that this early gingerbread was made of honey, flour, and ginger and probably resembled a bread more than a cake. Gingerbread was one of the awards given to medieval British knights for winning a tournament, and gingerbread stalls were one of the attractions at the fairs of this period.

One of the special holiday foods of the Middle Ages was gingerbread molded into fancy shapes. Some of these molds of men, birds, animals, and alphabet letters have survived and are now museum pieces. The importance of the occasion dictated the size of the gingerbread, with some weighing 150 pounds. For example, in 1672, the birth of Peter the Great of Russia was celebrated with huge gingerbread in various shapes depicting Russian symbols and landmarks.

Gingerbread was one of the desserts served by the early American settlers. In fact, George Washington's mother often served gingerbread to famous guests.

Although much of this early gingerbread resembled cookies rather than the cakelike gingerbread of today, during the early 1800s, soft gingerbread gained in popularity. In New England, gingerbread became one of the traditional foods at the annual military Training Day. Gingerbread was one of Abraham Lincoln's favorite desserts.

One of the first mixes, gingerbread mix was marketed in the United States in 1929.

Today, whether homemade or made from a mix, gingerbread is a family favorite. Serve it piping hot with a generous spoonful of whipped cream, vanilla ice cream,

Gingerbread

   ½ cup sugar
   ½ cup shortening
   ½ cup light molasses
   1 egg
   1½ cups sifted all-purpose flour
   ¾ teaspoon salt
   ¾ teaspoon baking soda
   ½ teaspoon ground ginger
   ½ teaspoon ground cinnamon
   ½ cup boiling water
   Citrus Fluff

Gradually add sugar to shortening, creaming till light. Add molasses and egg; beat thoroughly. Sift together flour, ¾ teaspoon salt, soda, ginger, and cinnamon. Add to creamed mixture alternately with ½ cup boiling water, beating after each addition. Bake in well-greased 8x8x2-inch baking pan at 350° till done, about 35 to 40 minutes. Spoon Citrus Fluff onto warm squares of cake. Twist and place an orange slice atop each serving, if desired.

Citrus Fluff: In small saucepan beat 1 egg; add ½ cup sugar, 1 teaspoon grated orange peel, 1 teaspoon grated lemon peel, and 2 tablespoons lemon juice. Cook and stir over low heat till thick, about 5 minutes. Cool thoroughly. Whip 1 cup whipping cream; fold into cooled mixture. Chill. Makes about 2 cups topping.

Ginger-Pear Cake

   2 tablespoons butter or margarine
   ¼ cup brown sugar
   ¼ cup dark corn syrup
   1 16-ounce can pear halves,
      well drained
   ½ cup walnut halves
   1 package gingerbread mix

Melt butter or margarine in 9x1½-inch round pan. Stir in brown sugar and corn syrup; blend well. Cut pear halves in half, forming quarters. Place one walnut half in the cavity of each pear quarter; arrange in pan spoke-fashion, cut side down. Arrange remaining nuts in center of pan.

Prepare gingerbread mix according to package directions; pour batter carefully over pears and nuts in pan. Bake at 350° till cake tests done, about 40 minutes. Let stand ½ minute before inverting onto serving plate. Serve fruit-topped cake warm with dollops of whipped cream, if desired.

Make both the gingerbread boys and house from Rolled Ginger Cookie dough, or use cardboard and frosting for the house.

or a fruit sauce, as a dessert. Or serve it warm with butter as a delicious lunch or supper bread to delight all the members of your family. (See also *Cake.*)

Ginger-Peach Squares

Mix and bake 1 package gingerbread mix according to package directions. Combine one 16-ounce can peach slices, drained, and ½ cup maple-flavored syrup; heat. Cut warm gingerbread in squares. To serve, top each gingerbread square with a scoop of vanilla ice cream and spoon the warm maple-peach sauce over. Makes 8 or 9 servings.

Ginger–Maple Alaska

A glamorous dessert for a special dinner —

Prepare 1 package gingerbread mix according to package directions, baking it in a 9x9x2-inch baking pan. Cool and remove from pan. Trim 2 pints *or* 1 quart brick maple nut ice cream and gingerbread so that cake is ½ inch larger than ice cream on all sides. Place gingerbread on wooden cutting board. Keep ice cream frozen till ready to use.

Beat 4 egg whites till soft peaks form; add 5 drops maple flavoring. Gradually add ½ cup sugar, beating till stiff peaks form. Center brick of ice cream on gingerbread layer. Spread meringue over ice cream and cake, sealing to edges of cake all the way around. Bake at 500° till meringue is golden, about 3 minutes. Serve immediately. Makes 8 servings.

GINGERSNAP—A flat, crisp cookie spiced with ginger and sweetened with molasses.

This cookie has long been a favorite of people of all ages. Children and adults alike will soon empty a cookie jar filled with crisp gingersnaps. In many homes, gingersnaps are traditionally baked at Christmas time. Even statesmen enjoy this spicy cookie. This was evidenced in 1947 when the Prime Minister of Canada served gingersnaps as the final course of a luncheon honoring one of President Truman's aides.

Like other cookies, gingersnaps are most popular as a dessert or snack with fruit or a glass of cold milk. However, crushed gingersnaps also add a delicious flavor to sauces and make a special crumb crust for cream or chiffon pies. (See also *Cookie*.)

A generous spoonful of fluffy citrus topping gives a new twist to an old favorite, Gingerbread. This delicious, spicy cake is best when served warm, so schedule your time accordingly.

Gingersnaps

In mixing bowl cream 1 cup brown sugar, $\frac{3}{4}$ cup shortening, $\frac{1}{4}$ cup molasses, and 1 egg till fluffy. Sift together $2\frac{1}{4}$ cups sifted all-purpose flour, 2 teaspoons baking soda, 1 teaspoon ground ginger, 1 teaspoon ground cinnamon, $\frac{1}{2}$ teaspoon salt, and $\frac{1}{2}$ teaspoon ground cloves; stir into molasses mixture.

Form cookie dough into small balls. Roll in granulated sugar; place 2 inches apart on greased cookie sheet. Bake cookies at 375° for 12 minutes. Makes about 5 dozen gingersnaps.

Ginger-Fruit Pie

Has a spicy crumb crust —

> 1 cup finely crushed gingersnaps
> 3 tablespoons butter or
>   margarine, melted
> 2 cups miniature marshmallows
>   *or* 20 large marshmallows
> 2 tablespoons milk
> 1 3-ounce package cream cheese,
>   softened
> 1 cup dairy sour cream
> 1 teaspoon vanilla
>   Dash salt
> 1 16-ounce can fruit cocktail,
>   drained

For crust combine crumbs and melted butter or margarine; press onto bottom and sides of 9-inch pie plate. Chill while making filling.

Melt marshmallows with milk in double boiler over hot water, stirring occasionally; cool 10 minutes. Combine cream cheese, sour cream, vanilla, and salt; beat smooth. Stir in marshmallow mixture and fruit cocktail. Pile into crust. Chill till firm, about 5 hours. Trim with additional fruit, if desired.

Gjetost cheese
is appetizer
or dessert fare.

GJETOST CHEESE *(jed′ ôst)*—A Scandinavian cheese made from goat's milk or a mixture of goat's and cow's milk. The name comes from the Norwegian words for goat (*gjet*) and cheese (*ost*). This firm, sweet, caramel-colored cheese is commonly thinly sliced and served on brown bread. It is popular throughout Scandinavia and is also found in many large cheese stores in the United States. (See also *Cheese*.)

GLACÉ *(gla sā′)*—1. The French word for something frozen, especially frozen desserts such as ice cream. 2. The French term for something covered with a glaze.

GLACÉ DE VIANDE *(gla sā′ duh vyand′)*—A jellylike meat extract with a concentrated flavor. It is used as a glaze or added to sauces or soups to enrich them. It can also be diluted and used as a stock.

GLACÉ FRUITS OR NUTS—Whole fruits such as grapes or strawberries or whole, shelled nuts such as almonds or walnuts coated with a crystal-clear sugar syrup.

GLASS—1. A tumbler used for beverage service. 2. A rigid product that has cooled without forming crystals. This material, which can be either transparent or translucent, is used in numerous cooking and dining items, including baking dishes, drinking glasses, and serving dishes.

Although the date and place of origin of glass are unknown, Egyptian glass objects dating back to about 2000 B.C. have been unearthed. The ancient Egyptians formed glass objects by a method called "coring." Using this method, layers of glass were formed around a piece of stone or clay; then this core was removed.

The development of glassblowing is generally classified as the most important event in the history of glassmaking. Since the earliest known articles made of blown glass were made by Syrian glassworkers, the development of glassblowing is generally credited to them in about 100 B.C. This technique opened the way for the production of numerous articles such as flasks and other hollow vessels that could not be formed by the previous molding methods. Luckily, Syrian glassblowers traveled wherever they could profitably practice their craft; thus, their beautiful art spread to many places throughout the world.

Although the basic technique of shaping molten glass by blowing through a hollow tube remained the same for centuries, glassmakers were constantly refining their materials and craft. From the Middle Ages to the nineteenth century, the important developments in glassmaking included the production of glass that could be blown very thin into intricate objects, the perfecting of glass hard enough to be engraved, and the development of lead glass which is especially beautiful when cut.

In the early 1800s glass manufacturing was given a boost with the introduction of a machine for pressing glass. Today, the majority of the manufactured glass is mechanically shaped by pressing, blowing, casting, or rolling it. The art of glassblowing, however, is still greatly in demand for producing intricate and beautiful handmade glassware and artwork.

Types of glass: Although there are several types of glass designed for specific uses, the glass used in table and cookware can be divided into four types—lime, lead, borosilicate, and glass-ceramic.

1. The largest proportion of glass articles are made of lime glass which is both durable and inexpensive. This type of glass is made by fusing sand, limestone, and sodium carbonate together at a high temperature. Bottles, jars, bowls, and drinking vessels are usually made of lime glass.

2. Lead glass is used in the manufacture of delicate table crystal. The characteristic sparkle of this type of glass is due to the lead oxide used in the formula.

3. Early in the twentieth century, scientists discovered that by using boric oxide and alumina in the formula, they could make a heat-resistant glass. Since borosilicate glass won't crack at high temperatures, it is used for baking dishes as well as top-of-the-range cooking utensils.

4. The last type of glass, glass-ceramic, is relatively new. Glass-ceramic cooking and baking ware can withstand extreme changes of temperature. It will not break even when taken directly from the freezer and put into an extremely hot oven.

A narrow paint brush is an ideal utensil for evenly brushing the honey-butter-lemon juice glaze onto Honey-Baked Bananas.

GLAZE—A smooth, glossy coating. A glaze, whether used on meats, vegetables, or desserts, should enhance both the flavor and the appearance of any food.

Glazes for roasted or grilled meat are usually brushed on the meat during the last part of cooking. The heat melts the glaze slightly to give a smooth, shiny coating. Baked ham is often glazed with brown sugar, jelly, or a fruit juice-honey mixture. Piquant, spicy, and fruity glazes give poultry an extra-special finish.

Vegetables such as carrots and squash can be cooked in a brown sugar mixture that adds shine as well as a special flavor. Molded cold meat or fish becomes an elegant buffet main dish when glazed with a crystal-clear, gelatin aspic.

A glaze is often used on pies, cakes, and other desserts to add a complementary flavor as well as a pretty finish. To achieve the desired lacquerlike finish, the glaze is usually poured onto the food where it hardens to a smooth, glossy finish. A sparkling, clear glaze full of fruit, such as pineapple or strawberries, gives a glorious finish to cheesecakes. Melted jelly makes an ex-

cellent glaze for fruit tarts. Fruitcake can be glazed with warmed corn syrup. A thin icing is often used as a sweet glaze for cookies, cakes, éclairs, cream puffs, sweet rolls, and yeast-raised doughnuts.

A glazed finish on pies is achieved by brushing the top crust with melted butter or beaten egg and then sprinkling it with sugar. As the pie bakes, the sugar melts to give the pie a glossy coating.

Peachy Glazed Ham

Roast a fully cooked ham at 325° to an internal temperature of 130°, about 2 to 2¾ hours. Half an hour before cooking time is up, pour off drippings. Score ham and stud with whole cloves. Spoon Glaze over. Cook 30 minutes more, spooning Glaze over 2 or 3 times. Remove to platter. Arrange peaches and oranges (from Sauce) atop ham; anchor with whole cloves. Serve with Spicy Peach Sauce.

Spicy Peach Sauce: Combine one 29-ounce can peach slices, undrained; ⅓ cup vinegar; ¾ cup sugar; 1 teaspoon whole cloves; 6 inches stick cinnamon; and 10 whole allspice. Add 1 unpeeled orange, cut in wedges. Simmer, uncovered, 5 minutes. Cover; cool. Remove spices.

Glaze: Drain 1 cup syrup from Spicy Peach Sauce; boil gently, uncovered, till liquid is reduced by half.

Honey-Baked Bananas

A glossy dessert —

    6 ripe bananas
    2 tablespoons butter or margarine
    2 tablespoons lemon juice
    ¼ cup honey *or* dark corn syrup

Peel bananas and place in shallow baking dish. Melt butter and combine with lemon juice and honey *or* corn syrup. Brush mixture on the bananas, coating them well. Bake at 325° till done and well glazed, about 15 minutes.

Succulent ham

←Give Peachy Glazed Ham a glossy finish by frequently spooning the glaze over it. A spicy sauce further enhances the flavor.

As soon as the Glazed Almonds are finished cooking, spread them in a thin layer on foil. Cool, then break into clusters.

Chocolate Glaze

    1½ 1-ounce squares unsweetened
        chocolate
    2 tablespoons butter or margarine
    1½ cups sifted confectioners' sugar
    1 teaspoon vanilla

Melt unsweetened chocolate and butter or margarine over low heat, stirring constantly. Remove from heat. Stir in confectioners' sugar and vanilla until crumbly. Blend in 3 tablespoons boiling water. Add enough water (about 2 teaspoons, a teaspoon at a time) to form medium glaze of pouring consistency. Pour quickly over cake; spread glaze evenly over top and sides of cake.

Glazed Almonds

    1 cup whole blanched almonds
    ½ cup sugar
    2 tablespoons butter or margarine
    ½ teaspoon vanilla

In heavy skillet heat and stir almonds, sugar, and butter till almonds are toasted and sugar is golden brown. Stir in vanilla. Spread on a sheet of foil; sprinkle lightly with salt. Cool candy; break into pieces consisting of 2- or 3-nut clusters.

GLOBE ARTICHOKE—A descriptive name for the most common type of artichoke; a green, thick-leaved vegetable of the sunflower family. This variety is also called French artichoke. (See also *Artichoke.*)

GLÖGG—A Christmas punch of Swedish origin made with spiced wine and aquavit or other liquor and often sprinkled with citrus peel, raisins, and almonds. This beverage may also be glamorously flamed, using liquor-soaked sugar cubes. Traditionally, the drinking of glögg is preceded by a toast to everyone's good health. (See also *Scandinavian Cookery.*)

Firetong Glögg

3¼ cups dry red wine
¾ cup granulated sugar
1 3x½-inch strip orange peel
1 2x½-inch strip lemon peel
½ cup orange juice
¼ cup lemon juice
3 whole cloves
½ cup sugar cubes
¼ cup rum, heated
Unpeeled orange slices

Heat wine with granulated sugar, fruit peels, juices, and cloves. *Do not* boil. Pour into heat-proof punch bowl. Soak sugar cubes in rum; place cubes in a strainer over punch.

Ignite sugar cubes; as they flame, spoon more heated rum from long-handled ladle over cubes. When sugar has melted into punch, add orange slices. Makes 8 servings. (Make 4 times recipe to match picture.)

American–Style Glögg

Combine 2 quarts apple juice; 3 sticks cinnamon; 2 tablespoons whole cloves; 8 whole cardamom, shelled and crushed; and dash ground nutmeg. Simmer, covered, for 30 minutes. Pour over 1 pound light raisins and let stand overnight.

Before serving, bring apple juice mixture to boiling. Reduce heat and let steep, uncovered, for 1 hour. Slice 2 unpeeled oranges. Cut slices in fourths and add to hot mixture. Add 1 fifth dark rum and 1 fifth brandy. Heat but do not boil. Serve in hot mugs. Makes about 30 servings.

GLOUCESTER CHEESE (*glos' tuhr*)—A firm, mild-flavored cheese similar to mild Cheddar. Originally, the rich milk from Gloucester cows was used exclusively, but in recent years, this breed has become extinct, so milk from other cows is now used.

Produced in Gloucester, England, this cheese is sold in two forms: single Gloucester, two to three inches thick, is aged less than two months; double Gloucester, twice as thick, is cured six to twelve months. Double Gloucester is often colored with red or brown dye. (See also *Cheese.*)

GLUCOSE—A sugar, also called dextrose or fruit sugar, that is found naturally in fruits, vegetables, and honey. Commercially prepared glucose is most often made by treating cornstarch with acid. If the reaction is stopped before completion, the resulting product is called corn syrup.

Although glucose is less sweet than sucrose (table sugar), it does not crystallize as readily. It is often used as an ingredient in commercial candies, baked goods, and wines. (See also *Sugar.*)

GLUTEN—A sticky, elastic protein found in flour. Gluten provides the greatest share of the structure of baked goods.

The amount and quality of gluten differ with the various types of flours. In cake flour, for example, the small amount of soft gluten present gives cakes their light, delicate texture. Bread flour, on the other hand, contains a larger amount of a more elastic gluten. This allows yeast doughs to expand without the cells breaking. During baking, the gluten coagulates, thus setting the familiar bread structure.

Kneading dough develops gluten, making it more elastic. This is a desirable characteristic in yeast-leavened breads. However, quick breads such as muffins are lightly mixed to avoid development of gluten which would make breads of this type tough.

A Scandinavian specialty

Rum-soaked sugar cubes produce the glow→ ing flame as they sizzle over Firetong Glögg, a punch served at Christmas.

GLUTEN BREAD—A specialty bread made with flour containing a higher proportion of gluten and a lower proportion of starch than is present in most other flours.

GNOCCHI (*nyôk′ kē*)—Italian-style appetizer or accompaniment dumplings that are made with puff pastry dough, potatoes, or semolina. They are formed into small balls, squares, or thin strips and are either poached or baked. Cheese is usually in the dough or is sprinkled over the cooked gnocchi. (See also *Italian Cookery.*)

Italian Gnocchi

Heat 3 cups milk with ¼ cup butter or margarine and 1 teaspoon salt just until scalding, stirring frequently (*do not boil*). Add ¾ cup farina in a fine stream, stirring constantly. Cook and stir mixture for about 5 minutes.

Remove from heat. Stir small amount of hot farina into 2 slightly beaten eggs. Return to hot mixture. Stir in ½ cup shredded Parmesan cheese. Pour into greased 8x8x2-inch pan. Chill.

Turn out of pan; cut chilled farina in 4x½-inch slices. Overlap the slices in a greased 13x9x2-inch baking dish. Sprinkle with another ½ cup shredded Parmesan cheese and dot with ¼ cup butter or margarine. Bake at 400° for 30 minutes. Makes 6 servings.

Italian Gnocchi is a versatile accompaniment for all meals. Serve it with Canadian bacon to give breakfast a different twist.

GOAT'S MILK CHEESE—Any of several distinctively flavored cheeses made largely or entirely from goat's milk. France is the largest producer of goat cheeses. The French forms available in the United States have been aged less than one month. Italy, Norway, Argentina, and Switzerland have their own varieties, but these are not on the American market. (See also *Cheese.*)

GOLD CAKE—The name for a yellow, shortening-type cake usually made with egg yolks rather than whole eggs.

GOLDEN SYRUP—A gold-colored syrup made with corn syrup, molasses, and sugar. It is especially popular in Great Britain and is primarily used as a topping.

GOLUBTSI—Meat and rice-stuffed cabbage leaves common to Russian cuisine. *Golubtsi*, which literally means "little pigeons," are rolled into a shape that resembles these birds. (See also *Russian Cookery.*)

GOOBER—Another name, often used in the South, for the peanut. (See also *Peanut.*)

GOOSE—A wild or domestic waterfowl with cone-shaped beak. A goose is larger than a duck but smaller than a swan.

The goose has long influenced folklore as well as peoples' eating habits. It has been a symbol of faithfulness to the Chinese and of spiritual freedom to the Hindus. Romans helped introduce the goose as a food to European cultures. Today, a goose is served at Christmas dinner in Germany, England, and Denmark and at St. Martin's Eve dinner in Sweden.

Nutritional value: In comparison to other poultry, goose is an equally good source of protein, but contains a higher proportion of fat. One serving of goose meat provides approximately 320 calories.

How to buy: Choose young birds for roasting, frying, or broiling. More mature geese are suitable for stewing purposes.

All domestic geese are inspected for wholesomeness. Some are also graded according to the USDA poultry standards, but grading is not required. Most geese are marketed while young, but the few older birds marketed are labeled mature.

How to store: A goose killed by a hunter should be cleaned, drawn, dressed, and chilled immediately. Whether wild or domestic, refrigerate the goose promptly when it reaches your home. Leave a store-purchased bird that has been wrapped in transparent material in its original packaging. If another packaging material has been used, unwrap and remove the giblets.

Place wild or domestic birds on a plate or tray, cover loosely, and refrigerate. Wrap and refrigerate the giblets separately. Fresh goose may be stored in the refrigerator for up to one or two days.

Freezing is recommended if the goose is to be kept for a longer time. Wrap the bird and giblets separately in moisture-vapor-proof material and freeze at 0° or less. A frozen goose may be stored up to six months; the giblets, three months.

How to use: Goose is a more popular food with Europeans than with Americans, but European cooking techniques are indicative of how you, too, can enjoy this waterfowl. Roasting and stewing are the most popular cooking methods. Apple, chestnut, sausage, or sauerkraut mixtures are favored for roast goose stuffings. Dried fruits are stewed with goose blood and giblets for the German *Schwarzsauer*. The Danes often stew goose in thyme-flavored water, then serve it sliced. For a French *cassoulet*, goose, sausage, and white beans are used.

In addition to goose meat, the goose liver is a renowned delicacy. Hungarians roast or stew the livers or use them in stuffing. In France the goose livers used in making the magnificent appetizer spread called *pâté de fois gras* are obtained from geese that are specially raised and fattened for this purpose. (See also *Poultry*.)

Roast Wild Goose

A hunter's delight —

Salt the cavity of one ready-to-cook wild goose. Stuff the goose cavity loosely with quartered onions and apples. Truss bird; place, breast side up, on rack in shallow roasting pan. Lay bacon slices over breast or rub with salad oil. Roast, uncovered, at 400° following Goose Roasting Chart given below. Cover loosely with aluminum foil, if necessary, to prevent excessive browning. Discard onion-apple stuffing. Allow 1 to 1½ pounds wild goose per serving.

Note: If bird has had a fish diet or may be old, stuff loosely with peeled carrot or quartered potato; precook in simmering water about 10 minutes. Discard stuffing. Prepare and roast as above.

Goose Roasting Chart				
	Ready-to-Cook Weight	Oven Temp.	Roasting Time Stuffed and Unstuffed	Special Instructions
Wild Goose	2-4 lbs. 4-6 lbs.	400° 400°	1½-3 hrs. 3-4 hrs.	Stuff loosely with quartered onions and apples; discard stuffing before serving. Baste frequently with drippings.
Domestic Goose	4-6 lbs. 6-8 lbs. 8-10 lbs. 10-12 lbs. 12-14 lbs.	325° 325° 325° 325° 325°	2¾-3 hrs. 3-3½ hrs. 3½-3¾ hrs. 3¾-4¼ hrs. 4¼-4¾ hrs.	Prick legs and wings with fork so fat will escape. During roasting, spoon off fat in pan. Do not rub with oil.

The fresh gooseberries shown in the lower left corner indicate the proper ripeness for use in pies, jams, jellies, and preserves.

Roast Domestic Goose

Salt cavity of one ready-to-cook goose. Stuff, if desired. Truss bird; place; breast side up, on rack in shallow roasting pan. Do *not* rub goose with oil. Prick legs and wings. Roast, uncovered, at 325°, spooning off fat following Goose Roasting Chart, page 1053.

GOOSEBERRY—A tart berry, related to the currant, from a spiny shrub belonging to the sassafras family. Depending on the variety, the ripe berries range in color from green to dark purple. Unsweetened, fresh gooseberries are very low in calories (39 calories in ⅔ cup) and are a fairly good source of vitamin C.

Fresh gooseberries are available only during June and July. Those from the most common American variety appear amber with a slight, red blush when they are ripe and are slightly soft to the touch. They can be loosely covered and refrigerated one or two days before being used.

Gooseberries are used more frequently on the European continent than they are in America. They are particularly popular in Great Britain where they were introduced in the 1500s. Gooseberries are most fre-quently used in pies, but they also make delicious jellies. When fresh berries are not available, substitute equally tasty canned gooseberries. (See also *Berry*.)

Fresh Gooseberry Pie

Plain Pastry for 2-crust 9-inch pie (See *Pastry*)

. . .

3 cups gooseberries
1½ cups sugar
3 tablespoons quick-cooking tapioca
¼ teaspoon salt
2 tablespoons butter or margarine

Roll out half of pastry for bottom crust and line pie plate. Crush ½ *cup* of the gooseberries. In a saucepan combine crushed gooseberries, sugar, tapioca, and salt. Cook and stir till mixture is thick and bubbly. Add remaining berries. Pour into pastry-lined shell. Dot with butter.

Roll out remaining pastry and adjust over top of pie, cutting slits for escape of steam; seal. Bake at 400° till crust is browned, about 30 to 40 minutes. Serve pie while still warm.

Gooseberry Cups

1 16-ounce can gooseberries
2 3-ounce packages lemon-flavored gelatin
½ cup sugar
2 cups orange juice

. . .

1 cup sliced celery
¼ cup broken walnuts

Drain gooseberries, reserving syrup. Add enough water to syrup to make 1½ cups; add gelatin and sugar. Heat to boiling, stirring till the gelatin and sugar are dissolved. Remove from heat. Stir in orange juice. Chill till partially set. Fold in drained gooseberries, celery, and nuts. Pour into ten ½-cup molds. Chill molds till firm. To serve, unmold on lettuce-lined plates. Makes 10 servings.

GOOSEBERRY FOOL—An English dessert consisting of stewed, sweetened gooseberries and light or whipped cream.

In rear are regular and baby Goudas. In foreground, Edam.

GOUDA CHEESE *(gou' duh, gŏŏ-)*—A semisoft to hard cheese with mild flavor. This cheese was first made near the town of Gouda in the Netherlands, but it is now made in many parts of the world, including the United States. It is similar in color, flavor, and texture to Edam cheese, differing only in its higher milk fat content.

Gouda may be molded into portions shaped like large, flat spheres, or it may be formed into small ovals and then enclosed in a red wax coating. These small units are often called "baby Goudas."

Wedges of this cheese make a pleasant addition to a cheese tray for appetizers or desserts. (See also *Cheese.*)

GOULASH—A Hungarian stew made of beef or veal and vegetables. Goulash is well seasoned with paprika and sometimes other spices. Its Hungarian name is *gulyas*. (See also *Hungarian Cookery.*)

GOURMANDISE CHEESE *(gŏŏr' muhn dēz', gōrm'-)*—A creamy, soft dessert cheese made in France. Flavored with kirsch or cherry extract, gourmandise is pasteurized or cooked after it is made. (See also *Cheese.*)

Gourmandise is primarily served as a dessert cheese.

GOURMET *(gŏŏr' mā)*—A person who is an expert in judging foods and beverages. Foods that appeal to the highly trained taste buds of such an epicure are often termed gourmet foods.

GRAHAM CRACKER—A sweet cracker or wafer made from whole wheat flour. Honey is often used as a portion of the sweetening. Served with milk, these crackers are delicious as a snack. Graham crackers are also frequently crushed for use in desserts or for piecrusts. (See also *Pastry.*)

Graham Cracker Pudding

A baked dessert —

Cream ¼ cup shortening, ⅓ cup sugar, and 1 teaspoon vanilla; add 1 egg yolk. Beat well. Stir in ½ cup raisins *or* snipped, pitted dates and ¼ cup chopped walnuts. Mix 2 cups fine graham cracker crumbs, 1 teaspoon baking powder, and ¼ teaspoon salt. Add to creamed mixture alternately with ⅔ cup milk. Fold in 1 stiffly beaten egg white.

Fill six greased 6-ounce custard cups. Bake at 350° for 25 to 30 minutes. Serve warm with whipped cream or a lemon sauce.

S'Mores

Toast marshmallows. Sandwich 2 hot marshmallows and one square of milk chocolate bar between two graham cracker squares.

Fruited Cheesecake

Combine 1 cup graham cracker crumbs and ¼ cup sugar; stir in ¼ cup butter or margarine, melted. Press on bottom and sides of 8- or 9-inch springform pan; chill. Combine 1 envelope unflavored gelatin (1 tablespoon) and ½ cup sugar; stir in one 6-ounce can frozen lemonade concentrate, thawed. Cook and stir till gelatin is dissolved; cool.

Beat 1½ cups cream-style cottage cheese till smooth; stir in gelatin mixture and 1 teaspoon vanilla. Chill till partially set. Whip 1 cup whipping cream; fold into cheese mixture along with one 16-ounce can fruit cocktail, drained. Spoon into crust. Chill cheesecake at least 6 to 8 hours or overnight. Makes 10 to 12 servings.

S'Mores have been a long-time favorite dessert at picnics. Both adults and children enjoy roasting the marshmallows, then sandwiching them with chocolate between graham crackers.

Chocolate-Mint Parfaits

1 4¼- or 4½-ounce package *instant* chocolate pudding mix
1 cup whipping cream
½ teaspoon peppermint extract
4 or 5 drops red food coloring
3 tablespoons crushed peppermint candies
½ cup graham cracker crumbs

Prepare pudding according to package directions. Cool. Whip cream; add extract, food coloring, and crushed candy. Layer pudding, crumbs, and whipped cream into 6 parfait glasses. Repeat layers. Garnish parfaits with additional crushed peppermint candy, if desired. Chill. Makes 6 servings.

Glorified Grahams

Line a 15½x10½x1-inch pan with 24 graham cracker squares. Mix together ½ cup butter or margarine, melted, and ½ cup brown sugar. Spoon over graham crackers. Sprinkle with 1 cup chopped pecans. Bake nut-topped crackers at 350° for 12 minutes. Break cracker squares apart. Makes 24 crackers.

GRAHAM FLOUR—A flour prepared from the whole kernels of wheat. The name honors Sylvester Graham, an American health-food advocate, who long ago recognized the nutritive value of whole wheat. Today, graham flour and whole wheat flour are considered synonymous. (See also *Flour*.)

GRAIN—Any seed or seedlike fruit from a grass plant. The most common edible grains are called cereal grains or cereals.

Grains, some of the first foods cultivated by early man, are believed to have been propagated 10 to 15 thousand years ago. Remains from an early civilization in what is now the Middle East indicate that wheat was being cultivated about 7000 B.C. Extremely old harvesting and pulverizing utensils that were used for wheat and other grains have also been uncovered by archaeological teams throughout the world.

These ancient people relied heavily on various grains as a source of food for both themselves and their livestock. In the Middle East, Greece, and Rome, the staple grains were wheat, barley, and millet. And as is true today, the orientals relied on rice. The American Indians, on the other hand, utilized many forms of corn (maize), the only type of grain that is indigenous to the Western Hemisphere.

How grains are produced and processed: Grains are planted in the spring or fall, depending on the variety of grain and the region where that grain is to be planted. In the northern United States, spring grain crops—wheat, corn, oats, grain sorghum, and rice—are most numerous; rye is the primary fall crop. Southern farmers, on the other hand, can often plant twice a year as in the case of oats since the milder winter does not harm some grain seeds. Corn, grain sorghum, and rice are the customary spring crops in this region; wheat and barley are fall crops.

Throughout the United States, grain production has become a highly specialized operation. The vast technological revolution of the last century has brought about improved crop quality, disease, pest, and weed control, and most importantly, mechanized grain farming and processing.

A need to feed the world's growing population has resulted in increased grain production. This has been accomplished by means of large-scale farming. Most grain crops are now planted and cultivated by farmer-operated machines, and are harvested, save for corn, by complex combines. Corn is mechanically picked from the stalks, husked, and then shelled off the cob.

From the raw grains harvested, innumerable grain products have been developed. For whole grain products, the grain is broken and recombined as in the case of whole wheat flour. For grain portions, the grain is broken and divided into bran, endosperm, and germ, and the parts utilized separately. For example, wheat bran is used by itself in some breakfast cereals.

Nutritional value: The composition of grains differs from one variety to another. In general, however, grains are composed primarily of carbohydrates and are relatively low in proteins. Although the quantities and types of vitamins and minerals present in whole grains also vary, their most notable dietary contribution is in the realm of B vitamins and iron.

When grains are processed, some of these natural nutrients are lost due to removal of portions of the grain kernels. Today, restoration and enrichment of processed grains with supplementary vitamins and minerals is widely undertaken according to legally defined limits. This improves the nutritive value of the processed foods.

Types of grains: Rice and wheat are the world's most important staple grains. These two along with barley, buckwheat, corn, grain sorghum, oats, rye, and wild rice are the best known grains used in one or more forms of food.

1. *Barley*—can be sown spring or fall because of its short growing season. Popular forms are pearl barley (the polished grain with outer shell or bran removed), barley flour, and barley malt (used in the manufacture of yeast and beer).

2. *Buckwheat*—is a quick-growing, easily milled grain. This pungent, strong-flavored grain is primarily processed into flour and blended with mild-flavored wheat flour.

3. *Corn*—consists of two main types: field or dent corn and sweet corn. Both can have yellow or white kernels. Field corn is processed into cereals, cornstarch, sugars, and corn oil. White dent corn is used for hominy; yellow and white corn, for cornmeal. Sweet corn with its higher sugar content and more tender kernels is the type eaten and enjoyed fresh, frozen, or canned either left on or cut off the corncob.

Potato-Corn Triangles

Good with creamed dried beef —

> ⅔ cup packaged instant mashed
> potatoes
> ⅓ cup shortening
> 1¼ cups sifted all-purpose flour
> 2 tablespoons sugar
> 4 teaspoons baking powder
> ½ cup cornmeal
> ½ cup milk

Combine dry instant potatoes and ⅔ cup hot water; stir till moisture is absorbed. Blend in shortening. Sift together flour, sugar, baking powder, and ½ teaspoon salt. Stir in cornmeal; add to potato mixture. Blend in milk.

Turn dough onto well-floured surface. Knead 3 or 4 times. Roll into 9-inch circle. Cut into 12 triangles. Place triangles on *ungreased* baking sheet 2 inches apart. Bake at 400° for 20 to 30 minutes. Makes 12.

4. *Grain sorghum*—has more protein and less fat than corn. In this country, it is used in the production of alcoholic beverages, oil, and starch. Asians and Africans utilize grain sorghum every day in porridges, breads, and cakes.

5. *Oats*—are primarily processed into oatmeal, either the ground or rolled form, and used for cereal. The low gluten protein content of oats makes this type of grain less suitable for use in flour form.

Lemon Crunch Parfaits

Combine 1 cup rolled oats; ½ cup brown sugar; and 6 tablespoons butter or margarine, softened. Mix well. Spread in 15½x10½x1-inch baking pan; bake at 350° for 10 minutes, stirring occasionally. Crumble oats mixture; cool.

With rotary or electric mixer, beat 1 cup cream-style cottage cheese till smooth. Add 1 cup milk, one 3¾ or 3⅝-ounce package *instant* lemon pudding mix, and 3 tablespoons lemon juice; beat 1 minute. Chill mixture thoroughly.

In parfait glasses alternate layers of pudding mixture and oatmeal crunch, beginning and ending with pudding mixture. If desired, top each with a dollop of whipped cream and a small amount of crunch. Makes 4 or 5 servings.

Cinnamon-Frosted Raisin Bars

> ¼ cup granulated sugar
> 1 tablespoon cornstarch
> 1 cup water
> 2 cups raisins
> ½ cup butter or margarine
> 1 cup brown sugar
> 1½ cups sifted all-purpose flour
> ½ teaspoon baking soda
> ½ teaspoon salt
> 1½ cups quick-cooking rolled oats

In saucepan combine granulated sugar and cornstarch. Stir in water and raisins. Cook and stir over medium heat till thickened and clear.

In mixing bowl cream together butter or margarine and brown sugar. Sift together flour, baking soda, and salt; stir into creamed mixture. Add quick-cooking rolled oats and 1 tablespoon water. Mix till the mixture is crumbly. Firmly pat *half* the mixture in a greased 13x9x2-inch baking dish. Spread with cooled raisin mixture. Stir 1 tablespoon water into the remaining crumbs. Spoon onto filling; pat smooth. Bake at 350° about 35 minutes. Drizzle with Cinnamon Icing. Cool; cut in bars.

Cinnamon Icing: Mix 1 cup sifted confectioners' sugar with ¼ teaspoon ground cinnamon. Stir in enough milk (about 1 tablespoon) to make mixture of drizzling consistency.

6. *Rice*—is utilized in two main forms: brown and polished. Brown rice consists of the rice kernels with only the husks removed. Both husks and bran are removed for polished rice. Brown and polished rice are sorted by length of the grains—long, medium, or short. Long-grain rice is preferred for home-cooking purposes. Rice flour, a less common product in the United States, is used chiefly by Asians.

Ham and Rice Casserole

> ¾ cup uncooked long-grain rice
> ½ cup chopped onion
> 2 tablespoons salad oil
> 2 cups cubed fully cooked ham
> 1 9-ounce package frozen cut
> green beans
> 1 10½-ounce can condensed beef
> broth

Cook rice and onion in oil till rice is lightly browned, stirring frequently. Add ham, beans, beef broth, and ½ cup water; heat to boiling. Turn into 2-quart casserole. Cover; bake at 350° till rice is done, about 45 minutes. Stir just before serving. Serves 5 or 6.

7. *Rye*—is usually milled into flour for bread due to its good proportion of structure-building protein. Light and dark rye flours are available.

8. *Wheat*—is the most popular grain in the United States. Some types are used for very definitive purposes. Durum wheat, for example, is the basis for all pasta products. But wheat's best known use is as flour. With controlled milling techniques, a variety of flour types can be produced—from high gluten bread flour to low gluten cake flour, from whole wheat flour to white flour. Other wheat products include farina (wheat kernel endosperms), bran (the outer kernel layer), and wheat germ.

Whole Wheat Rolls

Rich in nutrients and flavor —

> 2 packages active dry yeast
> 4 cups stirred whole wheat flour
> 3 cups sifted all-purpose flour
> • • •
> 2¼ cups milk
> ½ cup sugar
> 3 tablespoons shortening
> 2 beaten eggs
> Butter or margarine

In large mixer bowl combine yeast, *1½ cups* whole wheat flour, and *1½ cups* sifted all-purpose flour. Heat milk, sugar, shortening, and 1 tablespoon salt just till warm, stirring occasionally to melt shortening. Add to dry mixture in mixing bowl; add eggs. Beat at low speed with electric mixer for ½ minute, scraping sides of bowl constantly. Beat 3 minutes at high speed.

By hand stir in remaining whole wheat flour and enough remaining 1½ cups all-purpose flour to make a soft dough. Place in greased bowl, turning once. Cover; refrigerate. Two hours before serving, shape in rolls. Let rise till double (1½ hours). Bake at 400° for 15 to 20 minutes. Brush with butter or margarine. Makes about 48 rolls.

Banana-Bran Muffins

For best flavor, use fully ripe fruit —

Sift together 1 cup sifted all-purpose flour, 3 tablespoons sugar, 2½ teaspoons baking powder, and ½ teaspoon salt. Stir in 1 cup whole bran. Mix 1 well-beaten egg, 1 cup mashed *ripe* banana, ¼ cup milk, and 2 tablespoons salad oil *or* melted shortening; add all at once to flour mixture, stirring just to moisten. Fill greased muffin pans ⅔ full. Bake at 400° for 20 to 25 minutes. Makes about 10 muffins.

9. *Wild rice*—is harvested from a grass that grows in shallow lakes and marshes. It is not a true rice. Because wild rice is difficult to cultivate and harvest and because United States government regulates its production, wild rice is a luxury rather than a staple. (See *Cereal* and individual entries for additional information.)

Wild Rice and Beef Loaf

Surprise layer hides inside —

> ½ 6-ounce package long-grain and
>   wild rice mix (⅓ cup)
> ¼ cup chopped onion
> 1 tablespoon butter or margarine
> 1 3-ounce can chopped mushrooms
> 1 beaten egg
> 1 teaspoon Worcestershire sauce
> 2 beaten eggs
> 2 tablespoons fine dry bread
>   crumbs
> 2 pounds ground beef

Using 2 tablespoons of seasoning in rice mix package, cook rice following package directions. Cook onion in butter or margarine till tender. Drain mushrooms, reserving liquid. Mix the 1 egg, cooked rice, mushrooms, cooked onion, and Worcestershire sauce; set aside.

Mix 2 eggs, reserved mushroom liquid, crumbs, and 1½ teaspoons salt. Add meat; mix well. Pat ⅓ of meat into bottom of 9x5x3-inch baking dish. Top with rice mixture leaving ½-inch border on all sides. On waxed paper pat remaining meat to 11x7-inch rectangle. Invert over rice; discard paper. Press meat layers together. Bake meat loaf at 350° for 1¼ hours. Makes 8 servings.

GRAPE—An edible, juicy berry, ranging from pale green to deep purple in color, that grows in clusters on a vine. Its smooth skin is sometimes covered with a natural, white powdery substance called the bloom.

Although it is uncertain where this fruit was first grown, archaeologists know that *Vitis vinifera* grapes were grown by some early civilizations. It is believed this grape variety first grew in the Caspian-Black Sea region of Asia. Grape seeds have also been uncovered in Swiss archaeological finds and in the treasures of ancient Egyptian tombs. In addition, early writings of the Hebrews, Greeks, and Romans allude to the use and culture of grapes.

During these ancient times, completely different grapes were developing in the Western Hemisphere. Viking explorers finding such an abundance of grapes growing there called the region Vinland.

Later, settlers tried to plant European grapes on American soil. Attempts on the East Coast were unsuccessful because of unfavorable climate and soil conditions. In California, on the other hand, the European varieties flourished.

How grapes are produced: Grape production, called viticulture, is the world's largest fruit industry. Success in this venture, however, is not simple since grapevines will grow only under certain conditions.

Climate conditions followed by soil composition are the most important factors affecting growth and development of grapes. For optimum growth, grapes need a long, dry, warm summer and cold, yet mild winter. The soil should be a balance of fertile black soil and sand. European grapes are extremely sensitive to these conditions. In fact, some varieties will grow only in a few areas of the world. Most American varieties are more tolerant.

Grape production requires constant scrutiny. The vines are usually propagated by means of cuttings or grafts. Once planted, the vines are carefully trained by means of staking, trellising, pruning, and other complex techniques. When the grapes are ready to harvest, they are handpicked, although in the United States, mechanical pickers are rapidly replacing field hands for the task of gathering the grape harvest.

Grapes in an assortment of colors and flavors can complement poultry, fish dishes, and breads as well as other fruits.

Nutritional value: The largest portion of grapes' caloric content is in the form of sugars. One cup of grapes provides about 105 calories. Like all fruits, grapes also provide useful yet varying amounts of assorted vitamins and minerals.

Types of grapes: The numerous natural and intentional crossings of grape varieties account for over 8,000 varieties that are known today. These are differentiated according to how they will be used: for table use, wines, raisins, or juice.

The assortment of good table grapes for eating fresh is considerably wider than for more specific uses. For marketing purposes, the grapes must maintain fresh, good quality under shipping conditions. Some of the most popular varieties include the western varieties—Tokay, Emperor, Cardinal, red Malaga, Almeria, Ribier, and Thompson Seedless—and the eastern varieties—Niagara, Delaware, and Catawba.

Although most grapes can be fermented, only a limited number produce wines outstanding in flavor and bouquet. Most of these are of European origin. Some well-known types include White Riesling, Cabernet, Sauvignon, and Pinot Noir.

Even fewer grape varieties are suitable for drying into raisins. The two most popular are Thompson Seedless and Muscat.

A grape that is to be pressed for juice must withstand pasteurization or freezing without marked flavor change. In the United States Concord grapes are almost exclusively used for this purpose.

How to select: Grapes do not continue to ripen after the bunches are removed from the vines. The best tasting ones, therefore, are those picked fully ripe, then delicately handled from vineyard to market. High color for the variety usually indicates ripeness, sweetness, and full flavor. Dark varieties should be free of green casts. White ones are at their best when they have a decided amber tinge.

When selecting grapes, choose well-formed, nicely colored, good-looking bunches. Bunches with dry and brittle stems usually drop the grapes even with gentlest handling. Western grapes that have been injured by freezing have a dull appearance, become sticky, and drop from the stems easily. Similarly injured Eastern grapes shrivel and show milky or opaque pulp. Avoid those, too, with signs of decay indicated by mold, wetness, or staining of the packing containers. The appearance of a few small, sunburned, wrinkled grapes in a bunch does not indicate poor flavor or quality for the whole bunch.

There are grapes of some kind available in supermarkets about every month of the year. Perlette, the earliest, appears in early June followed by Cardinal and Thompson Seedless. Ribier ripens in August. Tokay in September, and Emperor in October. Because Emperor grapes can withstand controlled storage conditions, they are often available throughout the winter.

How to store: Grapes, being very perishable fruits, keep best when refrigerated, unwashed and uncovered, in the crisper. They will keep three to five days.

How to prepare: Wash all grapes before using. To separate them into small bunches, cut the stems with kitchen shears so that the clusters remain intact. Seedless grapes require no further preparation. For seeded varieties, halve the grapes and snip out the seeds with kitchen shears.

How to use: The popularity of grapes as a snack fruit equals that of apples or bananas. Grapes can add interest to many dishes, too, such as appetizer fruit cups and cheese trays, and fruit salads. Hot rolls seem incomplete without grape jelly. Even main dishes can include grapes as a sauce, stuffing, or garnish. And as a dessert, grapes excel in luscious fruit compotes and enticing fruit pies. (See *Fruit, Wines and Spirits* for additional information.)

Popular grape varieties

The varieties that are most frequently marketed are as follows:

Almeria—greenish yellow

Cardinal—reddish purple

Concord—blue; standard eastern variety

Emperor—red; late western variety

Tokay—red; large and oval

Lady Finger—pale green; very elongated

Malaga—white or red; round

Muscat—greenish yellow

Niagara—white; leading eastern table

Perlette—white; small and round to oval

Ribier—black; large and round

Thompson Seedless—white; small and oval; practically seedless

---

Fruit Sparkle Cup

Combine 1 cup honeydew balls; 1 cup halved, pitted, dark sweet cherries; 1 cup seedless green grapes; and ½ teaspoon snipped candied ginger. Chill. Spoon into 5 sherbet dishes. Slowly pour one chilled 7-ounce bottle lemon-lime carbonated beverage over the fruit mixture. Makes 5 servings.

Spiced Grape Punch

        6 cups water
        1 quart grape juice
        1 6-ounce can frozen lemonade
            concentrate
        1 6-ounce can frozen orange juice
            concentrate
        1 cup sugar
        4 inches stick cinnamon, broken
        6 whole cloves

In large saucepan combine water, grape juice, lemonade and orange juice concentrates, and sugar. Tie cinnamon and cloves in cheesecloth bag or place in tea ball and add to punch. Simmer about 15 minutes; remove cinnamon and cloves before serving. Serve punch hot. Makes 2½ quarts.

Refrigerated Fruit Salad

        1 13½-ounce can pineapple tidbits
        2 slightly beaten egg yolks
        1 tablespoon vinegar
        1 tablespoon sugar
            Dash salt
        1 cup pineapple-flavored yogurt
                . . .
        1 16-ounce can pear slices,
            drained
        1 11-ounce can mandarin oranges,
            drained
        1 cup seeded, halved red grapes
        ½ cup snipped, pitted dates
        ½ cup flaked coconut

Drain pineapple, reserving 2 tablespoons syrup. Combine reserved syrup, egg yolks, vinegar, sugar, and salt in 1-quart saucepan. Cook over low heat, stirring constantly, till mixture thickens *slightly* and *barely* coats a spoon. Cool to room temperature. Stir in pineapple-flavored yogurt.

Combine pineapple, pears, oranges, grapes, dates, and coconut. Fold in dressing. Cover and chill 3 to 4 hours. Makes 6 to 8 servings.

Cool midsummer finale

←Nectarine-Grape Compote can be served as a sparkling fruit dessert or fruit sundae sauce to be spooned over vanilla ice cream.

Fruity Ginger Ale Mold

        1 3-ounce package lemon-flavored
            gelatin
        1 7-ounce bottle ginger ale,
            chilled (about 1 cup)
        1 unpeeled apple, cut in wedges
        ½ cup chopped peeled apple
        ½ cup halved seedless green grapes
        1 8¾-ounce can pineapple tidbits,
            drained (⅔ cup)

Dissolve gelatin and dash salt in 1 cup boiling water. Cool to room temperature. Slowly add ginger ale. Chill till partially set.

Arrange apple wedges in 5½-cup mold. Pour in a little gelatin mixture. Chill till *almost* firm. Add chopped apple, grapes, and pineapple to remaining mixture. Pour fruit mixture over first layer. Chill gelatin till firm. Makes 5 or 6 servings.

Cranberry-Grape Salad

A flattering pink and red —

        2 cups fresh cranberries
        ¾ cup sugar
        1 cup seeded, halved red grapes
        ¼ cup broken walnuts
        2 cups miniature marshmallows
        ½ cup whipping cream

Grind cranberries through food chopper, using coarse blade. Stir in sugar. Cover; chill overnight. Drain, pressing lightly to remove excess juice. Add grapes, nuts, and marshmallows to *well-drained* cranberries. Whip cream; fold into fruit mixture. Mound in lettuce cups. Makes 6 to 8 servings.

Spiced Grapes

Select firm Tokay, Emperor, or Thompson grapes. Leave on stems. Snip into small clusters; wash and drain. Tightly pack grapes, 5 whole cloves, 5 whole allspice, and 2 inches stick cinnamon into one clean pint jar, being careful not to bruise fruit. (*Or* place the grapes in a small deep bowl.)

In saucepan combine 1½ cups sugar and 1 cup white vinegar; heat, stirring till sugar dissolves. Boil 5 minutes. Pour hot syrup over grapes; cover tightly. Refrigerate grapes for 1 or 2 days. Drain grapes well before serving. Makes 1 pint.

Fruited Chicken Breasts

> 3 large chicken breasts, skinned,
> boned, and halved
> 1 chicken bouillon cube
> ½ cup boiling water
> ¼ teaspoon grated orange peel
> ¼ cup orange juice
> 1 tablespoon chopped green onion
> 1 tablespoon cornstarch
> ½ cup seeded, halved red *or*
> green grapes
> Paprika
> Orange slices

Sprinkle chicken with salt; place in 10x6x1½-inch baking dish. Dissolve chicken bouillon cube in ½ cup boiling water; add orange peel, orange juice, green onion, and dash pepper. Pour over chicken. Cover with foil; bake at 350° till tender, about 50 to 60 minutes. Remove chicken breasts to warm serving dish.

Strain juices, reserving ¾ cup. In small saucepan blend together cornstarch and 2 tablespoons cold water; stir in reserved juice. Cook and stir till mixture is thickened and bubbly: cook 1 minute more. Stir in grapes; heat through. Spoon grape sauce over chicken; sprinkle with a little paprika. Garnish the sauced chicken with orange slices.

Burgundy Ham with Green Grapes

> 1 tablespoon butter or margarine
> 2 tablespoons sugar
> Dash ground ginger
> 1 2¼-pound fully cooked ham
> slice, cut 1½ inches thick
> · · ·
> ¾ cup red Burgundy *or* port
> 1 tablespoon cornstarch
> 1 cup seedless green grapes

Melt butter or margarine in large skillet; stir in sugar and ginger. Brown ham quickly on both sides in butter-sugar mixture. Remove ham. Blend wine into sugar mixture; cook and stir till mixture is boiling.

Combine cornstarch and ¼ cup cold water; add to wine mixture. Cook and stir till thickened and bubbly. Return ham to skillet; cover and cook over low heat for 15 minutes. Add green grapes; cook 1 to 2 minutes longer. Transfer ham to warm serving platter. Spoon green grapes and wine sauce over ham slice. Makes 6 servings.

Veal Veronique

> 6 veal chops, cut ¾ inch thick
> 2 tablespoons salad oil
> 1 chicken bouillon cube
> ½ cup boiling water
> ½ cup dry white wine
> 1 tablespoon cornstarch
> ¼ cup water
> 1 tablespoon snipped parsley
> 1 tablespoon chopped green onion
> 1 cup seeded, halved red *or*
> seedless green grapes
> 2 teaspoons lemon juice

Brown chops in hot oil; season with salt and pepper. Dissolve bouillon cube in the ½ cup boiling water; add to chops along with wine. Cover; simmer over low heat till meat is tender, 45 to 55 minutes. Remove chops to warm platter.

Skim fat from wine mixture. Combine cornstarch and the ¼ cup water; stir into wine mixture along with parsley and green onion. Cook and stir over medium heat till mixture is thickened and bubbly. Stir in red or green grapes and lemon juice; cook till grapes are heated through. Pour grape sauce over veal chops. Makes 6 servings.

Devonshire Green Grapes

> 3 cups seedless green grapes
> ½ cup dairy sour cream
> Crème de cacao *or* brown sugar

Wash grapes; drain well. Add sour cream; mix carefully, coating grapes well. Chill at least 2 hours. Serve in sauce dishes; pass crème de cacao or brown sugar. Makes 6 servings.

Nectarine-Grape Compote

> 8 nectarines, peeled and sliced
> 2 cups seedless green grapes
> 1 cup white grape juice
> 2 tablespoons orange-flavored
> liqueur
> 1 pint pineapple sherbet

In serving bowl, combine fruits. Add grape juice and orange liqueur; stir gently. Chill. To serve, spoon nectarine-grape mixture into dishes; top each serving with a scoop of sherbet. Makes 8 servings.

Green and Gold Ambrosia

    1 20-ounce can pineapple chunks
    2 large fully ripe bananas
    3 large Temple oranges
    ½ pound seedless green grapes
    ½ cup flaked coconut
    1 7-ounce bottle ginger ale,
        chilled (about 1 cup)

Drain pineapple, reserving syrup. Slice bananas on bias into pineapple syrup; drain. Peel and slice oranges, removing seeds. Wash grapes; snip into small clusters.

In large serving bowl arrange in sections, *half* the pineapple, bananas, and oranges; sprinkle with *half* the flaked coconut. Repeat to make second layer. Mound grape clusters in center. Chill. Just before serving, slowly pour chilled ginger ale over the fruit mixture. Makes 6 servings.

Concord Grape Pie

Slip skins from 1½ pounds Concord grapes (4 cups); set aside. Bring pulp to boil; reduce heat. Simmer, uncovered, for 5 minutes. Sieve pulp to remove seeds. Add grape skins.

In mixing bowl mix 1 cup sugar, ⅓ cup all-purpose flour, and ¼ teaspoon salt. Add 1 tablespoon lemon juice; 2 tablespoons butter or margarine, melted; and grape mixture. Pour sweetened grape mixture into one 9-inch *unbaked* pastry shell (see *Pastry*). Bake the pie at 400° for 25 minutes.

Meanwhile, sift ½ cup all-purpose flour with ½ cup sugar. Cut in ¼ cup butter till crumbly. Sprinkle atop pie. Bake 15 minutes more. Arrange Pastry Grape Leaves atop pie.

Pastry Grape Leaves: Cut leaf design from pastry with sharp knife. Mark leaf veins with the tip of a sharp knife. Bake pastry leaves on a cookie sheet at 450° for about 8 to 10 minutes.

Best "grapevine news" is a luscious dessert filled with succulent grapes. A crumbly baked-on topper and grape leaf-shaped cutouts dress up old-fashioned Concord Grape Pie.

For frosted grapes, brush clusters with slightly beaten egg white mixed with a little water. Sprinkle with sugar; dry on rack.

Grape-Syruped Crepes

1 cup sifted all-purpose flour
1 tablespoon sugar
1½ cups milk
2 eggs
1½ teaspoons grated lemon peel
2 teaspoons lemon juice
½ teaspoon vanilla

. . .

1 4-ounce container whipped cream cheese
⅓ cup chopped pecans
1 6-ounce can frozen grape juice concentrate, thawed (⅔ cup)
4 teaspoons cornstarch
2 tablespoons sugar

Combine flour, sugar, milk, eggs, ½ *teaspoon* lemon peel, juice, and vanilla; beat smooth. Lightly grease 6-inch skillet; heat. Remove from heat; spoon in 2 tablespoons batter. Rotate pan so batter is spread evenly over bottom. Return to heat; brown on 1 side only. Invert pan over paper toweling.

Repeat with remaining batter, greasing pan as needed. Spread unbrowned side of crepes with cheese; sprinkle with nuts. Roll up.

In large skillet gradually stir grape juice into cornstarch. Add ½ cup water. Cook, stirring constantly, till thickened and bubbly. Stir in sugar and remaining lemon peel. Add cream cheese- and nut-filled crepes; heat through. Makes 6 servings.

Grape Parfait Pie

Ice cream gives airiness —

1 envelope unflavored gelatin (1 tablespoon)
⅓ cup sugar
1¼ cups boiling grape juice
2 tablespoons lemon juice
1 pint vanilla ice cream
1 9-inch *baked* pastry shell, cooled (See *Pastry*)

Combine gelatin and sugar. Add boiling grape juice and stir till gelatin is dissolved. Add lemon juice. Add vanilla ice cream by spoonfuls, stirring till melted. Chill till mixture mounds when spooned. Turn gelatin mixture into baked pastry shell. Chill till firm.

Grape Conserve

Citrus fruits add tang —

Wash 4 pounds Concord grapes. Slip skins from pulp; reserve skins. Cook pulp till soft; sieve to remove seeds. Squeeze 1½ cups orange juice (about 5 medium oranges) and ½ cup lemon juice (about 3 medium lemons); reserve peels from 2 oranges and 1 lemon. Scrape excess white from the orange and lemon peels. Slice peel very thin. Cover with warm water and cook, uncovered, till tender; drain.

Add grape skins, 8 cups sugar, juices, and peels to grape pulp. Boil till mixture is thick and sheets from spoon, about 35 to 40 minutes. Add 1 cup broken walnuts. Pour into hot scalded jars. Seal at once. Makes ten ½-pints.

GRAPE LEAF—The large, tender, green leaf from the grapevine. Worldwide, there are many cuisines that utilize fresh grape leaves in cooking. Popular Near Eastern *dolmas* are simply grape leaves stuffed with any one of several meat mixtures.

GRAPEFRUIT—A somewhat round citrus fruit with a yellow skin and a juicy, acidic pulp. The word grapefruit, which originated in Jamaica, seems to have been coined because the fruits often grow in clusters, like grapes. As one of the largest fruits in the citrus family, grapefruit usually range from four to six inches in diameter.

Ancestor of the grapefruit is the pomelo or shaddock (so named for a Captain Shaddock who brought pomelo seeds from East India to Barbados). It is on the Malay Archipelago that the pomelo appears to have originated. By the 1300s, pomelo trees had been brought to Europe, but the fruits, then called Adam's apples, were not eaten. Instead the pomelo trees were used merely as decorative shrubbery.

Grapefruit, as we know them, were brought to America via the West Indies. Sometime after Captain Shaddock left the pomelo in Barbados, a natural mutation of the shaddock and the sweet orange occurred that produced the species most closely related to today's grapefruit. A Spaniard, Don Phillippe, then brought grapefruit seeds to America in the 1840s. For many years grapefruit were not popular eating fruit in this country. But early in the twentieth century, promotional attempts to increase their use were very successful.

Nutritional value: The grapefruit, along with many other citrus fruits, is outstanding in its contribution of vitamin C to the diet. And much to everyone's enjoyment, fresh grapefruit is low in sugars and, thus, low in calories, too. Half of a 4-inch grapefruit provides the day's requirement of vitamin C and contains only 40 calories.

Types of grapefruit: Grapefruit are categorized by the color of the pulp—white or pink —and by the seed content—seeded or seedless (less than five seeds). The most popular white varieties are the many seeded Duncan and the seedless Marsh. The Marsh, first grown in 1890 in Lakeland, Florida, is now the most widely produced variety. Popular pink grapefruit, mutations of the whites, include the seeded Foster and Thompson grapefruit, and the seedless Marsh Pink and Ruby Red grapefruit.

How to select: Some appearance characteristics of grapefruit are better selection guides than others. Juiciness is indicated by the heaviness of the grapefruit. A bright, smooth, fine-textured skin is another good indication of quality. Minor blemishes can be ignored, but bad bruises may indicate some interior damage.

Although grapefruit are not chemically treated to restore the natural color, grapefruit color cannot be relied on for quality. In other words, the fruit can be equally good whether the rind is pale yellow or russet. In addition, green-tinged grapefruit may be as ripe as full yellow ones. The extra chlorophyll that the grapefruit trees must produce for their new blossoms gives the ripe grapefruit already on the trees this greenish cast, technically known as "regreening."

Grapefruit are available throughout the year in the fresh, canned, or frozen state. Most fresh grapefruit found in stores from October through June are produced in Florida and Texas. California and Arizona grapefruit appear in markets from January through the summer months.

How to store: Grapefruit keep well. For best results, refrigerate them uncovered in the crisper. In this way, the grapefruit will stay fresh for one to two weeks.

How to use: The tangy flavor of grapefruit makes it an invigorating breakfast waker-upper, a first course, or a dessert. In place of the traditional sugaring, try sweetening the fruit with honey or brown sugar, then serve it chilled or broiled. Section or chop grapefruit to add refreshing flavor and texture to fruit cups, side dish or main dish salads, and desserts. Use grapefruit juice in beverage mixtures or as a recipe ingredient for molded salads and desserts. Or candy the leftover grapefruit peel for a piquant confection to serve at holiday time. (See also *Citrus Fruit*.)

Grapefruit-Crab Cocktail

A zesty appetizer —

Combine ½ cup mayonnaise or salad dressing, 2 tablespoons catsup, 1 tablespoon lemon juice, and dash bottled hot pepper sauce; chill.

At serving time sprinkle one 7½-ounce can crab meat, chilled, drained, flaked, and cartilage removed, with 1 tablespoon lemon juice. Alternate crab meat with one 16-ounce can grapefruit sections, chilled and drained, in lettuce-lined sherbet glasses. Pour the chilled mayonnaise-catsup dressing over the citrus-crab cocktails. Makes 8 servings.

Broiled Grapefruit

A cherry tops each half —

3 grapefruit
Butter or margarine
3 tablespoons sugar
¾ teaspoon ground cinnamon
Stemmed maraschino cherries

Have grapefruit at room temperature. Cut each in half; then cut a thin slice from the bottom of each half to make grapefruit sit flat. Cut around every section, close to the membrane — fruit should be completely loosened from shell. Remove core from each grapefruit half; dot with butter or margarine.

Combine the sugar and ground cinnamon; sprinkle over grapefruit halves. Place on broiler rack or in shallow baking pan; broil 4 inches from heat till heated through and bubbling, about 8 minutes. Garnish hot grapefruit with the stemmed maraschino cherries. Makes 6 servings.

Elegant Grapefruit

A variation of Broiled Grapefruit —

Prepare Broiled Grapefruit above, *except* omit dotting with butter, sugar, and spice.

Combine 6 tablespoons melted butter or margarine, 6 tablespoons orange-flavored liqueur, and 1 tablespoon sugar; drizzle butter mixture over cut fruit. Let stand at room temperature about 2 hours to marinate fruit. Broil the grapefruit as directed above or till the tops of the grapefruit are brown and bubbling hot. Makes 6 servings.

Apple-Grapefruit Molds

Lime gelatin adds refreshing flavor —

1 8-ounce can grapefruit sections
1 3-ounce package lime-flavored
   gelatin
1 cup diced unpeeled apple

Drain grapefruit, reserving syrup; cut up grapefruit sections. Dissolve gelatin in 1 cup boiling water. Add enough water to reserved syrup to make 1 cup; stir into dissolved gelatin. Chill till partially set. Fold in grapefruit and apple. Pour into six ½-cup molds. Chill till firm. Makes 6 servings.

Buffet Fruit Bowl

1 large banana
2 fresh medium pears
1 large apple
1 medium pink grapefruit
1 3-ounce package cream cheese,
   softened
2 ounces blue cheese, softened
½ cup chopped pecans

• • •

4 canned peach halves
Green grape clusters
Romaine
Cranberry-orange relish
Assorted salad dressings

Peel banana and score lengthwise with tines of fork; cut diagonally into crosswise sections. Halve pears; remove cores. Cut apple into wedges; remove core. (To keep fruits bright, use ascorbic acid color keeper or dip in lemon juice mixed with a little water.) Peel and section grapefruit. Blend cream cheese and blue cheese. Form into balls; roll in nuts.

Arrange fruits on bed of romaine in salad bowl. Top pear halves with cream cheese balls. Serve extra cheese balls on the side. Spoon relish into peach halves. Serve with assorted salad dressings. Makes 6 servings.

Grapefruit-Sherbet Ring

Refreshing lime flavor —

2 16-ounce cans grapefruit sections
2 3-ounce packages lime-flavored
   gelatin
1 pint lime sherbet
½ cup broken pecans

Drain and dice grapefruit, reserving syrup. Add enough water to syrup to make 2 cups. Add gelatin; heat and stir till dissolved. Stir in sherbet; chill till partially set. Fold in fruit and nuts; turn into 6½-cup ring mold. Chill till firm. Makes 8 to 10 servings.

Salad arrangement

Self-service is the key to successful buffet→ dining. Buffet Fruit Bowl presents fresh and canned fruits with a dressing assortment.

Grapefruit-Cheese Squares

Tart and tangy —

>   2 16-ounce cans grapefruit sections
>   2 3-ounce packages lemon-flavored
>   gelatin
>   . . .
>   1 8-ounce package cream cheese,
>   softened
>   2 tablespoons milk
>   1/3 cup chopped walnuts
>   1/4 cup halved maraschino cherries

Drain grapefruit, reserving syrup; add water to syrup to make 3½ cups. Heat *half* the syrup mixture to boiling, then add to gelatin and stir till dissolved. Add remaining grapefruit syrup mixture to the dissolved lemon gelatin; cool.

Arrange *half* the grapefruit in bottom of 9x9x2-inch pan. Carefully pour *half* the gelatin over fruit; chill till firm. Blend cream cheese with milk and walnuts; spread over firm gelatin layer. Chill.

Meanwhile, chill remaining gelatin till partially set. Arrange remaining grapefruit and cherries on top of cheese layer. Carefully pour partially set gelatin over fruit. Chill till firm. Makes 9 to 12 servings.

Immediately after Broiled Grapefruit have been cooked, garnish them with stemmed maraschino cherries. Serve while bubbly.

Citrus Perfection Salad

>   1 3-ounce package lemon-flavored
>   gelatin
>   1 tablespoon vinegar
>   1 16-ounce can grapefruit sections
>   1 cup finely shredded cabbage
>   1/4 cup finely chopped celery
>   2 tablespoons sliced pimiento-
>   stuffed green olives

Dissolve gelatin in 1 cup boiling water; add vinegar and ¼ teaspoon salt. Drain grapefruit, reserving syrup. Add water to syrup to make 1 cup; add to gelatin. Chill till partially set.

Fold in grapefruit, cabbage, celery, and olives. Turn into a 4½-cup mold. Chill till firm. Unmold on lettuce. Makes 6 servings.

Winter Fruit Soufflé

>   1 3-ounce package lime-flavored
>   gelatin
>   1/2 cup mayonnaise or salad dressing
>   1½ tablespoons lemon juice
>   2 tablespoons finely chopped
>   celery
>   1 16-ounce can grapefruit sections,
>   drained and diced
>   1 avocado, peeled and mashed

Dissolve gelatin in 1 cup boiling water. Add ½ cup cold water, mayonnaise, lemon juice, and ¼ teaspoon salt. Beat with rotary beater till smooth. Chill till partially set, then whip till fluffy. Fold in celery and fruit. Pour gelatin mixture into 4½-cup mold; chill till firm. Makes 6 servings.

Sunshine Citrus Cups

Bright color and perky flavor —

Drain one 8¾-ounce can crushed pineapple and one 16-ounce can grapefruit sections, reserving syrups. Combine reserved fruit syrups, ¼ cup sugar, 2 envelopes unflavored gelatin (2 tablespoons), and dash salt; heat and stir over low heat till gelatin is dissolved. Chill till cold but still liquid; stir in pineapple, grapefruit, and ⅓ cup broken walnuts.

Carefully stir in two 7-ounce bottles ginger ale, chilled (about 2 cups). Chill till partially set. Spoon into individual molds; chill till firm. Makes 8 servings.

Artichoke-Grapefruit Salad

Uses pink grapefruit for color variation —

> 1 15-ounce can artichoke hearts,
>   drained
> ¼ cup salad oil
> 2 tablespoons vinegar
> 1 tablespoon snipped parsley
> 1 teaspoon Worcestershire sauce
> ½ teaspoon salt
> ⅛ teaspoon pepper
> 3 cups torn iceberg lettuce
> 2 cups torn romaine
> 1 cup torn endive
> 2 pink grapefruit, sectioned

Cut each artichoke heart in half. Combine oil, vinegar, parsley, Worcestershire sauce, salt, and pepper; mix well. Pour dressing over artichokes in bowl; cover and chill 3 to 4 hours or overnight. In large bowl combine lettuce, romaine, endive, and grapefruit sections. Add artichoke hearts with dressing; toss lightly. Makes 6 to 8 servings.

Tangy Seafood Toss

> 1 16-ounce can grapefruit sections
> 1 tablespoon cornstarch
> 1 tablespoon sugar
> ½ teaspoon paprika
> ½ teaspoon dry mustard
> ¼ teaspoon salt
> ⅛ teaspoon pepper
> ¼ cup catsup
> 2 tablespoons salad oil
> • • •
> 4 cups torn lettuce
> 1 7-ounce can water-pack tuna,
>   drained and broken into
>   chunks
> ½ cup sliced cucumber
> ⅓ cup sliced radishes

Drain grapefruit, reserving 1 cup syrup. In small saucepan combine cornstarch, sugar, paprika, mustard, salt, and pepper. Gradually stir in grapefruit syrup. Cook and stir over medium heat till thickened and bubbly. Remove from heat; stir in catsup and oil. Chill thoroughly.

At serving time combine lettuce, tuna, cucumber, and radishes. Stir dressing then toss with salad mixture. Makes 4 servings.

Curried Chicken with Grapefruit

An inviting flavor combo —

> ½ cup water
> 1 12-ounce can vegetable juice
>   cocktail (1½ cups)
> • • •
> 1 chicken bouillon cube, crushed
> 1 2 to 2½-pound ready-to-cook
>   broiler-fryer chicken, cut
>   up and skin removed
> ½ cup chopped onion
> 1 teaspoon curry powder
> ½ teaspoon poultry seasoning
> ½ teaspoon salt
>   Dash pepper
> • • •
> 1 tablespoon all-purpose flour
> 1 8½-ounce can water-pack
>   grapefruit sections, drained

In 10-inch skillet combine water, ½ *cup* of the vegetable juice cocktail, and chicken bouillon cube. Add chicken, chopped onion, curry powder, poultry seasoning, salt, and pepper. Simmer, covered, till chicken is tender, about 45 minutes. Remove cooked chicken pieces from skillet.

Skim off excess fat from liquid, if necessary. Blend remaining vegetable juice cocktail into flour; add to skillet. Cook and stir till mixture is thickened and bubbly. Return chicken to sauce; top mixture with the drained grapefruit sections. Cover skillet and heat through. Makes 4 servings.

Apricot-Grapefruit Ice

A summer cooler —

> 1 12-ounce can apricot nectar
>   (1½ cups)
> 1 cup grapefruit juice
> 2 tablespoons sugar
> • • •
> 4 stemmed maraschino cherries

Combine apricot nectar, grapefruit juice, and sugar; stir till sugar is dissolved. Pour into a 3-cup freezer tray; freeze till *almost* firm. Using fork, break frozen mixture into small pieces. Spoon into four sherbets. Top each serving with a whole maraschino cherry. Serve the fruit ice immediately or freeze till serving time. Makes 4 servings.

GRASSHOPPER—1. A drink or dessert flavored and colored with green crème de menthe and often containing crème de cacao. 2. A small insect sometimes chocolate covered and served as an appetizer.

Grasshopper

1 jigger green crème de menthe
  (1½ ounces)
1 jigger white crème de cacao
  (1½ ounces)
1 tablespoon heavy cream
3 or 4 ice cubes

Shake all ingredients in a cocktail shaker. Strain into a cocktail glass. Makes 1 serving.

Lazy Grasshopper Parfaits

1 3¾-ounce package vanilla
  whipped dessert mix
2 tablespoons green crème
  de menthe
1 tablespoon white crème de cacao
½ cup chocolate wafer crumbs
  (8 wafers)
  Chocolate curls

Prepare whipped dessert mix according to package directions. Fold in crème de menthe and crème de cacao. Chill till mixture mounds when spooned, about 30 minutes. Layer in parfait glasses with chocolate crumbs, using about 1 tablespoon crumbs between each layer. Chill. Garnish each parfait with chocolate curls. Makes 4 servings.

Light, airy Grasshopper Pie garnished with whipped cream and whole strawberries is a luscious meal ending. Crème de menthe and crème de cacao combine in this mint green pie.

Grasshopper Pie

It's both pretty and delicious —

Combine 1 cup chocolate wafer crumbs (about 19 wafers), ¼ cup sugar, and 2 to 3 tablespoons butter or margarine, melted; press onto bottom and sides of 9-inch pie plate; cool.

For filling combine 6½ cups miniature marshmallows (¾ pound) and ¼ cup milk in top of double boiler. Heat, stirring constantly, over *hot, not boiling* water till marshmallows are melted. Remove from heat; cool, stirring every 5 minutes. Combine ¼ cup green crème de menthe and 2 tablespoons white crème de cacao. Add liqueurs to melted marshmallow mixture; blend together well.

Whip 4 cups whipping cream. Fold marshmallows into whipped cream. Chill till mixture mounds when spooned. Fill cooled crust; freeze till firm, 6 hours or overnight. Trim with whipped cream and whole fresh strawberries.

GRATE—To reduce a food to very fine particles by rubbing it against something rough. Grating a spice or citrus fruit peel releases its flavor. Cheese is grated so that it will melt more easily in a sauce.

GRATIN *(grat' uhn, grät-)*—A dish, such as a meat casserole, that has a golden brown crust. This crust is usually formed by baking the dish at high heat for a short time. The top of the dish is often sprinkled with bread crumbs or shredded cheese to give a browner and crisper crust.

Eggs au Gratin

An excellent brunch dish —

In skillet melt 2 tablespoons butter or margarine. Add 2 cups crisp rice cereal and mix gently. Spoon *half* the cereal mixture into bottoms of four 10-ounce casseroles.

In saucepan combine one 11-ounce can condensed Cheddar cheese soup, ¼ cup milk, and ¼ cup sliced ripe olives; heat through. Slice 6 hard-cooked eggs (reserve 8 slices for garnish). Fold eggs into soup mixture. Spoon into casseroles. Top *each* casserole with 2 hard-cooked egg slices; wreathe with remaining rice cereal. Bake casseroles at 400° till heated through, about 15 minutes. Makes 4 servings.

GRAVY—The name for the sauce, based on the meat juices, that is served with meat or poultry. Although the unthickened meat juices (*au jus*) are sometimes called gravy, this name is usually reserved for the sauce made by thickening these juices with flour, cornstarch, or another thickening agent.

Contrary to the opinion of many inexperienced cooks, good smooth gravy is not difficult to make. The one important step to making lumpless gravy involves separation of the starch particles in the thickening agent. When flour or cornstarch is added directly to a hot liquid, the starch particles clump together and form lumps. Once formed, these lumps are difficult to eliminate, but they can be prevented by initially coating the particles with fat or by mixing the starch with a cold liquid.

Although the end products are indistinguishable from each other, the two types of gravy—pan gravy and kettle gravy—differ in the way the starch is initially dispersed. Use pan gravy when there is a high proportion of fat to liquid. This method is very similar to making a white sauce. The flour, cornstarch, or other thickening agent is stirred right into the meat drippings, allowing the fat to coat the starch particles. The liquid is then gradually stirred in as the mixture cooks. On the other hand, use kettle gravy when there is a lot of liquid but not much fat in the meat juices. In this method the starch is first dispersed by mixing it with a cold liquid, usually water or

For smooth Pot Roast Gravy, shake cold water and flour together. Use wire whisk to slowly stir thickening into pan juices.

milk. The starch-liquid mixture is then stirred into the simmering meat juices.

With both types of gravy, constant stirring is also important in preventing lumps. If the gravy is cooked only until it thickens, it will have a raw starch taste. Therefore, simmer the gravy for a few minutes after the mixture starts to thicken.

If, despite every care, there are some lumps in the gravy you make, strain them out or whirl the gravy in a blender for a few seconds. If you measured the fat a bit too generously so that some rises to the top of your finished gravy, skim the excess off with a spoon or a piece of paper toweling, or with an ice cube that is wrapped in a piece of clean cloth.

In recent years, homemakers have welcomed the introduction of instant-type flour for making gravy. This flour has been pretreated so that it is less apt to lump than is regular flour. However, when making kettle gravy, the instantized flour still must be combined with some kind of cold liquid before stirring into the hot meat juices.

Probably the easiest way to ensure lumpless gravy is to use canned gravy or packaged gravy mix. These products are also very convenient when you are in a hurry or when you want to serve gravy with leftover meat or meat that does not have enough drippings to make gravy.

Gravy is probably most commonly served over potatoes as an accompaniment to meat, but this is by no means its only use. There are many other foods that are especially delicious when served with gravy. Try it over rice, dumplings, or stuffing; spoon hot gravy over a roast beef sandwich, and make it a hot entrée serving. Mushroom gravy served over meat loaf converts it from a plain to a special main dish. In fact, spooning the gravy over any meat dish makes the meat seem more moist.

Pot Roast Gravy

Lift cooked pot roast to hot serving platter, reserving pan juices. Skim most of fat from reserved pan juices. Add enough water to pan juices to make 1½ cups liquid.

Put ½ cup cold water in shaker; add ¼ cup all-purpose flour. Shake mixture well. Stir flour mixture into pan juices; cook, stirring constantly, till gravy is thickened and bubbly. Season the gravy with salt and pepper to taste. Simmer gravy for 2 to 3 minutes more, stirring occasionally. Makes 2 cups.

Perfect Pan Gravy is easy if you follow these hints. Pour pan juices into measuring cup. Skim off excess fat, reserving some.

Return reserved fat to pan. Use wire whisk to gradually blend in flour. Cook and stir till bubbly. Slowly stir in liquid.

Hurry-Up Gravy

Remove meat from roasting pan. Skim off excess fat from meat juices. Pour ¼ cup water into pan. Stir well to loosen crusty bits on bottom of pan. Blend in one 10½-ounce can condensed cream of chicken soup *or* cream of mushroom soup. Heat and stir over low heat. Thin with more water, if necessary. Makes about 1½ cups.

Sour Cream Gravy

Remove pot roast from pan. Skim fat from pan juices. Measure juices; add water, if necessary, to make 1½ cups. Blend 1 cup dairy sour cream and 3 tablespoons flour; gradually stir in juices. Return to pan. Cook and stir till thickened and bubbly. Season with salt and pepper to taste. Makes 3 cups.

Perfect Pan Gravy

Crusty meat bits add extra flavor —

Remove roast meat to hot serving platter. Leaving crusty bits in pan, pour meat juices and fat into large measuring cup. Skim off fat reserving 3 to 4 tablespoons. Add water or milk to meat juices to make 2 cups liquid; set aside. For 2 cups gravy, return reserved fat to pan. Stir in ¼ cup all-purpose flour. Blend reserved fat and flour together thoroughly. Cook, stirring constantly, over low heat till mixture is thickened and bubbly.

Important tip: Remove pan from the heat. Add reserved liquid all at once; blend well. Season with salt and pepper. If desired, add a dash of dried thyme leaves, crushed, and a few drops kitchen bouquet. Simmer, stirring constantly, for 2 to 3 minutes. Makes 6 to 8 servings.

Golden brown Giblet Gravy is the perfect accompaniment for stuffed turkey. The chopped giblets and giblet broth add meat flavor to the rich gravy. Serve it over mashed potatoes.

Giblet Gravy

Traditionally served with roast poultry, particularly chicken or turkey —

Place chicken or turkey giblets, *except* liver in saucepan. Add water just to cover giblets; salt lightly. Add a few celery leaves and onion slices to water, if desired. Cover; simmer for 1 to 2 hours for chicken giblets (2 hours for turkey giblets). Add the liver and continue to simmer for 5 to 10 minutes for chicken liver (20 to 30 minutes for turkey liver). Cool giblets in broth; remove and chop.

Remove roasted chicken or turkey to hot platter and keep warm. Leaving crusty bits in roasting pan, pour meat juices and fat into large measuring cup. Skim off fat reserving 3 to 4 tablespoons. For 2 cups gravy, return reserved fat to pan. Stir in 1/4 cup all-purpose flour. Blend together the reserved fat and flour. Cook and stir gravy over low heat till mixture is thickened and bubbly.

Remove pan from the heat. Add 2 cups liquid (meat juices plus giblet broth) all at once; blend thoroughly. Add chopped giblets. Season with salt and pepper. If desired, add a dash of dried thyme leaves, crushed, and a few drops kitchen bouquet. Simmer, stirring constantly, for 2 to 3 minutes. Makes 6 to 8 servings.

GRAY SOLE—A flatfish, often called witch flounder, belonging to the flounder family. It lives in salt water off the Atlantic coast and can grow to be 25 inches long. The meat of the gray sole is firm and white with a fine, delicate flavor. Most often this fish is purchased in fillets that vary in weight from two to four ounces each. Some of the smaller gray sole are sold as whole fish. (See also *Flounder*.)

GREASE—1. Animal fat obtained by heating meat until the fat melts out. 2. To cover with a thin layer of fat. Baking pans and skillets are commonly greased to prevent foods from sticking.

GREEK COOKERY—The foods, recipes, and serving styles that characterize the long-established cuisine of Greece.

As one of the first centers of civilization, Greece and its food culture has a history that can be traced back to antiquity. The ancient Greeks enjoyed food and dined quite lavishly. One of the special dishes of these people was a pudding made of gruel and animal's intestines.

In early Greece, only two meals a day were customarily eaten—a light meal at noon and a big meal later in the day. This second meal often consisted of enough food for a banquet and was usually divided into two parts—the first for eating and the second for drinking and conversing.

About 400 B.C., Hippocrates, an ancient Greek physician, treated disease with controlled diets. However, unlike the scientific nutrition of our era, this treatment was based primarily on imagination and superstition and often failed to produce the desired curative results.

The early Greek cuisine included several dishes that are still popular today. The Greeks claim that their ancestors developed the first white sauce and brown sauce as well as the first pastry. Surprisingly, one of the favorite dishes of the early Greeks was cheesecake. In fact, the most complete book on the early history of Greek food devotes a whole chapter to the praises of this delectable dessert dish.

Even in those days, the cook had trade secrets and the treasured position of master cook could be obtained only after working for years as a cook's helper. Through the centuries, Greek cooks have handed down recipes from generation to generation. Today, the Greek cuisine consists of many variations of recipes that have survived the centuries of Greek history as well as recipes that are new or have been adapted from the cuisines of other countries.

Characteristics of Greek cookery: As with all countries, Greece embraces many cooking styles. However, as a food style in general, several characteristics stand out—the wide use of olives, grapes, lemons, herbs, lamb, seafood, sauces, and vegetables and the famous Greek pastry.

Olive trees have grown in Greece so far back in ancient times that legend calls them gifts of the gods. Even recipes of other countries with à la Grecque in their names are understood to require olive oil as an ingredient. Olives (preferably ripe) as well as olive oil, find their way into many of the Greek rice dishes and salads.

The Greeks use both the fruit and leaves of their large grape crop. A portion of the fruit is used to make wine which is the common beverage at meals for Greeks from poor to rich. The tender grape leaves, stuffed with ground meat or other stuffings, make a delectable main dish.

Another indispensable ingredient in the Greek cuisine is lemon. Lemon halves or wedges or lemon juice are used as a matter of fact when cooking meats, fish, vegetables, and poultry. A lemon half impaled on a fork is used as a basting brush for roasted and broiled foods, and lemon wedges are always on the table at mealtime to be squeezed over foods at will.

Besides lemons, Greek cooks use herbs generously. Garlic and oregano are used in lamb dishes, thyme or oregano with fish, dill with eggplant and in spinach pie, marjoram and thyme with a bay leaf in tomato sauce. Baked fish, stuffed grape leaves, and rice stuffing for poultry are all, by Greek standards, improved with mint.

Lamb is the most popular meat of Greece. Traditionally at Easter, the Greeks roast a whole lamb over an open fire pit. Other favorite ways of serving lamb include stuffed, in casseroles, and in stews. Ground lamb and herbs are often mixed and used as a stuffing for grape leaves.

Since Greece is a peninsula, fresh seafood is readily available. This fact, coupled with the long periods of abstinence from meat in the Greek Orthodox church calendar, has resulted in the development of numerous seafood dishes as a part of the Greek cuisine. Although the Greeks frequently use the simple method of frying, they add a special touch to fried fish by marinating it before cooking. Fish is baked or broiled with lemon-oil sauce or stuffed with herbs, garlic, and onions. Squid is often stuffed with a mixture of cooked rice, dry red wine, and onions.

The Greeks are extremely fond of sauces. The most famous Greek sauce is an egg-lemon sauce called *avgolemono* sauce. This all-purpose sauce is used over meat, fish, vegetables, and in soups. Other basic Greek sauces include a tomato sauce and a very strong garlic sauce that is relished by garlic lovers but served only in the presence of understanding friends.

The Greeks love vegetables of all types. In fact, mixtures of vegetables layered in a baking dish then topped with crumbs are often used as a main dish with cheese and a salad. Tomatoes and green peppers are stuffed with a rice and meat mixture for baking. Artichoke hearts soaked in lemon water may be baked with onions and a lemon-oil sauce, or crumbed and deep-fat fried. Vegetable salads are another important part of this cuisine. Tossed salads often include wild chicory or dandelion greens as well as the standard lettuce, romaine, and tomatoes.

Eggplant is probably the most popular vegetable in Greece. It is served fried, stewed, and stuffed. Eggplant slices are also used in several *moussakas* with ground lamb or beef, white sauce, and cheese. On other occasions, eggplant halves are stuffed with a meat and cheese mixture, then topped with *avgolemono* sauce.

The Greeks are known for their rich sweet breads and pastries. Most of these mouth-watering delicacies are too rich to eat as dessert, so they are reserved for visitors and special occasions. In fact, most holidays are celebrated with a bread or pastry such as New Year's Bread for the first day of the year.

Phyllo or filo is the Greek all-purpose pastry. The dough is made of flour, water, and salt, then stretched into tissue-thin sheets. Stretching phyllo into sheets takes a lot of practice and so today, many Greek cooks buy it fresh from bakeries or frozen from specialty stores. To make the crust for cheese or spinach pie or for pastry triangles filled with cheese and egg, several sheets, all buttered, are used. *Baklava* is made by placing ground nuts between repeated phyllo dough layers, then bathing the layered dessert in a spicy honey syrup.

Although Greece has a cuisine dating from antiquity, Americans have not been aware of many Greek specialties until quite recently. Now, increased tourism to this land of the Spartans and Athenians has sparked an interest in Greek cookery. Since most Greek dishes use ingredients readily available in the United States, Americans can enjoy this cuisine, too. The following typical Greek dishes are sure to be interesting and delicious additions to your meals.

Karidopita (Walnut Cake)

A very special cake —

4 egg yolks
½ cup sugar
2 tablespoons orange juice
1½ tablespoons cognac
1½ cups ground walnuts
¼ cup fine dry bread crumbs
1 teaspoon shredded orange peel
½ teaspoon shredded lemon peel
1 teaspoon baking powder
¼ teaspoon ground cinnamon
⅛ teaspoon ground cloves

. . .

4 egg whites
¼ teaspoon cream of tartar
Whipped cream
Shredded orange peel

In mixing bowl beat egg yolks till light; gradually add sugar, beating till thick. Stir in orange juice and cognac. Combine ground walnuts, fine dry bread crumbs, the 1 teaspoon shredded orange peel, shredded lemon peel, baking powder, ground cinnamon, and ground cloves. Stir in egg yolk-sugar mixture.

Beat egg whites with cream of tartar till stiff peaks form. Gently fold egg whites into nut mixture till well distributed. Bake in well-greased and lightly floured 8x8x2-inch baking pan at 350° about 30 minutes. Cool slightly. Cut in small squares. Serve with whipped cream and shredded orange peel.

Tyropitakia (Cheese Pastries)

A unique cheese dessert —

1½ cups sifted all-purpose flour
1 cup shredded provolone cheese
½ cup butter or margarine
3 tablespoons milk
1 slightly beaten egg

In mixing bowl combine all-purpose flour and shredded provolone cheese; cut in butter or margarine. Stir in milk; mix well. Divide dough into 24 pieces. Roll each piece into a 5-inch strip. Shape dough strips into wreaths on *ungreased* baking sheet. Brush tops with slightly beaten egg. Bake at 350° till lightly browned, about 20 to 25 minutes. Serve pastries with an assortment of fresh fruit, if desired. Makes 2 dozen pastries.

Vasilopita (New Year's Bread)

2 packages active dry yeast
5½ to 6 cups sifted all-purpose flour
1½ teaspoons grated lemon peel
1 teaspoon crushed aniseed

. . .

1½ cups milk
6 tablespoons butter or margarine
⅓ cup sugar
1 teaspoon salt
3 eggs
1 slightly beaten egg yolk
1 tablespoon water
2 tablespoons sesame seed

In large mixer bowl combine yeast, *2 cups* of the flour, the lemon peel, and aniseed. Heat together milk, butter or margarine, sugar, and salt just till warm, stirring occasionally to melt butter. Add to dry mixture in mixing bowl; add the 3 eggs. Beat at low speed of electric mixer for ½ minute, scraping sides of bowl constantly. Beat 3 minutes at high speed. By hand, stir in enough of the remaining flour to make a moderately stiff dough.

Turn out onto lightly floured surface; knead till smooth and satiny, 8 to 10 minutes. Shape into ball; place dough in lightly greased bowl, turning once to grease surface. Cover and let rise till double, about 1 to 1½ hours. Punch down. Divide dough in 3 parts. Cover with the greased bowl and let the dough rest for 10 minutes.

Shape 1 part of dough in a flat, round loaf, 8 inches in diameter. Place in greased 9x1½-inch round pan. Repeat with second part, placing in another 9-inch pan. Divide remaining dough in half. Shape into 2 strands, each 18 inches long. Twist each strand like a rope and seal ends to form circle 7 inches in diameter. Place one dough rope atop each round loaf of dough.

Combine slightly beaten egg yolk and water; brush atop loaves. Sprinkle with sesame seed. Cover and let rise till double, about 30 to 45 minutes. Bake at 375° for 25 minutes. Remove from pans. Cool on rack. Makes 2 loaves.

Greek holiday breads

Vasilopita (New Year's Bread) and Chris-→ topsoma (Honey-Nut Bread) are traditional during the Christmas-New Year season.

Christopsoma (Honey-Nut Bread)

    1 package active dry yeast
 2½ to 3 cups sifted all-purpose flour
    ¾ cup milk
    4 tablespoons butter or margarine
    ¼ cup sugar
    ½ teaspoon salt
    1 egg
    ½ teaspoon grated lemon peel
          . . .
    ½ cup light raisins
    ½ cup chopped figs
    ½ cup chopped walnuts
    ¼ cup honey

In large mixer bowl combine yeast with *1 cup* of the all-purpose flour. Heat together milk, butter or margarine, sugar, and salt till just warm, stirring occasionally to melt butter. Add to dry mixture in mixer bowl. Add egg and grated lemon peel. Beat at low speed of electric mixer for ½ minute, scraping bowl constantly; beat 3 minutes at high speed. By hand, stir in enough of the remaining flour to make a moderately stiff dough.

Turn out onto lightly floured surface. Knead till smooth and elastic, about 5 to 10 minutes; shape into ball. Place in lightly greased bowl, turning once to grease surface. Cover, let rise till double, about 1 to 1½ hours. Knead in light raisins, chopped figs, and chopped walnuts. Let rest 10 minutes. Shape into round loaf. Place in greased 9x1½-inch baking pan. Let rise till double, about 45 minutes. Bake at 375° about 30 minutes. While still hot, remove bread from pan and brush with honey.

Kourabiedes (Butter Cookies)

Cognac provides a background flavoring —

In mixing bowl cream 1 cup butter or margarine thoroughly. Add ⅓ cup sifted confectioners' sugar gradually, creaming well. Stir in 1 tablespoon cognac and 1 teaspoon vanilla. Gradually work in 2 cups sifted all-purpose flour to make a soft dough. Chill 2½ to 3 hours.

Pinch off small pieces of dough and shape into oblong cookies. Center each cookie with a whole clove. Bake on *ungreased* cookie sheet at 325° for 25 to 30 minutes. (Cookies will not be brown.) Cool on cookie sheet, then remove. Dust cooled cookies generously and evenly with sifted confectioners' sugar. Makes about 2 dozen cookies.

Greek Salad

    1 medium head iceberg lettuce,
       chopped (6 cups)
    1 head curly endive, chopped
       (4 cups)
    2 tomatoes, peeled and chopped
       (1 cup)
    ¼ cup pitted ripe olives,
       sliced
    ¼ cup sliced green onion
    ⅔ cup olive *or* salad oil
    ⅓ cup white wine vinegar
    ½ teaspoon salt
    ¼ teaspoon dried oregano leaves,
       crushed
    ⅛ teaspoon pepper
    3 ounces feta cheese, cubed
       (¾ cup)
    1 2-ounce can anchovy fillets,
       drained

In mixing bowl toss together chopped lettuce and chopped curly endive; arrange on individual salad plates. Arrange tomato, sliced olives, and sliced green onion atop greens.

In screw-top jar combine olive *or* salad oil, wine vinegar, salt, crushed oregano, and pepper. Cover; shake vigorously to blend. Pour over salads. Top each salad with some cubed feta cheese and anchovy fillets. Makes 4 servings.

A bean slicer simplifies making French-style green beans After ends and strings are removed, just pull through bean slicer.

GREEN BEAN—A kind of kidney bean, also called snap bean and string bean, that is picked while green and immature. Unlike some members of this family which are first shelled before cooking and eating, green beans are used pod and all.

Some authorities believe green beans were native to Indonesia. On the other hand, there is strong evidence that the kidney bean family (of which green beans are a member) first grew in the Western Hemisphere. Whichever is true, the use and enjoyment of green beans as a food has spread throughout the world.

Nutritional value: As with many vegetables, green beans are low in calories, with one cup of cooked green beans adding only 31 calories. Since green beans are low in protein and fat, the primary energy source is in the form of carbohydrates. Green beans are also contributors of vitamins A and C and the B vitamin, riboflavin.

How to select and store: In some regions of the United States, fresh beans are available all year. Since the peak crops are harvested in spring and fall, however, fresh green beans may be a seasonal item in your area. Equally good choices are the canned and frozen forms of which there are several styles: whole, French-cut (sliced lengthwise), and kitchen- or home-cut (sliced diagonally) green beans.

To obtain quality fresh green beans, judge the beans by their appearance. Select bright green, blemish-free, and long, straight pods. Flatness or roundness of the pods varies with the variety of bean and is not a good quality indicator.

At home, put the unwashed fresh beans in plastic bags or covered containers and refrigerate. Use fresh beans as soon as possible for best eating flavor and texture.

How to prepare: To prepare the beans for cooking, wash them first in cold water. Cut off ends and remove any strings. Then either leave the beans whole or cut up in the desired style.

Green beans should be cooked in a small amount of boiling, salted water. To make sure that the beans retain their bright green color, do not cover the saucepan until the water returns to boiling. The time needed to cook green beans to the optimum eating stage, crisp-tender, will depend on how the beans are cut. Whole or one-inch cut pieces require from 20 to 30 minutes, while French-cut beans need 10 to 12 minutes.

How to use: Green beans, most commonly prepared as a side dish vegetable, may be an ingredient in other side dish and main dish recipes as well. When using them as a vegetable, vary the way in which *you* prepare green beans by adding seasonings, other foods, or sauces. The seasonings that enhance the flavor of green beans include butter, savory, basil, dill, tarragon, and oregano. To give the dish a southern flair, add a small dash of ham, bacon, or salt pork with green beans, or add butter and slivered almonds to make a gourmet amandine. Another time, give the beans added flavor by means of a hollandaise, cheese, or mushroom sauce. And for further menu variation, make green beans an addition to salads, soups and chowders, or meal-in-a-dish stews. (See also *Bean.*)

Dutch Green Beans

> 1 medium onion, sliced and
>   separated in rings
> 3 tablespoons butter or margarine
> 2 9-ounce packages frozen
>   French-style green beans
> 1/3 cup water
> 1 teaspoon salt

In saucepan cook onion in butter until tender, but not brown. Add beans and water; sprinkle with salt. Cover and bring to boiling; reduce heat and simmer the green beans till they are crisp-tender, about 5 to 7 minutes. Makes 8 servings.

Snappy Green Beans

In saucepan cook 4 slices bacon till crisp; drain, reserving 2 tablespoons drippings. Cook 1/4 cup chopped onion in reserved drippings till tender. Add 1 to 2 tablespoons tarragon vinegar, 1/2 teaspoon salt, and dash pepper. Pour vinegar mixture over 2 cups hot cooked, drained green beans. Crumble bacon atop beans for garnish. Makes 3 or 4 servings.

Mustard and Worcestershire sauce give Deviled Green Beans a robust flavor. Top with cornflake crumbs and a parsley sprig.

Creamy Green Beans

Zesty flavor —

> 2 9-ounce packages frozen cut
>   green beans
> 1 5-ounce can water chestnuts,
>   drained and sliced
>   . . .
> ½ cup finely chopped onion
> 2 tablespoons butter or margarine
>   . . .
> 1 cup dairy sour cream
> 1 teaspoon sugar
> 1 teaspoon seasoned salt
> 1 teaspoon vinegar
>   Dash pepper

Cook frozen green beans according to package directions. Add sliced water chestnuts; heat through. In saucepan cook chopped onion in butter or margarine till tender but not brown. Add sour cream, sugar, seasoned salt, vinegar, and pepper; heat through (do not boil). Drain beans; top with the sour cream sauce. Makes 6 to 8 servings.

Green Beans Caesar

> 1 cup bread cubes
> 3 tablespoons salad oil
> 1 tablespoon vinegar
> 1 teaspoon instant minced onion
> 1 16-ounce can cut green beans,
>   drained
> 2 tablespoons shredded Parmesan
>   cheese

Brown bread cubes lightly in the *2 tablespoons* salad oil. Remove from pan. In same skillet, mix remaining oil, vinegar, onion and ¼ teaspoon salt. Stir in beans; heat through. Add bread cubes and cheese. Toss gently. Serves 4.

Deviled Green Beans

> 1 16-ounce can cut green beans
> 1 tablespoon butter or margarine
> 2 teaspoons prepared mustard
> ½ teaspoon Worcestershire sauce
>   Dash *each* salt and pepper
> 2 tablespoons cornflake crumbs

Heat beans; drain. In small saucepan, melt butter. Stir in remaining ingredients *except* crumbs. Pour over hot beans; stir gently. Sprinkle with cornflake crumbs. Trim with parsley, if desired. Serves 4.

Tomato-Bean Combo

> 1 16-ounce can cut green beans,
>   drained
> 2 medium tomatoes, peeled,
>   chopped, and drained
>   (about 1½ cups)
> ¼ cup finely chopped onion
>   . . .
> ½ cup dairy sour cream
> ¼ cup Italian salad dressing
>   Romaine leaves
>   Tomato wedges

Combine cut green beans, chopped tomato, and chopped onion. Blend together dairy sour cream and Italian salad dressing; add to green bean mixture and toss lightly. Chill thoroughly, at least 2 to 3 hours. At serving time, spoon salad into romaine-lined salad bowl. Garnish salad mixture with tomato wedges. Makes 6 servings.

Vegetable-Meat Medley

Hearty home-cooking —

1 pound bulk pork sausage*
¼ cup chopped onion
3 tablespoons all-purpose flour
1 16-ounce can tomatoes, cut up
1 8¾-ounce can whole kernel corn
1 8-ounce can cut green beans

. . .

1 cup sifted all-purpose flour
1½ teaspoons baking powder
½ teaspoon dry mustard
2 tablespoons shortening
⅔ cup milk
3 ounces sharp process American
    cheese, shredded (¾ cup)

In skillet cook meat with chopped onion till meat is brown and onion is tender, breaking up meat as it cooks. Drain off excess fat. Blend in 3 tablespoons flour, ¼ teaspoon salt, and dash pepper. Stir in tomatoes and cook till slightly thickened. Drain corn and beans; add vegetables to meat mixture. Heat to boiling; spoon hot mixture into 4 individual casseroles.

Meanwhile, sift together 1 cup flour, baking powder, ½ teaspoon salt, and mustard. Cut in shortening; blend in milk and ½ *cup* of the cheese to form soft dough. Drop biscuit dough onto *boiling hot* mixture. Sprinkle with remaining ¼ cup cheese. Bake, uncovered, at 350° for 30 minutes, till brown. Makes 4 servings.

*Or, substitute ground beef for sausage and increase salt in meat mixture to ¾ teaspoon.

GREENGAGE PLUM—A round plum with greenish yellow skin and flesh. At full maturity, the sun-touched portion of skin may have a faint red blush. The name "greengage" is a derivation of the plum's characteristic green coloring and the last name of an English botanist, Sir William Gage, who imported this group from France. In France these plums are called *Reine Claudes.*

Because these are the sweetest of all plums, greengage plums are particularly suited for cooking and do well in desserts, jams, preserves, and salads. The fresh fruits can be purchased in late summer. Canned greengage plums are also available the year-round. (See also *Plum.*)

Greengage Plum Squares

1 30-ounce can greengage plums
1 3-ounce package *each* lemon- and
    lime-flavored gelatin
1 cup finely chopped celery
1 3-ounce package cream cheese,
    softened
3 tablespoons light cream
1 tablespoon mayonnaise

Drain plums, reserving syrup. Sieve plums. Add water to syrup to make 3½ cups; bring to boiling. Remove from heat; add lemon and lime gelatins. Stir till gelatin is dissolved. Add plums. Chill till partially set. Stir in celery.

Turn into 8x8x2-inch pan. Blend remaining ingredients. Spoon atop salad; swirl to marble. Chill till firm. Serves 9 to 12.

GREEN GODDESS SALAD DRESSING—A popular, creamy-rich salad dressing consisting of mayonnaise, chives, parsley, anchovies, vinegar, and spices.

Green Goddess Salad

1½ cups mayonnaise
¼ cup finely snipped chives
4 anchovy fillets, finely chopped
1 green onion, finely chopped
2 tablespoons snipped parsley
2 tablespoons tarragon vinegar
1 tablespoon crushed tarragon

. . .

6 cups torn romaine, chilled
3 cups torn curly endive, chilled
1 9-ounce package frozen artichoke
    hearts, cooked, drained, and
    chilled
½ cup pitted ripe olives, sliced
1 2-ounce can rolled anchovy
    fillets
2 medium tomatoes, cut in
    wedges (optional)

For dressing combine first 7 ingredients; mix well. Chill thoroughly.

In large salad bowl combine romaine, endive, artichokes, olives, rolled anchovies, and tomatoes. Top with desired amount of dressing. Toss until greens are well coated. Serves 6.

GREEN ONION—An immature onion, also called scallion and spring onion, that is identified by its enlarged white bulb and tubular green leaves. Five 5x1½-inch green onions contain 45 calories.

How to select and store: Fresh bunches of green onions are available to consumers throughout the year. Select those with fresh-looking, crisp, green tops and firm, bleached-white bulbs that extend two or three inches up the stem.

Green onions must be refrigerated in the crisper to retain freshness. Use a tightly covered container to prevent the onion odor from penetrating other foods.

How to prepare and use: Be sure to thoroughly wash the onions first in cold water. Only the root base and upper leaf portions of green onions need to be cut away prior to use.

Because of their relatively mild flavor, green onions may be used raw or cooked. Leave the onions whole and arrange them as part of a vegetable relish tray served with dips. As a topping for meats and vegetables or in salads and sandwiches, thinly sliced bulbs and lower stems double as a garnish and flavor additive. Cooked green onions are used in a variety of dishes just like other onions. (See also *Onion.*)

Salata

>   6 cups shredded lettuce
>   3 tomatoes, peeled and chopped
>   1 large unpeeled cucumber,
>   chopped
>   1 bunch watercress, chopped
>   1 medium green pepper, chopped
>   4 green onions, finely chopped
>   . . .
>   ¼ cup sliced pitted Greek *or*
>   ripe olives
>   3 tablespoons lemon juice
>   ⅓ cup olive *or* salad oil

Combine first 6 ingredients. Add olives, lemon juice, and 1 teaspoon salt; toss. Mound salad on platter. Garnish with additional tomato wedges, cucumber slices, and olives, if desired. Pour oil over all. Let stand 15 minutes to blend flavors. Serves 8 to 10.

Shrimp-Cucumber Ring

>   2 envelopes unflavored gelatin
>   3 vegetable bouillon cubes
>   ¾ cup mayonnaise or salad dressing
>   2 tablespoons lemon juice
>   1 cup whipping cream
>   1½ cups cooked, cleaned shrimp,
>   sliced
>   ¾ cup shredded cucumber
>   ¼ cup sliced green onion

Soften unflavored gelatin in ½ cup cold water; dissolve with bouillon cubes in 2 cups boiling water. Blend in mayonnaise and lemon juice. Chill till partially set; whip till light and fluffy. Whip cream; fold into gelatin with remaining ingredients. Turn into 6½-cup ring mold; chill till firm. Serves 8.

Polynesian Haddock

Place 3 pounds frozen haddock fillets, thawed, in greased 9x9x2-inch baking dish. Dot fish with butter or margarine. Bake at 375° for 25 minutes. Combine one 10-ounce can frozen condensed cream of shrimp soup, thawed; 1 cup dairy sour cream, 3 tablespoons lemon juice, ½ teaspoon salt, and ¼ teaspoon pepper. Blend thoroughly.

Spoon soup mixture over fish. Bake 5 minutes more. Sprinkle with 3 or 4 thinly sliced green onions before serving. Makes 8 servings.

Mushroom-Bacon Burgers

>   2 pounds ground beef
>   1 6-ounce can chopped mushrooms,
>   drained (1 cup)
>   8 slices bacon, crisp-cooked,
>   drained, and crumbled
>   ¼ cup sliced green onion
>   2 teaspoons Worcestershire sauce
>   1 teaspoon salt
>   8 hamburger buns,
>   split and toasted

Combine ground beef, mushrooms, bacon, green onion, Worcestershire sauce, and salt; mix well. Shape into 8 patties, ½ inch thick. Grill over *medium* coals 8 to 10 minutes. Turn; grill till desired doneness, 6 to 8 minutes. Serve in buns with additional sliced green onion and crumbled bacon, if desired. Makes 8 servings.

Planning a picnicking venture? Shape patties at home, then transport the chilled meat in a cooler to the campsite. Garnish grilled Mushroom-Bacon Burgers with additional green onion.

Hawaiian Ham Pie

Splendid for a special dinner —

Plain Pastry for 1-crust 9-inch
  pie (see *Pastry*)
1 pound ground fully cooked ham
⅓ cup fine dry bread crumbs
1 beaten egg
½ cup milk
2 tablespoons sliced green onion
1 tablespoon prepared mustard
1 20½-ounce can crushed pineapple,
  well drained
¼ cup brown sugar

Prepare pastry according to recipe. Flatten ball of dough on lightly floured surface. Roll ⅛ inch thick. Fit pastry into 9-inch pie plate; trim ½ to 1 inch beyond edge; fold under and flute.

Combine ham, crumbs, egg, milk, onion, mustard, and ½ *cup* of the pineapple. Spread mixture into pastry shell. Combine pineapple and brown sugar; arrange sugared fruit on ham mixture spoke fashion. Bake ham pie at 350° for about 45 minutes. Makes 6 to 8 servings.

GREEN PEPPER—A sweet, mild, capsicum pepper that is picked at the bright green stage of color. Green peppers are also known as mango peppers, sweet peppers, or bell peppers. Their thick-walled, pod-like structures may be oblong or bell-shaped, and may taper very slightly or more dramatically. Two of the popular varieties are California Wonder and Ruby King. When allowed to fully ripen, green peppers turn a brilliant red without flavor impairment.

Nutritional value: A serving of green pepper can add a substantial amount of vitamin C and a fair amount of vitamin A to the daily diet. At the same time, it is a delight to calorie-counters—one large, uncooked green pepper adds 22 calories.

How to select: Modern production has made possible year-round availability of green peppers. Largest supplies are harvested during late summer and early fall.

Select peppers that are firm, thick-fleshed, and well-shaped. The bright green skins should have an attractive gloss. Lower quality peppers can be identified by their thin walls which may be soft and wilted-looking. Pale color indicates immaturity. Cuts, blemishes, or punctures are signs of poor handling and will result in rapid decay.

How to store: Green peppers retain their good quality only for brief periods. Store them tightly wrapped or covered in the vegetable crisper of the refrigerator.

How to prepare: For use by themselves or as a recipe ingredient, green peppers should first be washed under cold water. Next, remove the stems, seeds, and white membrane. Green peppers may be left whole as the serving shell for exotic fillings or they may be cut up—chopped, sliced lengthwise or crosswise—when used for a relish mixture or other recipe ingredient.

Whole peppers are sometimes parboiled prior to baking in order to achieve overall tenderness. Immerse the green peppers in boiling, salted water, cook for three to five minutes, then drain thoroughly.

How to use: Green peppers are recommended for use in appetizers or main and side dishes. For appetizers and salads, they are most often used raw, while for hot dishes, cooking is preferred.

Appetizer uses of green peppers are varied. Slice them lengthwise as a vegetable relish or dipper. Finely chopped green pepper perks up the color and texture of dips, canapés, and hors d'oeuvres. For attractive serving, use whole pepper shells as containers for flavor-packed dips.

Popular main dishes using green peppers include pepper steaks, oriental sweet-sours, and Spanish-style meats and sauces, but peppers need not be limited to these. Add green pepper to meat loaves, omelets, casseroles, skillet dishes, and stuffings.

In salads and vegetable dishes, use green peppers as a flavor and texture additive as well as a garnish. Slice them crosswise to gain the look of the three- or four-lobed shape. (See also *Pepper*.)

Mapled Appetizers

Fruit, green pepper, and sausage links stay hot in a sweet-sour sauce —

Drain one 13½-ounce can pineapple chunks, reserving ½ cup syrup. Cut two 8-ounce packages brown-and-serve sausage links in thirds crosswise; brown lightly in skillet. At serving time blend together 4 teaspoons cornstarch, ½ teaspoon salt, reserved syrup, ½ cup maple-flavored syrup, ⅓ cup water, and ⅓ cup vinegar in blazer pan of chafing dish. Heat to boiling over direct heat, stirring constantly; cook and stir a few minutes more.

Add drained pineapple; cooked sausage pieces; 1 medium green pepper, cut in ¾-inch squares; and ½ cup drained maraschino cherries. Heat through. Keep appetizers warm over hot water (bain-marie). Spear appetizer pieces with cocktail picks. Makes about 150 appetizers.

Italian Anchovy Salad

Separate one 2-ounce can anchovy fillets, drained, into bowl. Add 2 large tomatoes, peeled and cut in thin wedges; 2 medium green peppers, cut in narrow strips; 12 pitted ripe olives; and 8 green onions, chopped.

Combine ¼ cup olive oil and 2 tablespoons vinegar. Drizzle over anchovy mixture. Sprinkle with freshly ground black pepper. Refrigerate about 1 hour. At serving time, spoon anchovy mixture over shredded lettuce. Makes 4 servings.

Parboil peppers first in boiling, salted water. Large muffin cups act as handy baking containers for stuffed peppers.

Turkey-Stuffed Peppers

On another occasion stuff sweet red peppers as well as green ones for a colorful look —

4 medium green peppers

. . .

1 tablespoon butter or margarine
¼ cup finely chopped onion
1 cup packaged precooked rice, cooked according to directions
1 8-ounce can tomato sauce with mushrooms
1½ cups diced cooked turkey *or* chicken
1 tablespoon snipped parsley
½ teaspoon Worcestershire sauce
Dash salt

. . .

¼ cup shredded Parmesan cheese

Cut off tops of green peppers; remove seeds and membranes. Precook pepper cups in boiling salted water about 5 minutes; drain.

Heat butter or margarine in saucepan. Add onion and cook until tender but not brown. Mix in the cooked rice, tomato sauce with mushrooms, turkey *or* chicken, parsley, Worcestershire sauce, and salt. Spoon filling into peppers; stand upright in small baking dish. Sprinkle tops with shredded Parmesan cheese. Bake stuffed peppers, uncovered, at 350° till hot, about 30 minutes. Makes 4 servings.

Indian-Stuffed Peppers

1 10½-ounce can condensed beef broth
1¼ cups water
1 6-ounce package long-grain and wild-rice mix

. . .

6 medium to large green peppers
1 3-ounce can broiled chopped mushrooms, drained
½ cup broken pecans, toasted

. . .

⅓ cup buttered bread crumbs

Combine beef broth, water, and rice mix. Cover and cook, stirring often, till rice is done, about 30 minutes. Meanwhile, cut tops off peppers, leaving shoulders on. Remove seeds and membranes. Precook peppers in boiling, salted water about 5 minutes; drain thoroughly.

Stir mushrooms and nuts into cooked rice mixture. Spoon about ½ cup rice mixture into each pepper. Place in 10x6x1½-inch baking dish. Sprinkle tops with bread crumbs. Bake at 350° about 25 minutes. Makes 6 servings.

Garden Pepper Boats

3 medium green peppers
¼ cup chopped onion
2 tablespoons butter or margarine
½ cup cooked baby limas
1 cup fresh-cut *or* canned corn
1 16-ounce can tomatoes, well drained and chopped
¼ teaspoon salt
Dash pepper

. . .

½ cup soft bread crumbs
1 tablespoon butter or margarine, melted

Remove tops and seeds from peppers. Cut in half lengthwise and cook in boiling, salted water 5 minutes; drain. Cook chopped onion in 2 tablespoons butter or margarine till tender but not brown. Add baby limas, corn, and chopped tomatoes. Mix well. Season pepper shells with salt and pepper; fill with vegetable mixture.

Combine bread crumbs with melted butter or margarine; sprinkle over stuffed peppers. Bake at 350° for 30 minutes. Makes 6 servings.

GREENS—The green leaves, and in some cases, stems of plants used as food. The most commonly used greens include spinach, cabbage, lettuce, endive, watercress, onion tops, and escarole. Others have long been used by southerners but less so by other people—dandelion greens, chicory, kale, turnip greens, collards, mustard greens, and chard are only a few.

Greens are highly nutritious as regards vitamin and mineral content. The dark green varieties are particularly outstanding sources of vitamin A.

Cooking greens is a matter of preference. They may be cooked and subtly flavored for a vegetable side dish. When harvested while still young, the tender, crisp leaves and stems also make tantalizing salads. (See *Afro-American Cookery* and individual entries for additional information.)

Green Salad Quintet

½ bunch watercress
6 romaine leaves
6 Boston lettuce leaves
4 escarole leaves
2 Belgian endives
6 radishes, sliced
1 green onion, finely chopped
2 tablespoons olive oil
2 tablespoons wine vinegar
    Dash *each* garlic salt, paprika,
    and pepper

Rinse first 5 ingredients; drain. Tear leaves in bite-sized pieces and slice Belgian endives. Combine greens with radishes and onion. Combine remaining ingredients. Toss salad dressing lightly with greens mixture. Makes 4 to 6 servings.

San Francisco Eggs and Spinach

Cook one 10-ounce package frozen, chopped spinach according to package directions; drain. Add dash *each* ground nutmeg and pepper. Blend ¼ *cup* of one 10-ounce can condensed frozen cream of shrimp soup, thawed, with 2 tablespoons milk. Mix remaining soup with spinach; heat through. Place in 4 greased 1-cup baking dishes. Break 1 egg into each. Spoon reserved soup-milk mixture over. Bake at 350°, about 15 to 20 minutes. Serves 4.

GREEN TEA—Tea that has been processed without allowing it to ferment. This tea, which is favored in the Orient, is characteristically paler in color (a greenish yellow) and milder in flavor than the fermented black tea that is preferred in the United States. Japan, Indonesia, and communist China are the major countries that produce green tea. (See also *Tea.*)

GREEN TURTLE SOUP—A delicate, clear soup made from the meat of a large sea turtle. The shell of this turtle is green, hence the name green turtle.

GRENADINE SYRUP (*gren' uh dēn', gren' uh dēn'*)—A bright red flavoring syrup. Although originally made of pomegranate juice, grenadine syrup now usually contains a mixture of fruit juices or artificial flavoring and coloring. This syrup is used primarily as an ingredient in cocktails and other beverages but can also be used in salads, desserts, and dessert sauces.

Trader's Punch

A sparkling drink —

2 cups orange juice
2 cups lemon juice
1 cup grenadine syrup
½ cup light corn syrup
3 28-ounce bottles ginger ale,
    chilled

Combine orange juice, lemon juice, grenadine syrup, and light corn syrup; chill thoroughly. Just before serving, rest bottom on rim of punch bowl and carefully pour chilled ginger ale down side of bowl. Makes about 4 quarts.

GRIBENE—The Jewish name for the crisp cracklings remaining after the fat of meat, especially poultry, has been rendered. A small amount of onion is sometimes added to flavor the cracklings. These crisp, crunchy bits, nicely browned and free of excess grease, are a treat when eaten and also when used as an appetizer with soup or crackers or as a between-meal snack food. (See also *Jewish Cookery.*)

How to season a griddle

Lightly grease griddle with unsalted fat. Heat slowly for several minutes. Cool, then wipe off excess fat with paper toweling.

GRIDDLE—A flat, almost rimless cooking utensil. Nonelectric and thermostatically controlled electric griddles are available.

A griddle is probably most commonly used to fry pancakes, but it may also be used to cook bacon, eggs, quick-cook steaks, French toast, and grilled sandwiches. It also doubles as a warming tray for rolls or hot appetizers. (See *Appliance, Utensil* for additional information.)

GRIDDLE CAKE—Another name for a pancake cooked on a griddle. Wheat flour, buckwheat flour, cornmeal, and oatmeal are all used to make griddle cakes.

During the days of the American pioneer, griddle cakes were extremely popular because they were one of the few hot breads that could be cooked over the campfire or in ovenless cabins. (See also *Pancake.*)

Cornmeal Griddle Cakes

    1½ cups yellow cornmeal
    ¼ cup all-purpose flour
    1 teaspoon baking soda
    1 teaspoon sugar
    2 cups buttermilk
    2 tablespoons salad oil
    1 slightly beaten egg yolk
    1 stiffly beaten egg white

Combine cornmeal, flour, baking soda, 1 teaspoon salt, and sugar. Add buttermilk, oil, and egg yolk; blend well. Fold in egg white. Let stand 10 minutes. Bake on hot, lightly greased griddle. Makes 16 four-inch griddle cakes.

GRILL—1. Cooking equipment consisting of parallel bars or a grid over a heat source. 2. To cook on a griddle, a charcoal grill, or under a broiler. Grilled food has a browned surface. (See also *Barbecue.*)

Grilled Tomatoes

At your next outdoor barbecue, grill these peppy tomatoes alongside the meat —

Cut tomatoes in half. Brush cut surfaces with bottled Italian-style salad dressing; sprinkle with salt, pepper, and dried basil leaves, crushed. Heat, cut side up, on aluminum foil or greased grill over *hot* coals till hot through, about 10 minutes (don't turn). Then serve with your barbecued meat.

Grilled Sausage Treats

A quick main dish —

Spread large slices of bologna or salami with prepared mustard. Center each with ½-inch cube sharp process American cheese *or* slice of candied dill pickle. Overlap two opposite sides of meat; repeat with 2 remaining sides. Insert skewer to hold meat together. Thread several meat foldovers on skewer; top with pimiento-stuffed green olive.

Broil over *hot* coals till meat is lightly browned, about 10 minutes, brushing frequently with bottled Italian-style salad dressing.

Turkey Double-Decker

Almost a meal in itself —

    18 slices rye bread
       Mayonnaise or salad dressing
    6 slices process Swiss cheese
    1½ cups finely chopped cabbage
    6 slices boiled ham

           • • •

       Mayonnaise or salad dressing
    6 slices cooked turkey
       Butter or margarine, softened

Spread one side of each slice bread with mayonnaise. On *each* of 6 slices bread stack 1 slice cheese, about 2 tablespoons cabbage, and 1 slice ham. Cover with second slice bread, mayonnaise-side down; spread top side with mayonnaise. Cover with 1 slice turkey, about 2 tablespoons cabbage, and third slice bread.

Spread top of sandwiches with butter or margarine. Place on medium-hot griddle, buttered side down. Spread top slices with butter or margarine. Grill sandwiches till browned, about 12 to 15 minutes, turning once. Makes 6 servings.

Grilled Salmonwiches

Sesame seed coats the outside —

> 1 7¾-ounce can salmon
> ⅓ cup milk
> 2 well-beaten eggs
>   Dash ground nutmeg
> ¼ cup finely chopped celery
> ¼ cup dairy sour cream
> 1 teaspoon prepared horseradish
> 1 teaspoon prepared mustard
> ½ teaspoon finely chopped green
>   onion
> ¼ teaspoon salt
> ¼ teaspoon dried tarragon leaves,
>   crushed
>   Dash pepper
>   • • •
> 8 slices bread
>   Sesame seed

Drain salmon, reserving liquid. Remove bones and skin from salmon; flake meat into bowl. In shallow dish combine salmon liquid, milk, eggs, and nutmeg. Blend together salmon, celery, sour cream, horseradish, mustard, green onion, salt, tarragon, and pepper. Spread salmon mixture evenly on 4 slices bread; top with the remaining bread slices.

Dip each sandwich into egg mixture; sprinkle with sesame seed. Cook on hot, lightly greased griddle, browning on both sides. Serves 4.

Grilled Beefwiches

A delicious use for leftover roast beef —

> 1 tablespoon dry onion soup mix
> 1 tablespoon prepared horseradish
>   Dash pepper
> 6 tablespoons butter or margarine,
>   softened
> 8 slices white bread
> 8 thin slices cooked roast beef
> 4 slices process Swiss cheese

Soften soup mix in 1 tablespoon water. Stir soup mix, horseradish, and pepper into butter or margarine. Spread on both sides of each slice bread. Top each of 4 slices bread with 2 slices beef, 1 slice cheese, then second slice of bread. Brown sandwiches on medium-hot griddle till cheese melts, about 10 minutes, turning once. Makes 4 servings.

GRIND—To reduce to small particles. Many products, such as ground beef, cornmeal, coffee, and grits, are purchased already ground. Other foods, such as cooked meats, fruits, vegetables, and nuts, can be ground at home using a grinder. Ground meats are popular for sandwiches and meat loaves, and fruits and nuts are often ground for use in cakes and cookies.

GRINDER—1. A piece of kitchen equipment used to grind foods. Both nonelectric and electric grinders have a variety of blades which can be used to vary the degree of coarseness. 2. A long sandwich on a roll containing meat and other ingredients such as cheese, lettuce, tomato, and pickles. Grinder sandwiches are often served with a spicy sauce. (See also *Sandwich.*)

GRISSINO (*gruh sē' no*)—The Italian name for long slender, very crisp bread sticks.

GRITS—Finely ground hominy, commonly used during American pioneer days and still popular in the Southern states. They are often served as a hot cereal and as an accompaniment to eggs and bacon.

A mixture of dry bread crumbs and Parmesan cheese sprinkled over Parmesan Grits Ring before baking gives it a crispy coating.

Parmesan Grits Ring

       5 cups water
 1½ teaspoons salt
 1¼ cups quick-cooking grits
       1 beaten egg
       1 tablespoon cooking oil
 ¼ cup fine dry bread crumbs
 ¼ cup grated Parmesan cheese

Combine water and salt; bring to boiling. Slowly stir in quick-cooking grits. Cook, covered, over low heat for 25 to 30 minutes, stirring occasionally; remove from heat. Pour hot mixture into 5½-cup ring mold which has been rinsed with cold water. Let stand 25 minutes.

Unmold onto large ovenproof platter. Combine egg and oil; brush on ring. Combine crumbs and cheese; sprinkle over ring. Bake at 375° till golden brown, about 8 to 10 minutes.

GROAT (*grōt*)—Coarsely ground, hulled cereal. Groats are commonly made from oats, wheat, buckwheat, barley, and corn. Corn groats are actually large grits.

GROOM'S CAKE—A dark fruitcake served at weddings. Traditionally, the white bride's cake is served at the wedding reception and small pieces of the groom's cake are sent home with the guests in remembrance of the celebration. (See also *Cake*.)

Groom's Cake

 3½ cups diced candied fruits and
             peels (1½ pounds)
 1¼ cups dark raisins (8 ounces)
 1¼ cups light raisins (8 ounces)
       1 cup chopped walnuts (4 ounces)
       1 cup chopped pecans (4 ounces)
       3 cups sifted all-purpose flour
       1 teaspoon baking powder
       1 teaspoon salt
       1 teaspoon ground cinnamon
       1 teaspoon ground allspice
 ½ teaspoon ground nutmeg
 ½ teaspoon ground cloves
       1 cup shortening
       2 cups brown sugar
       4 large eggs
 ¾ cup grape juice

These pieces of Groom's Cake are ready for the guests to take home. This dark fruitcake is full of fruits and nuts.

In mixing bowl combine candied fruits and peels, dark and light raisins, chopped walnuts, and chopped pecans. Sift together flour, baking powder, salt, ground cinnamon, ground allspice, ground nutmeg, and ground cloves. Sprinkle ¼ *cup* dry ingredients over the fruit mixture; mix well. Thoroughly cream shortening and brown sugar; add eggs, one at a time, beating well after each. Add remaining dry ingredients to creamed mixture alternately with grape juice, beating smooth after each addition. Pour the spicy batter over the fruit-nut mixture; combine the two mixtures thoroughly.

Line two 8½x4½x2½-inch loaf pans with paper, allowing ½ inch to extend above all sides. Pour fruit-nut batter into prepared pans, filling ¾ full. Bake at 275° till done, about 3 to 3½ hours. (If you place pan containing 2 cups water on bottom shelf of the oven, the fruitcakes will have greater volume and more moist texture.)

Cool cakes in the pans; remove. Enclose in foil or clear plastic wrap. (If you desire, first wrap cakes in brandy-soaked cloth.) Store in cool place several weeks. To prepare the packages, chill the cake thoroughly; cut the cake into tiny rectangles that will fit groom's-cake boxes. Makes about 80 pieces.

GROUND BEEF

Numerous ideas for preparing, storing,
and using this popular and versatile meat.

For hundreds of years, ground beef has been used around the world. The ancient Egyptians ground some of their meat and one of the favorite dishes of the medieval Russians was finely chopped beef which they ate raw. Today ground beef is the main ingredient in dishes of many countries. A sausage made of ground beef and veal is a Yugoslavian specialty. The Chinese combine meatballs made of ground beef with various sauces to make different dishes. Ground beef is also used to make Swedish meatballs, Italian lasagna, Mexican tacos, and German-stuffed cabbage rolls.

Ground beef is defined as meat ground from a steer or cow. Since steaks and roasts are very popular cuts, the homemaker may ask why some of the beef is ground instead of being used for these other cuts. The answer to this question is simple—grinding the meat makes it more tender. Any whole beef has muscles which are not tender enough to roast or broil. It is these cuts, such as the chuck, shank, brisket, short plate, and rib, which are commonly used for grinding into ground beef.

In the United States today, the popularity of ground beef is second only to that of beef steak. In fact, in recent years the demand for ground beef has risen to the point where the beef available for grinding after the steaks and roasts are cut off will not fulfill the demand. Consequently, grocers are purchasing extra wholesale cuts especially for grinding.

The popularity of ground beef is largely

due to its versatility, reasonable cost, and ease of preparation. It can be made into patties, meatballs, meat loaves, casseroles, spaghetti sauces, and sandwich mixtures. Its reasonable cost makes ground beef a relatively inexpensive source of protein and the ease of preparation enables the housewife to fix delicious and varied meals in a relatively short amount of time.

Nutritional value: Even though ground beef is generally made from less tender cuts, this does not affect its nutritional value for all cuts of beef contain approximately the same proportions and types of protein, vitamins, and minerals.

Like other meats, ground beef is a good source of high-quality protein. It's also a good source of minerals such as iron, copper, and phosphorus, and the B vitamins, thiamine, riboflavin, and niacin.

The caloric value of ground beef will depend on the amount of fat ground with the lean and also on the amount of fat added during cooking. As a general guide, a 4-ounce patty of uncooked ground beef yields about 245 calories when broiled.

Types of ground beef

When you stop at the meat counter of any supermarket, you are often confronted with hamburger, ground beef, ground chuck, ground round, and ground sirloin. Since all of these products look similar in the package and yet the prices vary widely, you no doubt wonder how these types of ground beef differ. Basically they differ in two ways—fat content and the cut from which the meat was ground.

1. If the package is labeled hamburger, the ground beef can contain up to 30 percent fat, according to government standards. This means that often additional fat

Giant meatballs

← Cheesy Stuffed Burgers hide a mushroom-onion stuffing inside. The quick-as-a-wink sauce starts with canned cheese soup.

has been ground with the meat since beef cuts usually do not have this much fat.

2. The same is not true with ground beef. This may contain up to 30 percent fat, but unlike hamburger no fat other than that normally attached to the beef cut may be added. This means that ground beef usually contains only about 20 to 25 percent fat. Ground beef cannot contain extenders such as nonfat dry milk, soybean products, cereal products, or water.

3. Meat ground from the chuck wholesale cut is called ground chuck and usually contains 15 to 25 percent fat. Since chuck steak and roast are both in demand, ground chuck is more expensive than beef ground from less popular cuts.

4. Some people like a leaner ground beef so they have round steak ground. This usually contains only about 11 percent fat. Because of this, ground round is often higher priced than ground chuck.

5. The most expensive ground beef commonly sold is ground sirloin. This type of ground beef makes up only a small part of the ground beef market and often must be specially ground since most people prefer to eat this fine-flavored meat as sirloin steak rather than ground beef.

How to select

When shopping for ground beef, base your selection on both the appearance of the meat and its intended use. Immediately after grinding, ground beef should be a bluish red color but after exposure to air for a short period of time the meat turns red, varying from pale red to bright red. Meat that is either bluish red or red identifies freshness. Ground beef that has been exposed to air for a prolonged period becomes brownish red. Although this meat may still be satisfactory when cooked, it is better to purchase ground beef that has no brownish color. Also avoid ground beef that appears dried out.

Since shrinkage during cooking is directly related to fat content, many homemakers assume that the leanest ground beef is the best buy. This is not always true. Actually, some fat (the U.S. Department of Agriculture's Consumer Marketing Service suggests between 15 and 30 percent) is necessary to give flavor and juiciness to the cooked ground beef.

When selecting ground beef, keep in mind the intended use. Shrinkage will be more apparent in patties or meat loaves than in skillet dishes, soups, and casseroles, so the leaner ground chuck and ground sirloin are most suitable for patties and loaves. Hamburger or ground beef, however, are fine for skillet meals, soups, and casseroles, if you drain off excess fat after browning the meat. Although the low fat content of ground round means shrinkage is slight, this meat makes a very compact patty unless there are any other ingredients that are added for moistness.

Because a pound of purchased ground beef is boneless, it will serve more people than a pound of T-bone steak. If the ground beef is to be used in patties, figure four servings per pound. However, if the meat is to be combined with other ingredients—soups, skillet meals, or casseroles—you can plan on six servings per pound of meat.

How to store

The refrigerator shelf life of ground beef is shorter than for steaks, roasts, and chops. In the grinding process more surface area is exposed to the air thus hastening drying out and spoilage of the meat, so one to two days is the maximum time that most ground beef should be stored in the refrigerator.

To keep the meat fresh, leave ground meat that has been prepackaged by the meat retailer in the original wrapper and store it in the coldest part of the refrigerator. Remove the market paper from ground meat not prepackaged and refrigerate it loosely wrapped in waxed paper.

However, if you have a home freezer, the storage life of ground beef can be lengthened to two to three months, but be sure to freeze the ground beef promptly after purchase before it has a chance to begin deteriorating. Wrap the meat tightly in any moisture-vaporproof material and freeze the wrapped meat at 0° or lower.

Ground beef may be thawed in the refrigerator or if tightly wrapped, under cold running water. The thawing method used usually depends on the amount of time you have. If time is really short, you can cook the ground beef without thawing it but be sure to allow a little extra time for cooking.

Although special sales on ground beef may sometimes seem irresistible, don't purchase the meat unless you have freezer space to store it. Without freezer storage, the short storage life of ground beef in the refrigerator can soon turn a bargain into a disaster of spoiled meat.

If you have freezer storage, purchase ground beef in quantities large enough for several meals and shape the unseasoned meat into patties, meatballs, or the desired amount for loaves before freezing. It is then easy to thaw only the amount of meat you need for one meal. Many seasonings intensify during freezing so it's recommended that meat be frozen without seasoning.

To freeze meatballs, place the shaped balls on a baking sheet, then freeze. When frozen transfer the meat to a plastic bag. Seal and return to freezer. An easy way to freeze ground beef patties is to seal the individually wrapped patties in a round container or plastic bag, then freeze.

Many casseroles, skillet dishes, and soups containing ground beef can be partially cooked and then frozen in meal-size portions. If you take advantage of this suggestion, the main dish for a meal can be ready in the time it takes to reheat the frozen dish. This is also a good way to take care of leftovers. The family will think they are eating a new ground meat casserole if you store leftovers in the freezer for a few weeks before serving them for a second meal.

How to shape

One of the simplest ways to vary a ground beef dish is to change its shape. Ground beef is equally delicious as patties, meatballs, meat loaves, and meat rolls and yet each variation of shape looks like a completely new dish.

No matter how you shape it, remember to handle the ground beef as little as possible. With minimum handling the loaf or patties will be juicy and light. Excessive handling makes a compact, drier product.

Patties: Probably the most common way to shape ground beef is into patties. Although patties are essentially quick and easy to shape, getting the patties the same thickness at the edges as they are in the center is often a problem.

There are several ways to make a uniform ground beef patty. Try using a ⅓- or ½-cup measuring cup. Gently pat the meat into the measuring cup then turn it out onto waxed paper and pat to a uniform thickness. Or, pat the meat mixture to an even thickness between two pieces of waxed paper and then cut the patties with a jumbo cookie cutter or large can with bottom and top removed. A third way is roll the meat into a long roll about three to four inches in diameter and then slice off patties ½ to ¾ inch thick.

Meatballs: If your family likes large meatballs, use a ¼-cup measuring cup to make each meatball the same size. You can also gauge the size of meatballs by making them a uniform diameter. Or, try patting the ground beef mixture out onto waxed paper and then cutting it into squares. Each square will make one meatball. About the only way to form the meat into balls is to roll it between your hands. If you wet your hands slightly with cold water, the meat mixture won't stick as much. Chilling the meat also helps prevent sticking.

Loaf or roll: The standard meat loaf is usually baked in a loaf pan but for a change, try making a meat loaf ring. After gently patting the meat mixture into a ring mold, turn it out into a shallow baking pan, if a crust is desired. However, if your family prefers a soft top, bake the meat loaf right in the ovenproof ring mold. The center of the meat ring makes a handy serving container for buttered peas, beans, carrots, potatoes, or other vegetables, sprigs of parsley, or a spicy tomato sauce.

If your family likes a meat loaf with lots of crust, a shallow pan is what you need. Shape the loaf so only the bottom is touching the pan. That way the top and sides will become crispy.

Or, make individual meat loaves in custard cups, muffin tins, or small casserole dishes. This way everyone is sure to get an equal-sized serving and preparation time is reduced because the smaller meat loaves will bake in less time than one large loaf.

Meat loaf shaping made easy

Sprucing up a plain meat loaf—Make slanting indentations across the top with the handle of a wooden spoon or spatula. Fill these grooves with a sauce or glaze, if desired.

Shaping a stuffed meat loaf or roll—Use waxed paper or foil as a guide. Pat the meat mixture out on waxed paper to the designated size. Spread the filling almost to the edge of the meat rectangle. Pick up two adjacent corners of the waxed paper and carefully pull it straight up and over. The waxed paper will act as a guide as the meat rolls over the filling. Seal the meat at the side seam and ends so the filling will not spill out.

Transferring a long meat roll to the pan—If this is your problem, once again the waxed paper comes in handy. Pick up all four corners of the waxed paper under the meat roll and lift the roll onto the baking pan. Then carefully slide the paper out.

How to prepare

When making ground beef patties, remember these basic points. A tender, juicy burger is achieved by handling the meat as little as possible, both before and during cooking. Avoid flattening the burger because this squeezes out the meat juices. As with any meat, overcooking dries out the ground beef patty and robs it of flavor.

In many recipes, the ground beef is browned before combining it with other ingredients. For even browning, break the meat up with a potato masher or fork. If the ground meat is shaped into meatballs before browning, brown only a few meatballs at a time and shake the skillet to keep them round and assure even browning.

Most of the ground beef purchased prepackaged is rather compact which can cause difficulty when mixing the meat with other ingredients. When mixing a meat loaf, this difficulty can be overcome by using this one-bowl mixing method. First, combine the dry extender such as bread crumbs or cracker crumbs with the liquid ingredients. Mix in any chopped vegetables and seasonings. Then, add the ground beef and mix lightly just until the ingredients are evenly combined. Overmixing the meat mixture will result in a compact loaf.

The tenderness of a meat loaf depends largely on the amount of other ingredients added. As ingredients such as chopped vegetables, bread crumbs, and liquid are added, the meat loaf becomes more tender. Although the preferences of your family will largely influence how tender you make the meat loaf, remember that a tender meat loaf is harder to handle than a compact loaf.

There are essentially four ways to cook ground beef—bake it, cook it on top of the stove, broil it, and grill it.

1. One of the easiest ways to cook ground beef is to bake it in the oven. Once the meat loaf or casserole is mixed up, it can be put in the oven to bake and it requires no tending while it is baking. Since the size and shape of meat loaves vary, a meat thermometer is the most accurate way to determine when the loaf is done. Follow the manufacturers' directions for thermometer use. If you don't have a meat thermometer, however, follow the time guides given in the recipe and gauge cooking time for the next meat loaf by noting how long it took to bake this loaf.

Meat and Potato Pie

Convenience foods make this dish quick —

Prepare 2 sticks piecrust mix according to package directions; roll out for 2-crust 9-inch pie. Line 9-inch pie plate with pastry.

Combine 1 pound ground beef, ½ cup milk, ¼ cup dry onion soup mix, dash pepper, and dash allspice. Lightly pat into pastry-lined pie plate. Top with one 12-ounce package loose-pack frozen hashbrown potatoes, thawed. Adjust top crust; seal and flute edge. Cut design in top pastry. Bake at 350° till browned, about 1 hour. Serve with warmed catsup. Makes 6 to 8 servings.

Reminiscent of Cornish pasties

This hearty Meat and Potato Pie is easy to →
fix with frozen hashbrowns and piecrust mix. Catsup adds the colorful finishing touch.

Cooking ground beef patties

Broiled

Cook 6 minutes on first side; turn and broil till done, about 4 minutes.

Panbroiled

Cook about 5 minutes on each side.

Grilled

Grill 6 minutes over medium hot coals; turn and grill till done, 4 minutes.

Beef-Mushroom Loaf

Drain one 3-ounce can broiled chopped mushrooms, reserving liquid. Add enough milk to liquid to make ½ cup. Combine liquid, 1 slightly beaten egg, 1½ teaspoons Worcestershire sauce, 1 teaspoon salt, ½ teaspoon dry mustard, 1½ cups soft bread crumbs, and dash pepper. Let stand about 5 minutes. Stir in 1½ pounds ground beef and mushrooms; mix lightly but thoroughly. Shape into loaf in 13x9x2-inch baking dish. Bake at 350° for 1 hour.

Combine 2 tablespoons catsup and 1 tablespoon light corn syrup; brush on loaf. Bake 15 minutes. Garnish with pimiento strips. Serves 6.

2. Probably the most versatile way to cook ground beef is on top of the range. Skillet meals, patties, soups, and meatballs can all be cooked by this method. Unless the ground beef is exceptionally low in fat, you won't need to add any fat. To keep patties from sticking, preheat the skillet, then sprinkle it lightly with salt. As the patties cook, pour off any excess fat.

Cheese and Beef Burgers

Combine ¼ cup catsup, 1 tablespoon finely chopped onion, and ½ teaspoon dry mustard. Add 4 ounces sharp process American cheese, shredded (1 cup), and 1 pound ground beef; mix well. Shape into 4 patties, ¾ inch thick. Panbroil in 1 tablespoon hot salad oil in skillet over medium-low heat for 6 minutes. Turn; cook 5 to 6 minutes longer. Serve the cooked burgers immediately in 4 hamburger buns, split and toasted. Makes 4 servings.

Vegetable-Meatball Soup

Rinse 1 cup large dry lima beans. In a large saucepan combine lima beans and 5 cups water; boil 2 minutes. Cover and let stand 1 hour. In skillet cook ½ cup chopped onion in 1 tablespoon butter till tender but not brown. Add onion to soaked lima beans with one 8-ounce can tomatoes, 1 cup sliced celery, 1 cup diced carrot, 1 bay leaf, and 2 teaspoons salt. Cover and cook slowly 2 hours.

Mix ¾ pound ground lean beef, ¼ cup fine dry bread crumbs, 3 tablespoons milk, ½ teaspoon salt, and ¼ teaspoon Worcestershire sauce. Shape into 1-inch balls; add to soup. Simmer 15 minutes longer. Makes 6 servings.

Skilletburgers

    1 pound ground beef
    1 cup chopped onion
    1 cup chopped celery
        . . .
    1 8-ounce can tomato sauce
    1 10¾-ounce can condensed
        tomato soup
    Dash bottled hot pepper sauce
    ¾ teaspoon salt
    ¼ teaspoon chili powder
    Hamburger buns, split and
        toasted

In skillet brown ground beef. Add chopped onion and chopped celery; cook till tender but not brown. Add tomato sauce, tomato soup, bottled hot pepper sauce, salt, and chili powder. Simmer, uncovered, about 30 minutes. Spoon ground beef mixture into toasted buns. Makes 8 to 10 servings.

Meatball Dinner

Soften 3 slices bread in ½ cup milk; add 1 beaten egg. In mixing bowl mix 1 pound ground beef, 3 tablespoons grated onion, 3 tablespoons snipped parsley, 1 teaspoon salt, and ⅛ teaspoon pepper. Combine bread and meat mixture. Form into 18 balls; roll in flour. In skillet brown meatballs in 2 tablespoons hot shortening; drain off excess fat.

Add 2 cups tomato juice, 1 cup water, ½ cup chopped carrots, ½ cup chopped celery, 1 teaspoon kitchen bouquet sauce, and ½ teaspoon salt. Cover; simmer 45 minutes. Serve meatballs and sauce with rice or mashed potatoes. Makes 6 servings.

3. Another popular way to cook ground beef patties is in the broiler. This method is relatively fast and gives a burger without a hard outer crust. Make the ground beef patties about ¾-inch thick and broil them 3 inches from the heat.

Mushroom Burgers

Combine ½ cup buttermilk *or* sour milk; ⅓ cup fine dry bread crumbs; one 3-ounce can chopped mushrooms, drained; 2 teaspoons instant minced onion; and 1 teaspoon seasoned salt. Add 1 pound ground beef; mix well.

Shape into 6 patties, ¾ inch thick. Broil 3 inches from heat for 6 minutes. Turn; broil 4 to 6 minutes longer. Serve in 6 hamburger buns, split and toasted. Makes 6 servings.

4. The arrival of warm weather means outdoor barbecues. One recent survey of homemakers' found that ground beef was the most popular meat for grilling. Plain beef patties are excellent for grilling because they are easy-to-prepare and cook quickly. However, for a change, try sandwiching shredded cheese and chopped onion or pickles between two thin patties. Seal the patties tightly before grilling.

Another popular way to barbecue ground beef is to combine it with other ingredients for a dinner-in-foil. This way the meat and vegetables all are cooked outdoors over the glowing coals.

Beef and Beans in Foil

Perfect on a camping trip —

Combine one 16-ounce can pork and beans in tomato sauce, ¼ cup catsup, 2 tablespoons brown sugar, 1 teaspoon instant minced onion, 1 teaspoon prepared mustard, and ½ teaspoon salt. Break up 1 pound ground beef with a fork. Stir into beans.

Tear off four 1-foot lengths of heavy foil. Divide bean-beef mixture in fourths and spoon onto foil. Top each mixture with a small cube of sharp process American cheese. Draw up 4 corners of foil to center; twist securely allowing room for expansion of steam. Bake over *slow* coals till meat is done, about 45 to 50 minutes. Makes 4 servings.

Uses of ground beef

The uses of ground beef are many and varied. Ground beef patties in a bun make a quick meal for the family and yet, a glazed ground beef loaf or ring is elegant enough to serve to company.

Seasonings: One of the easiest ways to fix up ground beef is through the use of seasonings. Salt and pepper are the standards used to season ground beef but also try seasoned salt or pepper, garlic salt, or hamburger seasoning. Onion, whether finely chopped, instant minced, or onion salt, is a natural partner for ground beef. Aside from spreading prepared mustard on your hamburger, you can get the mustard flavor by adding a little dry mustard to a ground beef mixture. Thyme, oregano, chervil, marjoram, basil, and chili powder all add distinctive flavors to ground beef. Fresh herbs such as parsley or dill can be used instead of the dried form. Since the fresh herbs are not as potent, substitute three times fresh for dried.

Ground beef patties take on a new dimension when you add a little tomato juice, broth, vegetable juice, milk, or club soda to the ground beef. This gives them a new flavor and also makes the patties juicier.

Another easy fix-up is to add a small amount of wine, Worcestershire sauce, broth, vegetable juice, or catsup to the skillet after the ground beef patties have been removed. Scrape the bottom of the pan to loosen all crusty meat bits, then heat the sauce and spoon over the patties. This quick sauce is bound to perk up the flavor and appearance of the ground beef patties.

Extenders: On one of those nights when there are unexpected dinner guests, it's easy to extend a pound of ground beef to serve six people. Just add ½ cup bread crumbs, oatmeal, cracker crumbs, or other extender to make a meat loaf. Or, add finely crushed cornflakes and an egg and make patties from the meat mixture. Or, mix in some rice and make porcupine meatballs. If you have more time to get dinner ready, extend the meat by making chili, goulash, a spaghetti sauce, a casserole, or one of the more elegant ground beef dishes.

Complementary ingredients: Of course, extending the meat is not the only reason for adding other ingredients to ground beef. Ground beef takes on a whole new dimension when combined with complementary ingredients. It can be used in sandwiches, meals-in-a-dish, casseroles, jiffy main dishes, and soups as well as special meat loaves and spaghetti sauces.

One of the favorite complementary ingredients for ground beef is tomato. Fresh tomatoes, canned tomatoes, tomato juice, tomato sauce, and tomato paste are all frequently used with ground beef. This compatible ground beef-tomato combination is essential in chili, beefburgers, lasagne, spaghetti sauce, many meat loaves, and numerous casseroles and meals-in-a-dish.

Savory Cabbage Rolls

       1 pound ground beef
   ½ pound ground pork
       1 cup cooked long-grain rice
       1 16-ounce can tomatoes, cut
           up (2 cups)
   ¼ cup chopped onion
   1½ teaspoons salt
           Dash pepper
     10 cabbage leaves
       1 tablespoon cornstarch
       1 tablespoon cold water

Combine ground beef, pork, rice, ¾ *cup* of the tomatoes, onion, salt, and pepper; mix well. Immerse cabbage leaves in boiling water for 3 minutes or just till limp; drain. Spoon meat mixture onto leaves; roll around meat, turning ends under.

Place cabbage rolls in large saucepan or Dutch oven; pour remaining tomatoes over rolls. Cover; simmer 30 minutes. Remove rolls to warm platter. Mix cornstarch with cold water; stir into liquid in saucepan. Cook over medium heat, stirring constantly, till mixture thickens and bubbles. Serve with cabbage rolls. Serves 5.

All made with oven meatballs

←Meatballs in Barbecue Sauce, Meatball Stroganoff, Meatballs in Sauerbraten Sauce, Spaghetti and Meatballs—try all four.

Another popular combination is ground beef and cheese. The simplest version of this combination is the cheeseburger which is merely a ground beef patty topped with cheese. The teen-age favorite, ground beef pizza, combines ground beef, cheese, and tomato. Cheese is also found in many ground beef casseroles and meals-in-a-dish.

Ground Beef Reuben

A favorite with a new twist —

   ½ pound ground beef
       2 tablespoons chopped onion
   ⅓ cup Thousand Island salad
           dressing
     12 slices pumpernickel bread
   ¾ cup drained sauerkraut, snipped
       6 slices process Swiss cheese
       6 tablespoons butter or margarine,
           softened

In skillet brown meat with onion; drain. Stir in salad dressing. Spread on *six* slices bread; top each with 2 tablespoons sauerkraut, 1 slice cheese, then remaining bread. Butter tops and bottoms of sandwiches. Grill sandwiches on both sides till the Swiss cheese melts. Makes 6 servings.

Ground beef can even become company fare when you add gourmet ingredients such as wine and sour cream. Meatballs in a wine sauce, ground beef stroganoff, or a fancy meat loaf are all ground beef dishes that are grand enough for company.

Teriyaki Miniatures

Let guests cook these at the table —

Combine 1 tablespoon soy sauce, 1 tablespoon water, 2 teaspoons sugar, ¼ teaspoon instant minced onion, dash garlic salt, dash monosodium glutamate, and dash ground ginger. Mix ½ pound lean ground beef and ½ cup fine soft bread crumbs; stir in soy mixture.

Shape into ¾-inch meatballs. Refrigerate till serving time. Spear on bamboo skewers; cook in deep hot fat (375°) in a fondue pot about 1½ minutes. Offer heated catsup and prepared mustard for dunking the meatballs, if desired. Makes 2½ dozen.

Planked Meat Loaf

A special occasion entrée —

> 2 beaten eggs
> 1 6-ounce can evaporated milk
> ½ cup finely crushed saltine
>   crackers (14 crackers)
> 2 tablespoons finely chopped onion
> ¼ teaspoon dried marjoram leaves,
>   crushed
> ¾ teaspoon salt
> 1½ pounds ground beef
>   Packaged instant mashed potatoes
>   (enough for 8 servings)
> 2 tablespoons sliced green onion
>   Grated Parmesan cheese
> 3 large tomatoes, halved crosswise
>   Italian-style salad dressing

Combine eggs, evaporated milk, cracker crumbs, onion, marjoram, and salt. Add meat; mix well. Pat into 8½x4½x2½-inch loaf dish. Bake at 350° for 1¼ hours. Remove from oven; let stand a few minutes. Remove from dish; place on seasoned plank or baking sheet. Prepare potatoes following package directions. Add green onion. "Frost" loaf with potatoes. Sprinkle with cheese.

Brush cut surfaces of tomatoes with Italian-style salad dressing; sprinkle with additional Parmesan. Arrange on plank with loaf. Broil 3 inches from heat for 5 minutes. Serves 6.

Sweet–Sour Glazed Loaf

Combine 2 beaten eggs; ¼ cup chili sauce; ½ cup crushed shredded wheat biscuit (1 large biscuit); ¼ cup chopped onion; ½ teaspoon salt; ¼ teaspoon dried marjoram leaves, crushed; and ⅛ teaspoon pepper. Add 1 pound ground beef; mix well. Shape into loaf in 11x7x1½-inch baking pan. Bake at 350° for 45 minutes.

Meanwhile, prepare sauce by draining one 8¾-ounce can pineapple tidbits, reserving syrup. Add enough water to syrup to make ¾ cup. In small saucepan combine 2 tablespoons brown sugar and 1 tablespoon cornstarch. Stir in reserved syrup, 1 tablespoon vinegar, and 1 teaspoon soy sauce. Cook, stirring constantly, till mixture thickens and bubbles. Stir in drained pineapple; heat to boiling.

Place meat loaf on serving platter. Spoon some of the sweet-sour sauce over top. Pass remaining sweet-sour sauce. Makes 4 or 5 servings.

Ground beef can also take on an international flair when you make lasagne, pizza, or Italian spaghetti sauce. However, the Italians are not the only ones who use this popular meat. From Mexico come ground beef tacos, enchiladas, and tamales. Versions of Chinese dishes such as chow mein and chop suey are often made with ground beef. This versatile meat is also used to make Hungarian goulash, Greek moussaka, or Swedish meatballs. Many other countries have their own special ground beef dish. Seasonings and other ingredients characteristic of a particular country are frequently combined with ground beef for a new dish with a foreign flavor.

Italian Meat Loaf

A delicious filled meat loaf —

> ½ cup coarsely crushed saltine
>   crackers (11 crackers)
> 1½ pounds ground beef
> 1 6-ounce can tomato paste
>   (⅔ cup)
> 2 eggs
> ½ cup finely chopped onion
> ¼ cup finely chopped green pepper
> ¾ teaspoon salt
>   Dash pepper
>   • • •
> ½ cup coarsely crushed saltine
>   crackers (11 crackers)
> 1 12-ounce carton small-curd
>   cottage cheese (1½ cups)
> 1 3-ounce can chopped mushrooms,
>   drained
> 1 tablespoon snipped parsley
> ¼ teaspoon dried oregano leaves,
>   crushed

In large mixing bowl combine the first ½ cup cracker crumbs, ground beef, tomato paste, eggs, onion, green pepper, salt, and pepper; mix well. Pat *half* of the ground meat mixture into the bottom of an 8x8x2-inch baking dish.

Combine remaining cracker crumbs, cottage cheese, chopped mushrooms, parsley, and oregano. Spread mixture evenly over meat in pan. Top with remaining meat mixture.

Bake at 350° for 1 hour. Let meat loaf stand 10 minutes before serving. Makes 8 servings.

As can be seen, these are multiple uses for ground beef. Almost every cook has a favorite casserole, meat loaf, or sandwich that uses this meat. But don't limit your cooking to the standard recipes. Try some new meat loaves, meatballs, spaghetti sauces, sandwiches, and other dishes made with ground beef. Include ground beef in the menu frequently and your family is sure to be pleased. (See also *Beef.*)

Oven Meatballs*

Keep these basic meatballs on standby in the freezer. It only takes a few minutes to heat them in one of the following sauces —

> 2 pounds ground beef
> 1½ cups soft bread crumbs
>   (3 slices bread)
> ½ cup milk
> ¼ cup finely chopped onion
> 2 eggs
> 1½ teaspoons salt

Combine all ingredients; mix lightly but thoroughly. Shape into 4 dozen *small* balls, about 1 inch in diameter. Place in 15½x10½x1-inch baking pan. Brown at 375° for 25 to 30 minutes. Divide meatballs into 4 portions. Wrap each portion separately in foil and freeze at 0° or less.

Meatballs in Sauerbraten Sauce

Thickened with gingersnap crumbs —

> ¾ cup water
> 1 beef bouillon cube
>
>   . . .
>
> 3 tablespoons brown sugar
> 2 tablespoons raisins
> 2 tablespoons lemon juice
> ¼ cup coarse gingersnap crumbs
> ¼ recipe Oven Meatballs* (12)
>   Hot cooked rice

Bring water and bouillon cube to boiling. Add remaining ingredients *except* meatballs and rice. Cook and stir to dissolve gingersnaps. Add frozen or not frozen meatballs. Cook, covered, over low heat for about 15 minutes, stirring occasionally. Serve over fluffy hot cooked rice. Makes 2 servings.

Meatball Stroganoff

> ¼ cup chopped onion
> 2 tablespoons butter or margarine
> 1 tablespoon all-purpose flour
> ¾ cup *condensed* beef broth
> 1 tablespoon dry sherry
> 1 tablespoon catsup
> ¼ recipe Oven Meatballs* (12)
> ¼ cup dairy sour cream
>   Hot cooked noodles

Cook onion in butter till tender. Stir in flour. Add broth, wine, and catsup. Cook and stir till bubbly. Add not frozen or frozen meatballs. Cover and cook over low heat 6 to 8 minutes (not frozen), or 10 to 12 minutes (frozen); stir occasionally. Stir in sour cream. Heat, but *do not boil.* Serve meatballs and sauce over noodles. Makes 2 servings.

Spaghetti and Oven Meatballs

> 2 tablespoons chopped onion
> 2 tablespoons chopped green pepper
> 1 tablespoon salad oil
> 1 8-ounce can tomatoes, cut up
> ½ cup tomato sauce
> 1 3-ounce can chopped mushrooms,
>   drained
> 1 teaspoon brown sugar
> ¼ teaspoon dried oregano leaves,
>   crushed
> ¼ teaspoon dried basil leaves,
>   crushed
> ¼ teaspoon garlic salt
> ¼ recipe Oven Meatballs* (12)
>   Hot cooked spaghetti

Cook onion and green pepper in oil till tender but not brown. Add next 7 ingredients; mix well. Add frozen or not frozen meatballs. Simmer, uncovered, 20 to 30 minutes, stirring occasionally. Serve over hot cooked spaghetti. Pass grated Parmesan cheese, if desired. Makes 2 servings.

Meatballs in Barbecue Sauce

In saucepan combine ½ cup catsup, 2 tablespoons butter, 2 tablespoons light molasses, 1 tablespoon vinegar, and 2 tablespoons water. Simmer, uncovered, for 15 minutes. Add ¼ recipe Oven Meatballs* (12); heat through. Serves 2.

Basic Ground Beef*

Use this frozen meat mixture as a shortcut to the following three recipes —

In skillet cook 2 pounds ground beef with 1 cup chopped celery, 1 cup chopped onion, and 1/2 cup chopped green pepper till ground beef is browned and vegetables are tender. Drain off excess fat. Cool quickly. Seal and freeze in three 2-cup portions in moisture- vaporproof containers. Makes 6 cups.

Beef and Rice Skillet

Meal-in-one dish —

Combine one 10 1/2-ounce can condensed cream of chicken soup, 1 3/4 cups water, 2 cups frozen Basic Ground Beef*, one 10-ounce package frozen peas, 1 cup uncooked packaged precooked rice, and 1/4 teaspoon salt. Cover and bring to boiling; reduce heat. Simmer till meat is thawed and peas and rice are tender, about 15 minutes; stir the meat-rice-pea mixture often. Makes 4 servings.

Speedy Beef Skillet

In saucepan combine one 10 3/4-ounce can condensed tomato soup; one 8-ounce can whole kernel corn, drained; 2 cups frozen Basic Ground Beef*; 1/2 teaspoon salt; and 1/4 teaspoon dried marjoram leaves, crushed. Cover and bring to boiling; reduce heat. Cook over medium heat, stirring frequently till meat is thawed, about 10 minutes. Add 4 ounces uncooked medium noodles and 1/2 cup water; cover and simmer till noodles are tender, about 15 minutes, stirring occasionally. Makes 4 servings.

Quick Chili on Buns

    1 15-ounce can chili with beans
    1 10 3/4-ounce can condensed
        tomato soup
    2 cups frozen Basic Ground Beef*
    1/2 cup chili sauce

    .   .   .

    8 hamburger buns, split and toasted

Combine first 4 ingredients. Cover: cook over medium heat till meat thaws, about 10 minutes. Serve the chili over buns. Makes 8 servings.

Cheesy Stuffed Burgers

    1 3-ounce can chopped mushrooms
    2 tablespoons chopped onion
    2 tablespoons butter or margarine
    1 cup dry bread cubes
    1 pound ground beef
    1 6-ounce can evaporated milk
    1 10 3/4-ounce can condensed
        Cheddar cheese soup

Drain mushrooms, reserving liquid. Cook onion in butter. Combine onion with 1/4 cup of the mushrooms, the bread cubes, 1/4 teaspoon salt, and dash pepper; toss with enough mushroom liquid to moisten (about 2 to 3 tablespoons).

Mix ground beef with 1/3 cup evaporated milk and 1/2 teaspoon salt. On waxed paper shape meat into five 6-inch circles. Spoon about 1/4 cup stuffing in center of each circle. Pull up edges over stuffing; seal. Bake in 1 1/2-quart casserole, uncovered, at 350° for 45 minutes.

Combine soup with remaining mushrooms and remaining evaporated milk; heat. Spoon over burgers. Garnish with parsley, if desired. Serves 5.

Hamburger Pie

Cook 1 pound ground beef and 1/2 cup chopped onion till meat is lightly browned and onion is tender. Add 1/2 teaspoon salt and dash pepper. Add one 16-ounce can cut green beans, drained, and one 10 3/4-ounce can condensed tomato soup; pour into greased 1 1/2-quart casserole.

*Mash 5 medium cooked potatoes while hot; add 1/2 cup warm milk and 1 beaten egg. Season with salt and pepper. Spoon in mounds over casserole. Sprinkle potatoes with cheese. Bake at 350° for 25 to 30 minutes. Serves 4 to 6.

*Or prepare 4 servings packaged instant mashed potatoes according to package directions *except reserve the milk.* Add 1 beaten egg and season with salt and pepper to taste. Add enough reserved milk so potatoes are stiff enough to hold their shape. Proceed with remaining recipe as above.

An elegant meat loaf

Planked Meat Loaf frosted with instant →
mashed potatoes is definitely company fare.
Accompany this loaf with grilled tomatoes.

Chili-Burger Stack-Ups

Pancakes are made from cornbread mix —

 1 pound ground beef
 ½ cup chopped onion
 1 clove garlic, minced
 . . .
 1 16-ounce can tomatoes, cut up
 1 6-ounce can tomato paste
 ¼ cup chopped green pepper
 1½ teaspoons seasoned salt
 1 teaspoon chili powder
 ¼ teaspoon dried oregano leaves,
    crushed
 . . .
 1 10-ounce package corn bread mix
 1¼ cups milk
 1 slightly beaten egg
    Grated Parmesan cheese

In medium skillet cook ground beef, chopped onion, and garlic till meat is brown and vegetables are tender. Stir in tomatoes, tomato paste, chopped green pepper, seasoned salt, chili powder, and oregano. Simmer, covered, for 15 minutes, stirring once.

For pancakes combine corn bread mix, milk, and slightly beaten egg; beat with rotary beater till smooth. Using 2 tablespoons batter for each pancake, bake on hot, lightly greased griddle. Keep baked pancakes warm in oven till all batter is used.

On serving platter, place 6 pancakes. Top with ⅓ of the meat mixture; sprinkle with about 4 teaspoons grated Parmesan cheese. Top each with second pancake, then with half the remaining meat mixture and 4 teaspoons grated Parmesan cheese. Repeat with remaining pancakes, meat mixture, and 4 teaspoons Parmesan cheese. Makes 6 servings.

Meal-in-a-Bowl Stew

 1 pound ground beef
 ½ cup chopped onion
 1 10½-ounce can condensed beef
    broth
 1 16-ounce can cream-style corn
 3 large potatoes, peeled and diced

In skillet brown ground beef and chopped onion. Add beef broth, cream-style corn, diced potatoes, 1 teaspoon salt, and dash pepper; mix well. Cover; cook over low heat for 20 to 25 minutes, stirring occasionally. Makes 4 or 5 servings.

GROUPER *(groo′ puhr)*—A saltwater fish belonging to the sea bass family. There are several kinds of groupers which are important—the red grouper, Nassau grouper, yellowfish grouper, black grouper, and gag. The red grouper is probably the most important of this group. All of these fish can be found on the southern Atlantic coast and along the coast of the Gulf of Mexico.

An interesting fact about the grouper is that it can change its skin color at will to match the water surroundings.

Grouper can be purchased whole, in fillets, or steaks. It is a lean fish and may be prepared by broiling, panfrying, or deep-fat frying. (See also *Fish.*)

GROUSE *(grous)*—A game bird of the Northern Hemisphere related to the pheasant. The prairie chicken, which was one of the popular meats of the American pioneer, is a member of the grouse family as is the ptarmigan of the Northern Hemisphere.

Grouse are not as brilliantly colored as pheasants. Instead, their reddish brown feathers provide a camouflage.

Today in the United States, the most popular member of this family is probably the ruffed grouse. This bird gets its name from the collar of feathers around its neck. When this grouse is showing off, it struts about and elevates these feathers until they resemble a ruffed collar.

Grouse are usually about the size of a small chicken and weigh from one to two pounds. Young grouse can be cooked by dry heat methods (roasted, broiled, and fried). Other grouse, however, may tend to be tough so are usually cooked using moist heat cookery methods (braised and stewed). (See also *Game.*)

GRUEL *(groo′ uhl)*—A thin porridge. In medieval Europe, gruel, made by boiling a cereal such as oatmeal with water, was one of the staple foods.

GRUYÈRE CHEESE *(groo yâr′, gri-)*—A pale ivory to yellow cheese with a nutlike, sweet flavor. It is made from cows' milk that is usually partially skimmed. This mild cheese was first made in the Gruyère Valley of Switzerland and today France and Switzerland export the majority of this cheese.

Natural Gruyère cheese is similar in shape, appearance, and flavor to Emmenthaler cheese (Switzerland Swiss cheese) but the "eyes" in Gruyère are smaller. Other differences between these two cheeses are the higher butterfat content of Gruyère and the brown wrinkled rind of Gruyère as contrasted with the smooth rind of Emmenthaler.

In the United States, process Gruyère cheese is more widely available than natural Gruyère. This process cheese which usually comes in foil-wrapped triangles may be made domestically or may be imported from Switzerland.

Gruyère cheese is an excellent cheese for cooking and is traditionally used in cheese fondue. Gruyère cheese is also a delicious dessert cheese. (See also *Cheese*.)

Nutty-flavored Gruyère cheese is ideal for dessert.

GUACAMOLE (*gwä kuh mō'lē*)—A Mexican dish made of mashed or puréed avocados, lemon juice, and minced onion. Tomatoes, bacon, olives, chilies, and seasonings such as chili powder or cayenne pepper are sometimes added to the basic mixture.

Blender Cheese Fondue

    8 ounces Gruyère cheese, diced
       (2 cups)
    2 cups dry white wine
    1 pound natural Swiss cheese,
       diced (4 cups)
  1½ tablespoons all-purpose flour
    ¼ teaspoon ground nutmeg
    ¼ teaspoon freshly ground pepper
    1 clove garlic
       French bread or hard rolls, torn
         in bite-size pieces, each with
         one crust

Place Gruyère cheese in blender container; cover and blend at high speed 20 seconds. Scrape down sides. Blend till cheese is in tiny bits, about 10 seconds more; remove from blender.

Warm the wine without covering or boiling. Put *2 cups* of the Swiss cheese in blender along with flour, nutmeg, pepper, and garlic. Cover; blend at high speed 20 seconds. Scrape down sides; blend till cheese is in tiny pieces, about 10 seconds more. Keeping blender at low speed, pour in warm wine; slowly add remaining Swiss cheese. Blend smooth.

Pour wine-Swiss cheese mixture into saucepan. Add the blended Gruyère cheese. Cook and stir over low heat till smooth and thick, about 15 minutes. Quickly transfer to fondue pot; keep warm over fondue burner. Spear bread cube with fondue fork piercing crust last. Dip bread into fondue, swirling to coat. Serves 10.

Guacamole

    2 medium ripe avocados
        • • •
    2 teaspoons lemon juice
    1 tablespoon onion juice
    1 clove garlic, crushed
    ½ teaspoon salt
    1 tablespoon chopped canned green
       chilies

Cut avocados in half and remove seeds; peel. Sieve avocado or blend smooth in electric blender. Add lemon juice, onion juice, garlic, salt, and green chilies; blend well. Cover and chill. Serve as appetizer dip garnished with bacon curls, meat accompaniment, or salad. To serve as a salad, spoon into lettuce cups. Top with chopped tomatoes, crisp toasted croutons, and grated Parmesan cheese. Makes about 1¼ cups.

Deviled Guacamole

    2 avocados, halved and peeled
    1 2¼-ounce can deviled ham
    2 tablespoons chopped green chilies
    2 teaspoons lemon juice
    1 teaspoon grated onion

Mash avocados with fork. Stir in deviled ham, green chilies, lemon juice, grated onion, and dash salt; chill. Serve as relish or dip. Makes 1½ cups.

Guacamole is usually served as a dip for crisp tortillas or potato chips but may also be used as a salad dressing or meat accompaniment. (See also *Mexican Cookery.*)

GUAVA *(gwä' vuh)*—A juicy, yellow to orange red, tropical or subtropical fruit. All varieties of guavas are thin-skinned and have numerous small seeds which need not be removed before eating the fruit.

The common guava is oval and about the size of a large plum. This fruit has a sweet, distinctive flavor and a strong, almost pungent aroma. The common guava is an excellent source of vitamin C. Although they may be eaten raw when very ripe, guavas are most frequently used in jellies and preserves. Guavas are not usually transported but are available any time of the year near the regional growing areas.

Because it is hardier than the common guava, the strawberry guava can be grown in subtropical regions. This fruit is smaller than the common guava and its flavor is reminiscent of strawberries.

Fresh guavas should be just starting to soften, yet still firm when purchased. Do not purchase fruit that is soft or has a spotted skin. (See also *Fruit.*)

Guacamole garnished with bacon curls and cream cheese topped with caviar give guests a choice. Serve with crackers.

GUGELHUPF, GUGELHOF, KUGELHOFF *(gŏŏ' guhl huf, -hôf)*—A sweet yeast cake that contains raisins and is topped with almonds. This cake is popular in Germany and Austria and is traditionally baked in a fluted mold with a hole in the center.

Gugelhupf

A golden coffee bread —

 1 **package active dry yeast**
2½ **cups sifted all-purpose flour**
 ¾ **cup milk**
 ¼ **cup butter or margarine**
 ½ **cup sugar**
 1 **teaspoon salt**
 2 **eggs**
 ½ **cup light raisins**
 1 **teaspoon grated lemon peel**

   . . .

 1 **tablespoon butter or margarine, melted**
 3 **tablespoons fine dry bread crumbs**
 Blanched whole almonds

In large mixer bowl combine yeast and 1½ *cups* of the sifted flour. Heat milk, the ¼ cup butter or margarine, sugar, and salt just till warm, stirring occasionally to melt butter. Add to dry mixture in mixer bowl; add eggs. Beat at low speed with electric mixer for ½ minute, scraping sides of bowl constantly. Beat 3 minutes at high speed.

By hand, beat in remaining flour. Stir in raisins and lemon peel. Cover batter; let rise till double (about 2 hours). Meanwhile, prepare a 1½-quart Turk's Head Mold or Bundt pan: Brush mold liberally with melted butter or margarine; sprinkle with fine dry bread crumbs, coating well. Arrange blanched whole almonds in a design in bottom of mold. Stir down batter; spoon carefully into mold. Let rise till almost double (about 1 hour). Bake at 350° till done, about 25 minutes. Cool 10 minutes. Carefully remove mold.

An elegant molded bread

Gugelhupf is an impressive as well as delicious bread. Subtly flavored with lemon, it's perfect served with coffee or tea.

How to roast guinea hens

Lay bacon over breast before roasting. Cover loosely with foil. Use 375° oven. For a guinea hen weighing 1½ to 2 pounds, allow ¾ to 1 hour roasting time. For a 2 to 2½ pound bird, allow 1 to 1½ hours. Uncover during last 20 minutes of roasting.

GUINEA HEN (*gin' ē*)—A female guinea fowl. Guinea hens, originally from western Africa, were quite frequently served at ancient Greek and Roman banquets. Today, this domesticated bird is eaten in a great many parts of the world; many Europeans also eat guinea hen eggs.

The slate gray feathers of this small bird are spotted with white. Their most striking feature is their bright crest feathers which range from blue to pink in color.

These delicately flavored birds can be prepared like chicken or other small game birds. To prevent the meat from drying out, cover the breast with bacon strips or a thin sheet of pork fat before roasting the guinea hen. (See also *Poultry*.)

Guinea Hens and Kraut

Pineapple introduces a sweet flavor —

> 1 27-ounce can sauerkraut, drained
> 1 13½-ounce can pineapple tidbits, drained
> 2 2- to 2½-pound ready-to-cook guinea hens
> 4 slices bacon
> 1 tablespoon all-purpose flour
> 2 tablespoons cold water

Combine sauerkraut and pineapple. Place mixture in bottom of shallow roasting pan. Rinse guinea hens; pat dry. Salt birds inside. Truss and place, breast side up, on top of mixture.

Lay bacon over breasts. Follow directions for roasting guinea hens (see above directions). Transfer birds to a warm platter. Remove bacon. Blend flour into water; stir into sauerkraut. Cook and stir till mixture thickens and bubbles. Makes 4 or 5 servings.

GUMBO—1. Another name for the vegetable okra. 2. A Creole soup made of meat, poultry, or seafood and vegetables and thickened with okra or gumbo filé. This dish is a New Orleans specialty. (See *Creole Cookery, Soup* for additional information.)

Tomato-Gumbo Soup

A quick fix-up for canned soup —

In saucepan cook ½ cup finely chopped onion and ¼ cup chopped green pepper in 2 tablespoons butter or margarine till tender. Add 1 tablespoon chopped canned pimiento, one 10½-ounce can condensed chicken gumbo soup, ½ cup water, ½ cup tomato juice, and ½ cup finely diced, cooked chicken. Heat through, stirring occasionally. Makes 2 or 3 servings.

GUMBO FILÉ (*fi lā'*)—Finely ground, dried sassafras leaves, used as a thickening agent in Creole cookery. When using filé powder, it is necessary to remove the mixture from the heat before the gumbo filé is stirred in. If this is not done, the mixture is overthickened and becomes a sticky, gluey mass. (See also *Creole Cookery*.)

GUMDROP—Sugar-coated, jellylike candy made of sugar, water, flavoring, coloring, and gum arabic. (This gum is responsible for the typical chewy texture of gumdrops.) Gumdrops are traditionally shaped like flat-nosed cones, but they are available also in various other shapes including rings, bars, and decorative fruit-shaped slices.

Gumdrops make attractive cake decorations and can also be used to add chewy texture and bright color to cookies, sweet breads, cakes, and other desserts.

Gumdrop-Nut Wreath

Truly holiday fare —

> 1 13¾-ounce package hot roll mix
> ½ cup snipped red and green gumdrops
> ½ cup chopped walnuts
> Confectioners' Icing
> Gumdrop Holly

Prepare roll dough from mix according to package directions. Stir in snipped red and green gumdrops and chopped nuts. Cover and let rise in warm place till double, about 30 to 45 minutes. Punch down; divide dough in half. Cover and let rest 10 minutes. Roll each half into a rope about 24 inches long.

Twist the ropes together; transfer to greased baking sheet and form into a ring. Cover and let rise till almost double, about 30 to 45 minutes. Bake at 375° for 25 to 30 minutes. (Cover with foil after first 20 minutes if browning too quickly.) Cool. Frost the coffee bread with Confectioners' Icing; decorate with red and green Gumdrop Holly.

Confectioners' Icing: Add light cream to 2 cups sifted confectioners' sugar till of spreading consistency. Add 1 teaspoon vanilla and dash salt; blend the icing mixture thoroughly.

Gumdrop Holly: Use red gumdrops for berries; roll green gumdrops flat with rolling pin and trim to look like dainty leaf shapes.

Gumdrop-Coffee Squares

Fruit-filled cake is delicately spiced —

> ¾ cup gumdrops
> Granulated sugar
> 1 cup brown sugar
> ½ cup shortening
> 1 egg
> ½ cup water
> 1 teaspoon instant coffee powder
> 1 teaspoon vanilla
> 1½ cups sifted all-purpose flour
> ½ teaspoon baking soda
> ½ teaspoon baking powder
> ¼ teaspoon salt
> ¼ teaspoon ground cinnamon
> ½ cup finely chopped walnuts
> Vanilla ice cream

Cut gumdrops into *very small* pieces; shake in small amount granulated sugar to keep pieces separate. In mixing bowl cream together brown sugar and shortening till light and fluffy. Add egg; beat well. Combine ½ cup water, coffee powder, and vanilla.

Sift together flour, soda, baking powder, salt, and cinnamon; add to creamed mixture alternately with coffee mixture, stirring after each addition. Stir in gumdrops and walnuts. Spread in well-greased 13x9 x2-inch baking pan. Bake at 350° for 25 to 30 minutes. Cool; cut in squares. To serve, top each square with a scoop of ice cream. Makes 12 servings.

Gumdrop Cookies

> ½ cup shortening
> ½ cup brown sugar
> ½ cup granulated sugar
> 1 egg
> ½ teaspoon vanilla
> ¾ cup sifted all-purpose flour
> ½ teaspoon baking powder
> ¼ teaspoon baking soda
> ¼ teaspoon salt
> ¾ cup quick-cooking rolled oats
> ½ cup flaked coconut
> ½ cup gumdrops, cut in small
>   pieces

Thoroughly cream shortening and sugars; add egg and vanilla; beat well. Sift together flour, baking powder, baking soda, and ¼ teaspoon salt; add to creamed mixture. Add oats, coconut, and gumdrops. Drop from teaspoon onto *ungreased* cookie sheet. Bake at 375° for 10 to 12 minutes. Makes 36.

Gumdrop Gems

> 1 cup butter or margarine
> 1½ cups sifted confectioners'
>   sugar
> 1 teaspoon vanilla
> 1 egg
> 2½ cups sifted all-purpose flour
> 1 teaspoon baking soda
> 1 teaspoon cream of tartar
> ¼ teaspoon salt
> 1 cup small gumdrops, sliced*

Cream butter, confectioners' sugar, and vanilla; beat in egg. Sift together dry ingredients; gradually stir into creamed mixture. Mix well.

Shape dough into roll 2 inches in diameter and 12 inches long. Wrap in waxed paper; chill several hours or overnight.

Cut ¼-inch-thick slices. Place on *ungreased* cookie sheet. Decorate tops with gumdrop slices. Bake at 375° till lightly browned, about 12 minutes. Cool gumdrop cookies slightly before removing from pan. Makes about 4 dozen cookies.

*Remove black candies.

GUNPOWDER TEA—A type of green tea made by rolling young tea leaves into small balls or pellets. (See also *Tea.*)

H

HADDOCK—A saltwater fish with very white meat, firm flesh, and pleasant flavor. This fish is a relative of the cod. The whole haddock can be easily recognized in the market because of its distinctive markings. One of these markings is a black line that runs the length of the fish on each side. Beneath this line is a small black patch, another distinguishing feature.

The haddock lives deep in the water and close to the bottom. Main producing areas are in the northeastern Atlantic Ocean from Nova Scotia to Cape Hatteras.

This fish averages about 20 inches long and weighs between 1½ and 7 pounds. Large haddock weigh 2½ pounds and more, while the young haddock, also called scrod, weigh 1½ to 2½ pounds.

Nutritional value: Haddock is a lean fish. A 100 gram uncooked fillet adds about 80 calories to the meal. When this same fillet is dipped in egg, milk, and bread crumbs, then fried, the calories are increased to 165. A similar-sized piece of smoked or canned haddock equals about 100 calories.

Haddock, like other fish, is a good source of protein. It also contains potassium, phosphorus, and some of the B vitamins.

How to select: Haddock can be purchased whole, cut into fillets, smoked, salted, or flaked. (Haddock flakes are canned.)

The fillets are available as fresh or frozen products. The smoked haddock fillets that are cut from the largest-sized fish are marketed as finnan haddie.

When choosing a whole fresh haddock, look for a fish with a firm flesh and bright clear eyes. The aroma should be fresh and the gills should be free from slime.

Haddock fillets must also have a fresh appearance with no drying around the edges. They should have a fresh odor and must be properly wrapped when purchased.

Frozen haddock must be solidly frozen with no freezer burn or fishy odor. The frozen fish also needs to be correctly packaged in moisture-vaporproof wrap.

How to store: All fish is very perishable and haddock is no exception. It should be refrigerated in the original wrapping as quickly as possible after purchase and then must be used within a day or two. Or fish can be frozen, tightly wrapped, and sealed. Frozen products will keep up to six months if properly wrapped

How to prepare: A dressed haddock can be stuffed and baked, while the fillets can be poached, broiled, fried, or baked. Since haddock is a lean fish, it needs to be basted with some kind of melted shortening or sauce, especially if it is to be baked or broiled. (See also *Fish.*)

Haddock-Shrimp Bake

2 pounds frozen haddock fillets
1 10-ounce can frozen condensed
cream of shrimp soup, thawed
¼ cup butter or margarine, melted
½ teaspoon grated onion
½ teaspoon Worcestershire sauce
¼ teaspoon garlic salt
1¼ cups rich round cracker crumbs
(30 crackers)

Slightly thaw fish. Place in greased 13x9x2-inch baking dish. Spread with thawed soup. Bake at 375° for 20 minutes. Combine butter, onion, Worcestershire sauce, and garlic salt. Mix with cracker crumbs. Sprinkle over fish. Bake 10 minutes longer or till fish flakes easily when tested with a fork. Makes 6 to 8 servings.

Herbed Fish Bake

1 pound frozen haddock fillets,
partially thawed
⅓ cup chopped onion
1 small clove garlic, minced
2 tablespoons butter or margarine
½ teaspoon dried tarragon leaves,
crushed
¼ teaspoon dried thyme leaves,
crushed
¼ cup cornflake crumbs

Place the haddock fillets in a greased 10x6x1½-inch baking dish. Cook onion and garlic in butter till tender but not brown. Stir in tarragon, thyme, ¼ teaspoon salt, and dash pepper. Cook 1 minute. Spread mixture over fish. Top mixture with cornflake crumbs. Bake at 500° till the haddock fillets flake easily when tested with a fork, about 12 minutes. Makes 4 servings.

Fried Haddock

Cut 1 pound haddock fillets in serving-sized pieces; dip in ¼ cup all-purpose flour then in 2 beaten eggs mixed with 2 tablespoons water. Roll in 1 cup crushed cornflakes.

In skillet heat ¼ inch of shortening till very hot. Add fish; fry till done, about 5 minutes, turning once. Drain on paper toweling. Serve haddock with lemon wedges. Makes 3 or 4 servings.

Lemon twists and bright green parsley add a colorful note to Haddock-Shrimp Bake. For special occasions, serve in shell dishes.

HAGGIS *(hag' is)*—A famous national meat specialty of Scotland made by stuffing the stomach of a sheep. To make haggis, the thoroughly cleaned stomach is stuffed with oatmeal, meat fat, and a seasoned mixture of chopped heart, liver, and lung. The pouch is tied shut and then it is boiled in water like a bag pudding. Traditionally, it is served to the sound of bagpipes.

HAKE *(hāk)*—A lean, saltwater fish from Atlantic waters. It is related to the haddock and cod, although it has a different appearance. The hake is a small, slender, soft-bodied fish with a reddish or olive brown color. It has only two dorsal fins. Hake usually weigh from one to four pounds and are marketed whole, filleted, smoked, or salted. Most often it is sold mixed with cod and haddock as deep sea fillets. The meat of hake is soft, white, and delicate in flavor; to some people it seems almost bland. Hake is good for frying, poaching, or baking in a sauce. (See also *Fish*.)

HALF AND HALF—1. A cream that is made up of a mixture of half milk and half cream. It contains not less than 10.5 percent milk fat. Most often half and half is used in coffee or poured over cereal or warm fruit desserts. 2. In England a mixture of two malt liquors. (See also *Cream.*)

HALIBUT—A saltwater fish with firm, white meat. Halibut is the largest member of the group of fish known as flatfish.

Halibut is caught in the cold waters of the North Atlantic, North Pacific, and Arctic Oceans. Some halibut is caught in the Atlantic all year long, with the peak months being from March to September. It used to be very abundant along the East Coast, but because of overfishing, halibut has become more scarce. Fishing for halibut along the Pacific coast starts in May and lasts for about two months.

The size of halibut ranges from about five to 100 pounds, but some can be as large as 400 or 600 pounds. The smaller halibut, from five to ten pounds, is called a chicken halibut; when ten to sixty pounds in weight, it is referred to as medium; a sixty to eighty pound halibut is called large; and one that weighs over eighty pounds is known as a whale halibut.

Nutritional value: Halibut is a lean fish and one 3x2x1-inch uncooked piece adds 100 calories. A 3½-ounce portion of smoked halibut is 224 calories.

Halibut is a very good source of easily digested protein and contains some vitamin A and some of the B vitamins. It also contains some of the minerals—sodium, calcium, potassium, and phosphorus.

How to select: Most of the halibut is marketed as steaks which have a cross-section of the backbone in them. Sometimes, halibut fillets or chunks are also available. Smoked halibut is another product that can be purchased occasionally.

Halibut has good keeping qualities and can be frozen successfully. Most of the halibut found in stores is frozen and may be cooked without thawing if extra cooking time is allowed. Look for steaks with a fresh appearance. The odor should be fresh and the package properly wrapped.

How to store: Keep frozen halibut solidly frozen in the freezer till ready to use, or store in the refrigerator if not frozen. Use fresh fish within a day or two after purchase and frozen fish within six months.

How to prepare: Halibut steaks or fillets can be fried, broiled, baked, steamed, or poached. If one of the dry-heat methods—baking or broiling—is used, be sure to baste or cook the fish with butter or a sauce during cooking. (See also *Fish.*)

Crumb-Crowned Halibut Steaks

Thaw two 12-ounce packages (1½ pounds) frozen halibut steaks. Place steaks on rack of broiler pan. Brush with 1 tablespoon melted butter. Sprinkle with salt and pepper. Broil 5 inches from heat for 5 minutes. Turn fish, brush with 1 tablespoon melted butter and sprinkle with salt and pepper. Broil the fish 5 minutes longer.

Stir 1 tablespoon melted butter into one 2-ounce package seasoned coating mix for fish. Spread on fish. Return to broiler for about 5 minutes or till brown. Makes 4 servings.

Fisherman's Luck

A summer barbecue idea —

  ½ cup chopped green pepper
  ½ cup chopped onion
  3 tablespoons butter or margarine
  ½ cup catsup
  ½ teaspoon garlic salt
  1½ pounds frozen halibut steaks, thawed and cut in 4 serving-sized pieces
  4 small bay leaves

Cook green pepper and onion in butter till tender. Add catsup and garlic salt. For each serving, cut a 28-inch length of foil and fold it in half. Place 1 serving of halibut in foil, just off center. Sprinkle both sides lightly with salt and pepper. Pour a *fourth* of the sauce over each serving; top each with bay leaf. Bring edges of foil together; seal well with double fold. Grill over *hot* coals about 2 inches from heat until fish flakes easily, turning once. Allow about 15 minutes per side. Remove bay leaves before serving steaks. Makes 4 servings.

Tartar sauce and lemon wedges are good accompaniments for the mildly flavored Halibut Royale. Halibut, as well as other fish, requires little cooking and must be handled gently.

Halibut Royale

   3 tablespoons lemon juice
   ½ teaspoon paprika
   6 halibut steaks
   ½ cup chopped onion
   2 tablespoons butter or margarine
   6 green pepper strips

In shallow dish combine lemon juice, 1 teaspoon salt, and paprika. Add halibut and marinate for one hour, turning steaks after 30 minutes. In a skillet, cook chopped onion in butter or margarine till tender but not brown.

Place steaks in greased 10x6x1½-inch baking dish. Top with green pepper strips and sprinkle with cooked, chopped onion. Bake at 450° till the halibut steaks flake easily when tested with a fork, about 10 minutes. Makes 6 servings.

Grilled Halibut

   1 16-ounce package frozen halibut
     fillets
   2 tablespoons soy sauce
   1 teaspoon lemon juice

     · · ·

   ½ cup dairy sour cream
   ½ cup fine cornflake crumbs
   2 tablespoons toasted sesame seed

Thaw fillets until they come apart. Brush with a mixture of soy sauce and lemon juice. Season fish with salt and pepper. Coat both sides of fillets with sour cream. Combine crumbs and sesame seed. Roll fillets in crumb mixture. Place fish in a greased, wire broiler basket. Broil over *medium* coals till fish flakes easily when tested with a fork, about 10 minutes, turning once. Makes 3 or 4 servings.

HAM

*How cured and smoked pork was developed, plus
the terminology and types associated with it.*

When man learned that salt water would preserve the meat of the wild boar and smoke from an open fire would improve its flavor, he was able to provide food for his family when meat was scarce. Later, he learned to trade his surplus of food for other needed goods.

No one knows specifically where ham processing originated, but one account places it along the Baltic Sea when man was a hunter who roamed the area in search of game. Wild boars were hunted and butchered in the late fall. Meat that couldn't be consumed at that time was buried in the sand along the shore to prevent it from falling into the hands of enemy tribesmen. Later, when the meat was dug up, a remarkable transformation had occurred. The salt water in the sand had preserved the meat and given it a new flavor. The making of ham was completed when the meat received a thorough smoking as it was suspended and cooked over the open fire.

As years passed, wild boars were domesticated, and their descendants known as hogs were raised in many parts of the ancient world. Both fresh pork and ham were common throughout Europe and Asia. Around the first century B.C., the Gauls, living in what is now France, were particularly successful in breeding hogs. It was natural that they should develop skills in processing ham, too. In fact, so popular were the hams they produced that the meat was shipped as far away as Rome.

Ham for elegant entertaining

←Decorate a baked ham with fruits and nuts to produce a luscious Ham Tropicale. Sauce does double duty for basting and topping.

Although the rich flavor of ham added welcome variety to the menu, the meat's chief advantage was that the salt acted as a preservative; the meat would keep reasonably well for several months. Consequently, armies carried ham, and sailing vessels were well provisioned with heavily salted pork before setting out for new lands and new conquests. Ships transporting colonists to America also carried live hogs as a source of meat for the family to use in the new land. Once the new settlements were established, the hogs and meat they produced became important commodities for trade. In the 1640s settlers in the northern colonies "salted down" meats in barrels and carried on extensive commerce with the West Indies. William Pynchon of Springfield, Massachusetts, is thought by many people to have been the first man to pack meat this way as a full-time business.

Home curing of hams became part of the fall work on farms and plantations, and, as the frontiers opened up, the pioneers, like their fathers before them, carried ham and bacon as important staples when they set out for a new land. Later, as the pioneers cleared land for homes, hogs were raised and farmers smoked their own hams in the newly prepared locations.

Packing and shipping salt pork and ham became commercially profitable as river boats opened trade inland. Shipments of ham went down the Ohio and Mississippi rivers by boat as early as 1820. Some of the meat was sold in New Orleans. Other shipments were sent to the Atlantic coast markets or abroad. Twenty years later pork packing began in Chicago and became one of the major industries of that city.

Originally, curing was done as a means of preserving the meat. Consequently, the meat was very salty and the texture quite dry. However, with the advent of adequate refrigeration in the home and at all stages of commercial production and distribution, hams are now cured for enjoyment of their cured flavor and not for preservation.

In earlier times ham commonly referred to several cuts of cured and smoked pork. Today, to be labeled ham according to United States government standards, the ham must come from the thigh (hind leg) of a hog. Although other parts of the hog are cured and smoked, they cannot be labeled ham. For example, the corresponding cut from the front leg, the smoked pork shoulder, is called a picnic.

How ham is processed

The first hams were very salty and probably tough. The animals had developed strong muscles from running wild, and the men of that time had no way of gauging the concentration of the sea water. Today, hogs are specially bred to be lean and tender, and the amounts of salt and other curing ingredients can be controlled.

Although the principles learned by early attempts at processing ham still apply, today's tender flavorful hams are vastly different from earlier varieties. Nevertheless, curing, smoking, and aging are still the basic steps in the production of the flavorful and nutritious ham.

Curing: Salt is the principle ingredient used to cure ham. It may be used alone or in combination with saltpeter to set the color and with white or brown sugar to add sweetness. Originally, the salt used came from salt water. Later, granular salt mixture was rubbed over the surface of the meat instead. This is known as a dry cure and is still used today in a limited way. After salting, the hams are packed into barrels or other large containers and allowed to stand until the curing action has worked its way to the center of the meat.

Another method of curing ham involves submerging the meat in a brine or pickling solution. Because sugar is usually added, the mixture is referred to as "sweet pickle." Just as in dry curing, the brine-cured hams are allowed to stand in the pickle several weeks until the desired change in color and texture has been achieved. Except for small specialty packers, most ham processors use the brine or sweet pickle method.

In large commercial operations, the pickle is pumped into the ham mechanically by means of rows of needles which penetrate deep into the meat and distribute the solution evenly throughout the ham. Pumping has two main advantages: it is faster than waiting for the brine solution to be absorbed into the center of the meat, and the final product is more uniformly cured. At this point most hams are placed in the smokehouse for further processing.

Smoking: The old saying "where there's smoke there's fire" takes on special meaning in the smokehouse. In this case, the appropriate phrase is "where there's smoke, there's heat." In the smokehouse the ham not only acquires a wonderful, smoky flavor but also cooks as it hangs suspended in the smoke from hardwood fires.

Hickory, apple, cherry, and other fruitwoods are burned to provide the smoke. Each type of wood smoke imparts its own special flavor. The amount of cooking and the intensity of the smoke-flavor depend upon the temperature in the smokehouse and how long the meat is there. Commercially, these times and temperatures are carefully regulated so that the ham reaches the desired internal temperature before moving on to the next phase of processing.

After smoking, some hams are ready to be chilled, wrapped, labeled, and shipped to market in refrigerated cars or trucks. Other hams are ready to be canned. These hams receive less cooking in the smokehouse because they will be fully cooked during canning. Still others go on to be aged. Of the total production of hams in the United States, only a few are aged.

Aging: Ham processors with the facilities for specialty hams such as country- or Virginia-style will allow the hams to hang or age from a few months up to a year. Aging is only practical for hams which have received a heavy cure, usually dry, and a long period of smoking. Because these hams require long periods of time for curing, smoking, and aging, the meat is expensive to produce and market.

Nutritional value: In these days when dietary emphasis is on lean meat, the modern ham is right in style. First, the meat comes from new breeds of hogs that are exceptionally lean and meaty with very little internal fat. Then, at the packing plant, much of the external fat is trimmed away. This is particularly evident in the formed hams. Most of them are made to specifications which allow no more than one-quarter inch of fat on the outside surface of the meat. A three-ounce serving of cooked, lean ham contains about 245 calories, much of which is protein.

The protein in ham is of high quality and, like all pork, ham is an outstanding source of the B vitamin, thiamine. In addition, it contains significant amounts of iron and the other B vitamins, niacin and riboflavin. Since ham is cured with salt, a considerable percentage of sodium is present in ham portions, too.

Types and styles

Although the curing, smoking, and aging of ham governs the flavor of the meat, two other factors influence the market form.

Ham Facts At A Glance									
Styles	Cure		Smoke			Amount of Bone		How Purchased	
	Heavy	Mild	Heavy	Mild	None	Bone in	Boneless	Fully Cooked	Cook Before Eating
Whole		X		X		X		X	*
Halves		X		X		Both available		X	*
Portions		X		X		Both available		X	*
Slices		X		X		Both available		X	*
Semiboneless		X		X		**		X	
Formed		X		X			X	X	
Canned		X	*		X		X	X	
Boiled		X			X			X	
Regional Specialties									
Scotch		X			X	X			X
Country-style	X		X			X			X
Prosciutto	X		X			X			Not cooked
Smithfield	X		X			X		*	X
*small number marketed **aitchbone removed									

1. Dry-cured *Prosciutto Ham*, heavily smoked and aged for a deep, rich flavor. Another distinction is a coating of spices.

2. Familiar *Mild-Cured Ham*. Shank portion upper left; Butt portion, upper right, and center slices or ham steaks, foreground.

3. *Semiboneless Hams* contain a single round bone giving football shape to whole ham, top. Ham pieces are at bottom.

These are the amount of cooking the ham received during processing and whether it contains a bone or is boneless.

Fully cooked ham: As the name implies, this ham is completely cooked when purchased. Serve it cold right from the can or package. If you prefer, heat the meat to the desired serving temperature. An internal temperature of 135° to 140° as shown on a meat thermometer is a good choice.

All canned hams and more than 90 percent of the hams marketed in the United States are fully cooked during processing. These hams may be purchased either as bone-in or boneless styles.

Cook-before-eating: During processing this type of ham is only partially cooked. Cook-before-eating hams from federally inspected plants receive sufficient cooking to make the meat safe to eat, but further cooking is needed to bring about a cooked-meat texture and flavor. Before serving, the ham should be cooked to an internal temperature of 160° as indicated on a roast meat thermometer.

The small number of cook-before-eating hams on the market today usually have the bone in. Some of the country-style and specialty hams are in this group. Also, some vacuum-sealed, packaged ham slices intended for grilling or panfrying will be labeled cook-before-eating.

Bone-in: This is the style of ham with the traditional fiddle shape that is associated with ham. At least part of the shank bone is present although the bone may be cut short. Bone-in hams are marketed whole, in halves, butt or shank portions, and as center-cut slices. The latter are frequently designated as ham steaks.

Country-style, *Virginia-style*, *Smithfield*, and *Prosciutto* (photo 1) are dry-cured hams which have been heavily smoked, and aged. They are the hams marketed today which most closely resemble those hams made by the early settlers and pioneers. Some of the hams have a coating of black pepper or spices on the surface. These are cook-before-eating hams which must be thoroughly scrubbed, soaked, skinned, and simmered before baking or panfrying.

Country-style hams are a tradition of the southern United States. After dry curing, the hams are smoked over hickory logs and then aged two or three months.

Virginia-style and genuine Smithfield hams, while similar to country-style, do have specific requirements. Both these hams must be processed in a particular locality; Virginia-style hams must come from Virginia; Smithfield hams must be processed within the city limits of Smithfield, Virginia. In addition to the dry cure and hickory smoking, Smithfield hams must age at least six months. Sometimes, the hogs are peanut fed which produces a meat that is rich and lean. A coarse, black pepper is used on the surface.

Prosciutto is the Italian version of the Virginia-style ham. Instead of pepper, a spice mixture is pressed into the surface of the ham before it is aged.

Whole hams, halves (photo 2) *and center slices* are the bone-in style of ham most familiar at the supermarket. All but a small percentage of these hams are fully cooked. The mild cure and the amount of smoking they receive is given careful attention by the commercial meat packer. Each company varies the curing solution and smoking procedure to produce a unique ham which will carry the packer's brand name.

The whole hams range in weight from 9 to 18 pounds. Butt and shank halves and pieces are marketed in the 6- to 9-pound range. Ham slices are usually marketed according to thickness of slice with ½- to 1-inch thicknesses being the most popular. Extra-thick slices are cut to order.

One of the lesser-known styles of ham is in a category by itself. Some New England processors occasionally market a cook-before-eating ham that is cured but not smoked. It has a variety of local names including "sweet pickle ham" and "scotch ham." It is interesting to note that its very mild flavor and delicate, pink color are almost the exact opposite of the country-style hams popular in the South.

The *semiboneless* ham (photo 3) has only the round leg bone remaining in this compact 8- to 12-pound piece of meat. Some retailers cut this ham in half crosswise, thus making a 4- to 6-pound piece available. Semiboneless hams are fully cooked.

4. Boneless *Formed Hams* are produced from lean muscles of large pork legs. Whole ham, top; halves and pieces, bottom.

5. *Canned Hams* come in convenient sizes, but only the smallest are shelf stable; the others require refrigerator storage.

6. Sliced *"Boiled" or Cooked Hams* are marketed either in vacuum-sealed packages or sliced to order at the meat counter.

Boneless ham: With the bones removed and the outside fat trimmed away, the lean, meaty muscles of the pork leg are shaped in a casing, stockinette, or can during processing. Most are fully cooked. Carving is simply a matter of slicing the meat across the grain into attractive meaty slices of the desired thicknesses.

Formed hams (photo 4, page 1121) are the newest of the boneless hams. Each is produced from one or more muscles from large pork legs. The finest of the formed hams is made from a single muscle, weighing 8 to 12 pounds, which is carefully trimmed of outside fat Only enough remains to keep the surface of the ham moist should the homemaker decide to bake the ham and serve it hot. Formed hams are always fully cooked and usually vacuum packaged in a transparent wrapping material before dispatched from the plant to allow for visual inspection.

Several meat packers also produce vacuum-packed slices and sections cut from these single-muscle, formed hams. These pieces of ham are especially convenient to prepare when the family is small or when meals must be prepared singly.

Canned hams (photo 5, page 1121) are solid, boneless pieces of ham that are fully cooked during canning. All are cured, but not all are smoked. Many specialty packs are available including those with sauces and glazes built in. A small number of Smithfield ham pieces are also canned and available in some grocery stores.

Except for the smallest sizes, canned hams are not shelf stable. They are, in fact, perishable and must be refrigerated. The reason is that the amount of heating necessary to make a canned ham shelf stable would so overcook the meat as to make it undesirable. Instead, canned hams are processed for a shorter time and become pasteurized rather than shelf stable when treated in this way.

Sliced *"boiled"* or *cooked* ham (photo 6, page 1121) is not really boiled. Instead, the meat is gently simmered, steamed, or slowly baked to enhance the delicate ham flavor. This boneless meat can be purchased sliced by the pound at delicatessen counters or in preweighed, vacuum-sealed packages displayed at grocery meat counters.

How to select and store

Choosing the style of ham best suited for your needs depends on the menu planned and your budget. Maintaining the quality of the meat depends on proper handling both at the market and at home. When making menu plans, a good rule to follow is to allow one-quarter pound per serving of boneless ham and one half pound per serving of bone-in ham. This will give you a basis for comparing the price of boneless ham versus that of bone-in ham.

The boneless formed hams are easy to slice and have almost no waste. Even though the price per pound is higher, they are frequently an excellent buy. Canned hams are another meaty choice. At other times, when the bone-in hams are attractively priced, this familiar style will provide the most economical servings. When buying a butt or shank piece, be sure to ask the meatman whether or not the center ham slice has been removed. The price for a piece without the center slice should be less per pound than a ham with center slice.

Become a label reader when shopping for ham. Besides brand and price, the label should tell you whether the ham is fully cooked or cook-before-eating. From time to time you may find other terms on the label. For example, the amount of water in the pickling solution is regulated. A meat packer may choose to exceed this amount by up to 10 percent, but the ham must be labeled "water added." If more than 10 percent water is added to the solution, the meat must then be labeled as "imitation ham."

Refrigeration is needed for all hams except the very small canned ham pieces. Larger canned hams just like those in other types of wrappings should be purchased from refrigerated cases and stored in the refrigerator at home.

Whole or half hams should be used within seven days; ham slices within three. Canned hams can usually be stored for several months in the refrigerator without a loss in their eating quality as long as the can has never been opened.

Freezing longer than one month is not recommended for cured and smoked meats because quality deteriorates during long storage at freezer temperatures.

How to prepare

Since the majority of hams are fully cooked, serving them hot is a matter of heating rather than cooking in the usual manner. Nevertheless, the basic techniques of roasting, broiling, and panfrying still apply. You will, however, find that the term "baking" is generally used instead of the word roasting. Should you purchase a cook-before-eating ham, the same directions apply, only the length of cooking time needed increases. The exceptions to this are the dry-cured hams. Because of the type of curing and the long aging, these hams must be scrubbed and simmered several hours before being skinned and baked. Most processors of these specialty hams pack instructions with the ham or print them on the packaging wrapper.

Roasting or baking: Place whole hams or ham pieces fat side up on a rack in a shallow pan. It is not necessary to add water or cover the ham as it bakes. The fat covering the meat browns beautifully. Many homemakers like to score the surface of the ham with a diamond patten (see page 1124). This lends an added attractiveness to the ham when it is served.

	Ham Roasting Chart		
Cut	Approximate Weight (Pounds)	Internal Temp. on Removal from Oven	Approximate Cooking Time (Total Time)
Roast meat at constant oven temperature of 325°.			
Ham (fully cooked)			
half, boneless	4 to 5	135° to 140°	1½ to 2 hrs.
whole, boneless	8 to 10	135° to 140°	2 to 2¼ hrs.
half	5 to 7	135° to 140°	1¾ to 2¼ hrs.
whole	10 to 14	135° to 140°	2½ to 3 hrs.
Ham (cook-before-eating)			
shank or butt	3 to 4	160°	2 to 2¼ hrs.
half	5 to 7	160°	2½ to 3 hrs.
whole	10 to 14	160°	3½ to 4 hrs.
To broil* or panfry fully cooked ham slices			
Ham Slices, Bone-in ¾ inch thick	1 to 1¼ pounds		Broil 10 to 12 minutes Panfry 12 to 15 minutes
Ham Slices, Bone-in 1 inch thick	1¼ to 1¾ pounds		Broil 14 to 16 minutes Panfry 16 to 18 minutes
Ham Slices, Boneless ⅜ inch thick	3 ounces		Broil 4 to 5 minutes Panfry 4 to 5 minutes
Ham Slices, Boneless ¼ inch thick	2 ounces		Broil 3 to 4 minutes Panfry 3 to 4 minutes
To broil* or panfry cook-before-eating ham slices			
Ham Slices, Bone-in ¾ inch thick	1 to 1¼ pounds		Broil 13 to 14 minutes Panfry 15 to 20 minutes
Ham Slices, Bone-in 1 inch thick	1¼ to 1¾ pounds		Broil 18 to 20 minutes Panfry 20 to 22 minutes
* Broil 3 inches from heat			

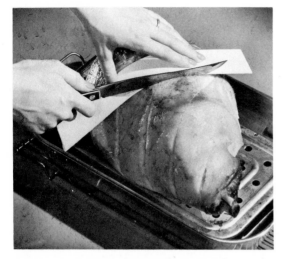

Score ham fat in diamond pattern by making cut ¼ inch deep with a sharp knife. Use a 12x2-inch paper strip as a guide.

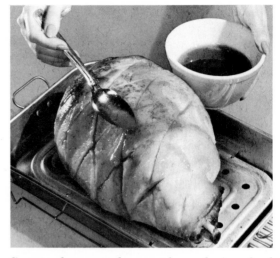

Spoon glaze evenly over ham during final 30 minutes of baking time. For a heavier coating, baste several times with glaze.

Insert a roast meat thermometer into the center of the thickest part of the meat, being sure that the point doesn't touch bone or fat. This is the best way to know when the ham is done. Then, bake according to Ham Roasting Chart (page 1123).

Hams, even those containing a bone, can, with practice, be balanced on a spit and heated on a rotisserie. Tying in several places is recommended when heating canned or boneless formed hams on the turning spit of the rotisserie.

About 30 minutes before the roasting time either in the oven or on the rotisserie is complete, brush the surface of the baked ham with a glaze or barbecue sauce, if desired. This is also the time to insert whole cloves into the squares of a ham that has been scored. The glaze may be as simple as a generous sprinkling of brown sugar or as complicated as a cooked sauce with many ingredients. The final 30 minutes heating sets the glaze and makes the surface bubbly and brown. The ham is then ready to transfer to a large meat platter and serve with a glorious flourish.

Broiling: Ham slices or steaks cut at least one inch thick are the most satisfactory for broiling in an oven broiler or grilling over charcoal. Begin by slashing the fat at intervals to prevent the meat from curling during cooking. Be careful to cut only the fat, not into the meat itself. When using a broiler oven, place the meat on a rack in a broiler pan and broil about three inches from the heat, turning once. When cooking over charcoal, place the meat directly on a lightly greased grill. (See chart on page 1123.) When thinner steaks are broiled over direct heat, they must be watched carefully to avoid overcooking or drying out. Many homemakers prefer to panbroil or panfry ham slices which are cut less than one inch thick.

Panbroiling and panfrying: Actually, ham slices of any thickness can be prepared by panbroiling or panfrying. The only difference is that panbroiling means cooking the ham without adding fat to the skillet or griddle, while panfrying does involve using a small amount of hot fat.

Slashing the fat on the ham slice is important for panbroiling, too. Place the steak in a skillet or on a griddle over medium heat. Cook the steak until well heated through. (See chart on page 1123.)

Panfrying is the traditional method of cooking the country-style or other dry cured ham slices. The ham slices are usually soaked, and/or simmered before they are cut and fried. Red-eye gravy is a frequent accompaniment for this style of ham. The gravy is made by pouring boiling water over the drippings left in the pan after cooking the meat. These juices are not thickened before being spooned over the cooked ham.

Ham Tropicale

This beauty is pictured on page 1116 —

> 1 fully cooked, boneless whole ham
> 1 15-ounce can sliced peaches
> 1 8¾-ounce can crushed pineapple
> 2 tablespoons cornstarch
> ½ teaspoon ground cinnamon
>   Dash ground cloves
> 1 cup water
> ⅓ cup frozen orange juice
>   concentrate, thawed
> ½ cup whole maraschino cherries
> ¼ cup light raisins
> ½ cup broken pecan halves

Place ham on rack in shallow roasting pan. Score ham in diamonds, cutting only ¼ inch deep. Insert meat thermometer into center of ham. Roast according to Ham Roasting Chart (see page 1123).

Drain peaches and pineapple, reserving syrups. In saucepan combine cornstarch and spices. Stir in reserved syrups, water, and orange juice concentrate. Cook and stir till mixture thickens and bubbles. Spoon some sauce over ham last 30 minutes of baking time. Continue baking; baste occasionally.

Reserve a few peach slices and whole cherries for garnish. Cut up remaining peaches and slice remaining cherries. To the cooked sauce, add cut up peaches, pineapple, and cherries, along with raisins and pecan halves. Simmer 10 minutes. Garnish ham with reserved fruit; spoon on some sauce. Pass remaining.

Mustard Glaze for Ham

> Whole cloves
> ½ cup brown sugar
> ½ teaspoon dry mustard
> 2 tablespoons fruit juice

The last 30 minutes of heating time, remove ham from oven. Stud ham surface with cloves. Combine brown sugar, dry mustard, and fruit juice. Spoon over ham. Return to oven. Baste occasionally.

Cranberry-Topped Ham Slices

> 1 fully cooked ham slice, cut
>   1 inch thick (about 1½ pounds)
> 1 8-ounce can whole cranberry
>   sauce (1 cup)
> ½ teaspoon prepared mustard
>   Dash ground cloves

Slash fat edge of ham slice. Place in a shallow baking pan. Combine the cranberry sauce, mustard, and cloves; spread over ham. Bake at 350° for 40 to 45 minutes. Makes 6 servings.

Ham Steak Barbecue

> ¾ cup catsup
> 3 tablespoons brown sugar
> 1 to 2 tablespoons Dijon-style
>   mustard
> 2 tablespoons Worcestershire sauce
> 2 tablespoons lemon juice
> 2 teaspoons chili powder
> 2 slices fully cooked ham, cut ½
>   inch thick (about 1½ pounds)

Combine first 6 ingredients for sauce. Slash fat edges of ham at intervals. Brush meat liberally with sauce and let stand 1 hour. Broil over coals, turning once and brushing with sauce 5 to 6 minutes per side. Watch closely. Serves 4 to 6.

Ham and Fruit Kabobs

> 2 to 2½ pounds fully cooked
>   boneless ham, cut in 1½-inch
>   cubes
> Spiced crab apples
> Pineapple slices, quartered
> Orange wedges (with peel)
>   • • •
> ½ cup extra-hot catsup
> ⅓ cup orange marmalade
> 2 tablespoons finely chopped onion
> 2 tablespoons salad oil
> 1 tablespoon lemon juice
> 1 to 1½ teaspoons dry mustard

Thread ham and fruits alternately on skewers. For sauce, combine remaining ingredients. Broil ham and fruit over *slow* coals 12 to 15 minutes, brushing often with sauce. Use a rotating skewer or turn skewers frequently during broiling. Serves 6.

Hawaiian Ham Slices

　　1 8½-ounce can sliced pineapple
　　2 tablespoons soy sauce
　　¾ teaspoon ground ginger
　　½ clove garlic
　　　　. . .
　　1 pound fully cooked formed ham,
　　　　cut into 4 slices

Drain pineapple, reserving syrup. Combine syrup, soy sauce, ginger, and garlic. Pour over ham slices in shallow container. Marinate ham 30 minutes; turn once. Discard the garlic clove.

Grill ham slices over *hot* coals just till heated through, about 2 minutes on each side, brushing with marinade once or twice. Heat pineapple slices on grill with ham during last 2 minutes. To serve, top each ham slice with a drained pineapple slice. Makes 4 servings.

Broiled Ham Dinner

　　½ cup apricot preserves
　　½ teaspoon dry mustard
　　¼ teaspoon ground ginger
　　¼ teaspoon salt
　　1 tablespoon water
　　1 fully cooked ham slice, cut
　　　　¾ inch thick
　　　　. . .
　　1 8-ounce package frozen potato
　　　　patties
　　3 tablespoons butter, melted

Mix preserves, dry mustard, ginger, salt, and water. Slash fat edge of ham. Place ham and potato patties on rack in broiler pan. Spread *half* the apricot glaze on ham; brush potatoes with *half* the butter. Broil 3 inches from heat 6 minutes. Turn ham and patties. Spread ham with remaining glaze. Butter patties; season with salt and pepper. Broil 6 minutes. Makes approximately 4 servings.

Ham steaks for the grill

←Bring a touch of the Islands to your backyard by serving Hawaiian Ham Slices. The ginger-soy sauce marinade is a favorite, too.

More ways to serve

Fine cooks know that ham is as versatile as it is convenient. Even leftover pieces can be used attractively in appetizers, salads, sandwiches, and main dishes.

The simplest appetizers are cubes of ham arranged on a platter and passed with a cocktail sauce for dipping. Or try strips of sliced, cooked ham wrapped around marinated artichoke hearts and serve hot.

Ham on rye bread spread with mustard or horseradish will always be a favorite of sandwich lovers. A new, crunchy version of the grilled cheese and ham sandwich sports a coating of crushed potato chips.

Tart apples, mellow diced pears, pineapple cubes, or halved grapes combine with cubed ham in imaginative salads. Cutting ham in thin strips is another attractive way to prepare the ham.

Few meats rival the good flavor that ham brings to casseroles. Likewise, it goes well with vegetable medleys and assorted pastas.

Artichoke–Ham Bites

　　1 15-ounce can artichoke hearts
　　½ cup garlic Italian salad dressing
　　6 ounces sliced boiled ham, cut in
　　　　1½-inch strips

Drain artichoke hearts; cut in half. Marinate in dressing several hours; drain. Wrap one ham strip around each artichoke half. Spear with cocktail pick. Bake at 300° till hot, about 10 minutes.

Apple and Ham Salad

Tossed with a blue cheese dressing —

　　3 cups sliced, tart apples
　　1 cup cubed fully cooked ham
　　½ cup diced celery
　　¼ cup mayonnaise or salad dressing
　　2 tablespoons light cream
　　2 tablespoons crumbled blue cheese
　　1 tablespoon lemon juice

Combine apples, ham, and celery. Blend together remaining ingredients. Toss dressing mixture lightly with apple-ham mixture. Serves approximately 5 or 6.

Ham-Stuffed Tomatoes

There's asparagus in the salad, too —

With stem ends down, cut 8 medium tomatoes into 6 wedges, *cutting to, but not through*, bases. Spread wedges apart slightly. Chill. Cook ½ cup macaroni following package directions; drain. Combine macaroni; 1½ cups cubed fully cooked ham; ½ of 10-ounce package frozen asparagus tips, cooked and drained; and ⅓ cup chopped celery.

Blend together ½ cup mayonnaise or salad dressing, ¼ teaspoon salt, ¼ teaspoon onion salt, and ⅛ teaspoon pepper. Add mayonnaise mixture to macaroni mixture; toss lightly. Chill. Just before serving, fill tomatoes with ham mixture. Makes 8 servings.

Sour Cream-Ham Omelet

Try this for Sunday brunch —

> 5 egg yolks
> 1 cup dairy sour cream
> ¼ teaspoon salt
> 5 stiffly beaten egg whites
> 1 cup finely diced fully cooked ham
> 2 tablespoons butter or margarine

Beat egg yolks till thick and lemon-colored, about 5 minutes. Beat in *half* of the dairy sour cream and the salt. Fold in stiffly beaten egg whites and diced fully cooked ham.

Heat butter in 10-inch oven-going skillet. Pour in omelet mixture, leveling gently. Cook over low heat until lightly browned on bottom, about 10 minutes. Finish cooking at 325° till top is golden brown, about 12 to 15 minutes. Loosen omelet; slide onto warm plate. Separate into wedges with two forks. Garnish with remaining sour cream. Makes 4 servings.

Creamed Ham

In saucepan melt ¼ cup butter or margarine; blend in ¼ cup all-purpose flour and ¼ teaspoon salt. Add 2 cups milk all at once. Cook and stir till mixture is thick and bubbly. Add 2 cups diced fully cooked ham; one 3-ounce can sliced mushrooms, drained; 2 tablespoons chopped green pepper; and ½ teaspoon prepared mustard. Heat through. Serve over hot toast points, fluffy rice, or baking powder biscuits. Trim each serving with some diced, canned pimiento. Makes 4 or 5 servings.

Ham and Potato Scallop

> 5 cups thinly sliced, peeled
>   potatoes
> 1 pound fully cooked ham, cut in
>   ½-inch cubes
> 1 10½-ounce can condensed cream
>   of mushroom soup
> ¼ cup milk
> ½ cup chopped onion
> ¼ cup chopped green pepper
>   Dash pepper
> 2 tablespoons butter or margarine

Place *half* the potatoes in the bottom of a greased 2-quart casserole. Cover with ham pieces. Top with remaining thinly sliced potatoes.

Combine soup, milk, onion, green pepper, and pepper; pour over potatoes. Dot with butter. Cover; bake at 350° 1 hour. Uncover; bake till potatoes are done, about 45 minutes. Makes 6 servings.

Ham-Cheese Crunch Sandwich

Potato chip-coated servings —

> 8 slices white bread
>   Butter or margarine, softened
>   Prepared mustard
> 4 slices boiled ham
> 4 slices process American cheese
> 1 tomato, thinly sliced
> 2 slightly beaten eggs
> 2 tablespoons milk
>   Dash onion salt
> 1¼ cups crushed potato chips

Spread each slice of bread on one side with butter or margarine, then mustard. Top four slices of bread with ham, cheese, and tomato. Cover with remaining bread. Combine eggs, milk, and onion salt. Dip sandwiches in egg mixture, then in crushed potato chips, patting to secure chips to bread and turning to coat both sides. Brown in buttered skillet or griddle till coating is crisp. Makes 4 servings.

Home-style casserole favorite

Enjoy the smoky goodness of Ham and→ Potato Scallop, a great way to use leftovers from a country-style or mild-cured ham.

Cauliflower-Ham Bake

1 medium head cauliflower
2 cups cubed fully cooked ham
1 3-ounce can sliced mushrooms,
drained (½ cup)
. . .
2 tablespoons butter or margarine
2 tablespoons all-purpose flour
1 cup milk
4 ounces sharp process American
cheese, cubed (1 cup)
½ cup sour cream
1 tablespoon fine dry bread crumbs

Break cauliflower into flowerets (about 4 cups). Cook in boiling, salted water till tender; drain. Combine with ham and mushrooms.

In medium saucepan melt butter or margarine. Stir in flour. Add milk all at once and stir constantly till mixture thickens and bubbles. Add cheese and sour cream to sauce; stir till cheese is melted, but do not bring to boil. Combine with vegetables and ham. Turn into a 1½-quart casserole. Top with bread crumbs. Bake, uncovered, at 350° till heated through, about 40 minutes. Makes about 6 servings.

Sweet-Sour Ham over Rice

2½ cups packaged precooked rice
1 16-ounce can apricot halves
1½ pounds fully cooked ham, cut in
strips (about 3 cups)
2 green peppers, cut in 1-inch
pieces
1 cup chicken broth
⅓ cup sugar
¼ cup vinegar
3 tablespoons butter or margarine
3 tablespoons soy sauce
¼ cup cornstarch

Cook rice according to package directions. Meanwhile, drain apricots, reserving syrup. In saucepan combine apricot syrup, ham, green pepper, ¾ *cup* of the chicken broth, sugar, vinegar, butter, and soy sauce. Bring ham mixture to boiling; cover and simmer the mixture for 10 minutes.

Blend cornstarch and the remaining ¼ cup *cold* chicken broth; add to ham mixture. Cook and stir till boiling; boil 2 minutes more. Add apricots and remove from heat. Spoon the sweet-sour sauce over servings of hot cooked rice. Makes 6 servings.

Ham-Turkey Sauce on Egg Puffs

Tasty as well as hearty —

Egg Puffs
. . .
⅓ cup chopped onion
2 tablespoons butter or margarine
3 tablespoons all-purpose flour
1½ cups milk
. . .
1 cup diced cooked turkey
1 cup fully cooked ham, cut in
julienne strips
½ cup diced sharp process American
cheese
2 tablespoons chopped, canned
pimiento
Dash ground nutmeg
Dash pepper

For *Egg Puffs:* Melt 2 tablespoons butter or margarine in saucepan. Blend in 3 tablespoons all-purpose flour and ½ teaspoon salt. Add 1 cup milk. Cook, stirring constantly, till mixture thickens and bubbles. Slowly add hot mixture to 4 well-beaten egg yolks stirring constantly. Fold in 4 stiffly beaten egg whites. Turn into greased 9x9x2-inch baking dish. Bake at 350° till done, about 30 minutes. Cut in squares. Serve at once with Ham-Turkey Sauce.

Ham-Turkey Sauce: Cook onion in butter till tender; blend in flour. Add milk. Cook and stir till mixture thickens and bubbles. Add remaining ingredients. Heat meat sauce through, stirring frequently. Makes 6 to 8 servings.

Ham and Vegetable Stew

Serve with homemade biscuits —

In Dutch oven brown 1 pound fully cooked ham, cut in 1-inch pieces, in 2 tablespoons shortening. Remove ham. Cook ¾ cup chopped green pepper, ½ cup chopped onion, and 1 clove garlic, minced, in Dutch oven till tender but not brown.

Add ham, one 10-ounce package frozen green beans; 3 medium potatoes, cut in 1-inch cubes; one 28-ounce can tomatoes, cut up; 1 cup water; and 1 teaspoon salt to Dutch oven. Bring to boiling; cover and simmer till tender, about 35 minutes. Combine 3 tablespoons all-purpose flour and ¼ cup cold water; stir into stew. Cook and stir till mixture thickens and bubbles; cook 1 minute longer. Serves 6.

Upside-Down Ham Loaf

Pineapple-crowned meat loaf —

    2 beaten eggs
    ½ cup milk
    1½ cups soft bread crumbs
        (about 2 slices)
    1 teaspoon salt
    ½ teaspoon poultry seasoning
    ¼ teaspoon pepper
    1 pound ground fully cooked ham
    1 pound ground beef
    1 8¾-ounce can pineapple tidbits
    ¼ cup brown sugar
    2 teaspoons prepared mustard
    1 teaspoon cornstarch

Combine first six ingredients. Add meats and mix well. Drain pineapple, reserving 2 tablespoons syrup. Arrange tidbits on bottom of 9x5x3-inch loaf pan. Pat meat on top. Bake at 350° for 1½ hours.

Drain off pan juices and reserve. Turn loaf out upside-down onto platter. Skim fat from pan juices. In saucepan combine pan juices, brown sugar, reserved syrup, and mustard. Blend cornstarch and 1 tablespoon cold water; add to brown sugar mixture. Cook and stir till thick and bubbly. Cook 1 minute longer. Spoon over loaf. Serves 8.

Ham Loaf

    1 10¾-ounce can condensed
        tomato soup
    1 beaten egg
    ⅓ cup milk
    ¾ cup coarsely crushed saltine
        cracker crumbs (17 crackers)
    ⅓ cup chopped onion
    1 pound ground fully cooked ham
    1 pound ground beef
    Mustard Sauce

Reserve *half* the soup. Combine remaining soup, egg, milk, crumbs, and onion. Add meats; mix well. Pat into 9x5x3-inch loaf pan. Bake at 350° for 1½ hours. Drain off excess fat. Let stand 5 minutes; turn onto a serving platter.

Serve with *Mustard Sauce:* Mix reserved soup with 1 beaten egg; 1 tablespoon sugar; 2 tablespoons prepared mustard; 1 tablespoon vinegar; and 1 tablespoon butter or margarine, melted. Cook, stirring till mixture is thickened and bubbly.

Glazed Ham-Raisin Balls

    1 cup raisin bran flakes
    1 6-ounce can evaporated milk
    1 egg
    1 tablespoon finely chopped onion
    Dash salt
    Dash pepper
    Dash dried thyme leaves, crushed
    ½ pound ground fully cooked ham
    ½ pound ground fresh pork
    ¼ cup brown sugar
    ¼ cup corn syrup
    1 tablespoon vinegar
    ½ teaspoon dry mustard

Combine bran flakes, milk, egg, onion, and seasonings. Add meats and mix well. Shape into 8 to 10 meatballs, using ¼ cup meat for each ball. Place in an 11x7x1½-inch baking pan. Bake, uncovered, at 350° for 30 minutes.

In a small saucepan combine brown sugar, corn syrup, vinegar, and dry mustard; bring to boiling. Pour over ham balls and bake 20 minutes more, basting with the sauce once or twice during baking. Makes 4 or 5 servings.

Ham Puffs

    1½ cups ground fully cooked ham
    4 ounces process American cheese,
        grated (1 cup)
    ¼ cup finely chopped green pepper
    ¼ cup finely chopped onion
    1¼ cups milk
    2 beaten egg yolks
    2 cups soft bread crumbs
    2 stiffly beaten egg whites
    Mushroom Sauce

Combine first four ingredients. Stir in milk, egg yolks, and crumbs. Fold in egg whites. Fill six, greased, 6-ounce custard cups. Bake in a pan of hot water at 350° about 40 to 50 minutes till set. Turn out on plates; top with Mushroom Sauce. Serves 6.

Mushroom Sauce: In saucepan melt 3 tablespoons butter or margarine. Blend in 3 tablespoons all-purpose flour. Stir in 1 cup milk and 1 3-ounce can broiled, sliced mushrooms with liquid. Cook, stirring till mixture thickens and bubbles. Add 1 tablespoon grated onion and 1 tablespoon snipped parsley. Season the mushroom sauce with ¼ teaspoon salt and dash pepper. Makes 1½ cups sauce.

Top Hat Ham and Turkey Pie

Pastry toppers can be made ahead —

> Puff Pastry
> 1 slightly beaten egg white
>   .   .   .
> ½ cup chopped onion
> 6 tablespoons butter or margarine
> ½ cup all-purpose flour
> 3 cups chicken broth
> 1½ cups cubed fully cooked ham
> 1½ cups cubed cooked turkey
> 1 10-ounce package frozen peas and
>   carrots, cooked and drained
> ¼ cup chopped, canned pimiento

Prepare Puff Pastry. Roll to 15x9-inch rectangle, ¼ inch thick. Cut in 3-inch circles. Place pastries on *ungreased* baking sheets Chill thoroughly. With very sharp knife, score tops, cutting only through top layer. Brush with mixture of 1 beaten egg white and 1 tablespoon ice water. Bake at 450° for 6 minutes. Reduce temperature to 300°. Bake till lightly browned and crisp, 30 to 35 minutes.

Meanwhile, cook onion in butter till tender but not brown. Blend in flour and 1 teaspoon salt. Add broth. Cook and stir till thickened and bubbly. Add ham, turkey, vegetables, and pimiento; heat to bubbly. Pour into 6 heated individual casseroles. Top each with baked Puff Pastry circle before serving. Freeze remaining circles. Serves 6. (If pastry toppers have been baked in advance, heat to crisp at 300° for 10 minutes before serving.)

Puff Pastry

> 1 cup butter, chilled
> 1¾ cups sifted all-purpose flour
> ½ cup ice water

Reserve two tablespoons butter; chill. Work remaining chilled butter with back of wooden spoon just till pliable. Pat or roll between sheets of waxed paper to 8x6-inch rectangle, ¼ inch thick. Chill sheets of butter at least 1 hour. (Keep all utensils cold — chill before using.)

Measure flour into mixing bowl; cut in reserved butter till mixture resembles coarse meal. Gradually add ice water, tossing with fork to make stiff dough. Shape into ball. Turn out onto lightly floured surface; knead till smooth and elastic, about 5 minutes. Cover dough; let rest 10 minutes.

On *lightly* floured surface, roll dough to 15x9-inch rectangle, ¼ inch thick. Peel top sheet of waxed paper from chilled butter; invert on half the dough. Peel off other sheet of waxed paper. Fold over other half of dough to cover butter. Seal edges by pressing with heel of hand. Wrap in waxed paper; chill thoroughly, at least 1 hour. Unwrap. On lightly floured surface, roll dough from center to 15x9-inch rectangle, ¼ inch thick. Dough should be of even thickness. Brush excess flour from pastry. Fold in thirds; turn dough and fold in thirds again. There now will be 9 layers of pastry dough.

Seal edges with heel of hand. Wrap in waxed paper; chill thoroughly, at least 1 hour. Repeat rolling, folding, and chilling 2 or 3 times more. Bake as directed in recipes.

Black Magic Ham Towers

> Puff Pastry
> 3 cups diced fully cooked ham
> ½ cup chopped onion
> 2 tablespoons butter or margarine
> ½ cup sliced pitted ripe olives
>   .   .   .
> 1 10¾-ounce can condensed cream
>   of chicken soup
> 1 cup dairy sour cream
> ⅓ cup milk
> ½ teaspoon paprika
>   .   .   .
> ⅓ cup slivered almonds, toasted

Prepare Puff Pastry. Roll to 15x9-inch rectangle. Cut into 12 squares. Place on *ungreased* baking sheets. Chill thoroughly. Bake at 450° for 6 minutes. Reduce temperature to 300°. Bake till lightly browned, 30 to 35 minutes. Split 6 squares horizontally.

Cook ham and onion in butter till onion is tender but not brown. Stir in olives. Combine soup, sour cream, milk, and paprika; stir till smooth. Add to ham mixture. Cook and stir till heated. On serving plate, spoon some ham mixture over half of pastry squares. Add top and more ham mixture. Top with toasted almonds. Makes 6 servings.

Ham leftovers with style

Bake Puff Pastry in squares or rounds for→ the glamorous settings—Black Magic Ham Towers and Top Hat Ham and Turkey Pie.

To make uniform hamburger patties, gently mold the ground beef in ½-cup measure. Turn out; flatten gently to shape.

Filled burgers are easy to make. Just seal mustard, onion, relish, and cubes of cheese tightly between two ground beef patties.

HAMANTASCH *(hä′ muhn täsh′, hum′ uhn-, hŏŏm′-)*—A three-cornered filled pastry traditionally served in Jewish homes during the ancient festival of Purim. The filling is usually made of prunes or poppy seeds. (See also *Jewish Cookery*.)

HAMBURGER *(meat)*—By government regulations, hamburger is made of ground beef that contains no more than 30 percent fat. Since the beef commonly ground usually has about 20 to 25 percent fat naturally attached to it, as much as 10 percent additional fat may be ground with the meat to supplement its juiciness. Because it is produced from lower priced cuts of beef and contains a higher percentage of fat than other beef, hamburger is normally lower in price than other types of ground beef.

Hamburger gets its name from Hamburg, Germany. The people of this city apparently refined the Russian habit of eating raw, finely chopped beef and adopted this grinding of meat. In fact, the Germans became so fond of ground beef that they gave it the name of their city. This hamburg steak was originally eaten raw but by the time it was introduced into the United States, more than likely by some German immigrants, the hamburger meat was usually cooked before being eaten.

Since shrinkage is directly proportional to the amount of fat in meat, hamburger is apt to shrink in cooking more than the other types of ground beef. Therefore, allow for this shrinkage when making patties and meat loaves from hamburger. In casseroles, one-dish meals, soups, and other dishes where the hamburger is first browned, shrinkage is less critical and you can pour off any excess fat before adding the other ingredients to the hamburger. (See also *Ground Beef*.)

HAMBURGER *(sandwich)*—A ground beef patty in a bun. The credit for the origin of this sandwich is usually given to an enterprising merchant at the St. Louis Exposition of 1904. Today, this American favorite is famous around the world.

The two essential ingredients of this sandwich are ground beef and a bun. Al-

Flavorful burgers

←Three variations of the ever popular hamburger sandwich—Iowa Corn Burgers, German Burgers, and Orange-Topped Burgers.

Tips for making hamburgers

For juicy patties, handle the ground beef as little as possible. Mix the meat gently when adding seasonings or other ingredients and don't pack the meat down.

Shaping patties
Assure evenly sized patties by shaping them one of these three ways.

1. Use a ⅓- or ½-cup measure to divide the ground beef. Turn the meat out of the measuring cup and gently form it into patties of uniform size.

2. Pat the meat between two sheets of waxed paper to a ½- to ¾-inch-thick rectangle. Then, use a large, round cookie cutter to cut out patties.

3. Form the ground beef into a roll about 3 inches in diameter. Slice off patties ½ to ¾ inch thick.

Timesaving hints
Save meal preparation time by shaping a large quantity of hamburger patties at one time and freezing them. Wrap the patties separately in clear plastic wrap or waxed paper before freezing so you can use one or two patties at a time as needed. Seal the wrapped patties in a plastic bag or round container.

Frozen hamburger patties do not need to be thawed before cooking but remember to allow a little extra cooking time.

Keep hamburger buns in the freezer also so you can assemble a hamburger sandwich in just a few minutes.

---

though the sandwich may be square, rectangular, or any shape you want, it is usually round. In fact, special round hamburger buns are commonly used and the ground beef patties are shaped so that they fit these round buns.

How to cook: Hamburger patties may be panbroiled, broiled, or grilled. Since all three methods will yield juicy, flavorful burgers, family preference should determine which method you use. To assure a tasty hamburger, avoid flattening the ground beef patty as it cooks since meat juices will seep out; learn to judge cooking time to give the degree of doneness desired; and remember that overcooking results in a dry and flavorless patty.

Although hamburger buns are ready to eat as purchased, many people prefer to make their sandwiches with toasted buns. These buns may be toasted in a broiler, on a griddle, or on a grill. The buns will brown more evenly when lightly buttered. Since the buns brown quickly, be sure to watch the buns very closely.

How to serve: There are many ways to perk up this meat patty in a bun. Toppers such as catsup, mustard, onion, pickle, and pickle relish are for some diners a must with hamburgers. Offer an assortment of these toppers so that each person can make his own combination. Cheese, another popular topper, is so frequently linked with a hamburger that this combination is called a cheeseburger. If you top the hamburger with cheese during the last few minutes of cooking, the cheese melts slightly.

Adding ingredients to the ground beef before making it into patties is another way of varying hamburgers. Try adding a little tomato juice, vegetable juice cocktail, beef broth, club soda, catsup, or milk to add not only an enticing flavor, but moistness as well. Or add crushed crackers or cornflakes and a beaten egg to the ground beef for meatloaf-like patties.

Stuff hamburgers for a scrumptious variance. Simply enclose shredded cheese, onion, pickles, or other ingredients between two thin ground beef patties. Then press the edges together to seal tightly.

Basic Hamburgers

Skillet: Shape 1 pound ground beef into 4 patties, ¾ inch thick. Heat skillet till sizzling hot; sprinkle skillet lightly with salt. Cook burgers over medium-high heat 5 minutes; turn and cook 4 to 5 minutes longer. Partially cover if meat spatters.

Broiler: In mixing bowl lightly combine 1 pound ground beef, ½ teaspoon salt, dash pepper, and ¼ cup finely chopped onion (optional). Shape into 4 patties, ¾ inch thick. Broil 3 inches from heat 6 minutes. Turn; broil till done, about 4 minutes.

This tasty burger trio is barbecue-grilled to perfection. For large barbecues, grill several of each and let guests choose a Burger Montain, Burgundy Beef Burger, or Square Burger.

Cheeseburger Towers

  2 pounds ground beef
  2 teaspoons salt
    Dash pepper
       . . .
  6 slices process American cheese
    Catsup
    Mustard
    Pickle relish
  6 hamburger buns, split and toasted

Combine meat, salt, and pepper; mix lightly. Shape into 12 4-inch patties. Cook on lightly greased griddle about 3 minutes on each side.

  Place cheese slices on waxed paper. With a 2-inch cookie cutter, cut a circle from center of each cheese slice. (Slices with holes go between patties, circles atop.) Place a patty on bottom half of *each* bun. Add cheese slice; fill hole with catsup, mustard, and pickle relish. Add second patty, then cheese circle; top meat towers with remaining hamburger bun halves. Makes approximately 6 servings.

Orange-Topped Burgers

The meat is mixed with zesty seasoning —

  ½ cup dairy sour cream
  2 tablespoons chopped green onion
  1 teaspoon Worcestershire sauce
  ¾ teaspoon salt
  1½ pounds ground beef
  2 large oranges, peeled and cut
      into 6 slices each
  1 medium green pepper, cut into
      6 rings
  6 hamburger buns, split and
      toasted

Combine dairy sour cream, green onion, Worcestershire sauce, and salt. Add ground beef; mix well. Shape into 6 patties. Broil 3 inches from heat for 6 minutes. Turn; broil 4 to 6 minutes longer. Top each with 2 orange slices and a green pepper ring. Broil till meat is done, about 2 minutes longer. Serve in toasted hamburger buns. Makes 6 servings.

Burger Mountains

  1½ pounds ground chuck*
    1 cup dairy sour cream
   ¼ cup Worcestershire sauce
    1 tablespoon instant minced onion
  1½ teaspoons salt
    1 cup corn flakes
      Butter or margarine
    2 hamburger buns, split
    1 medium tomato, thinly sliced
    1 medium unpeeled cucumber,**
      thinly sliced
   ½ cup dairy sour cream
    3 tablespoons milk
    1 tablespoon crumbled blue cheese

Combine first 5 ingredients; blend thoroughly. Crush corn flakes slightly; gently stir into meat mixture. Let stand ½ hour. To shape burgers, divide meat mixture in 4 portions and from each shape a 3½-inch patty and a 3-inch patty. (Patties will be about ¾ inch thick.) Broil in a wire broiler basket over *slow* coals, about 5 minutes per side.

Meanwhile, butter buns and toast, cut side down, on grill. Place a large burger on each toasted bun half; then top each with a tomato slice and 3 cucumber slices. Add a smaller burger; spear with skewer to keep "mountain" in place. Drizzle with *Blue Cheese Sauce:* In small saucepan blend the ½ cup sour cream, milk, and blue cheese; heat through, stirring constantly. Serves 4.

*If beef is lean, have 3 ounces of suet ground with this amount of meat.

**To flute cucumber edges as shown, run tines of a fork lengthwise down all sides of a whole unpeeled cucumber.

Pinwheel Burgers

Shows off swirls of cheese —

Combine 1½ pounds ground beef, ⅓ cup milk, 1 egg, ½ cup finely crushed saltine crackers (10 crackers), ¼ cup minced green pepper, ¼ cup minced onion, 1 tablespoon prepared mustard, ½ teaspoon salt, and dash pepper.

On waxed paper pat meat mixture to a 12-inch square shape. Spread with one 5-ounce jar process blue-cheese spread *or* pimiento-cheese spread. Roll meat as for jelly roll; seal edge. Cut in twelve 1-inch slices. Broil till done, about 12 to 14 minutes, turning once. Makes 6 servings.

Square Burgers

Patties with a different shape —

    1 teaspoon instant minced onion
   ½ cup evaporated milk
  1½ pounds ground chuck*
    1 slightly beaten egg
    4 slices white bread, toasted
      and buttered
    1 3½-ounce can onion rings
      or 1 4-ounce package frozen
      onion rings

Soak onion in milk 5 minutes; lightly mix with meat, egg, 1 teaspoon salt, and dash pepper. Place meat mixture on large sheet of waxed paper; lightly pat into a 9-inch square.

Cut meat in 4 squares. With scissors, cut through paper between burgers. Place, meat side down, on grill; peel off paper. Broil over coals 4 to 5 inches from heat 5 minutes; turn and broil 3 to 4 minutes longer. Meanwhile heat onions according to label directions. Place each burger on a slice of toast; top with onions. Serves 4.

*If beef is lean, have 3 ounces of suet ground with this amount of meat.

Iowa Corn Burgers

Drain one 8-ounce can whole kernel corn. Mix corn, ¼ cup catsup, 1 tablespoon grated onion, 1 tablespoon snipped parsley, 1 teaspoon salt, and ⅛ teaspoon pepper. Add 1½ pounds ground beef; mix well. Shape into 8 patties, ¾ inch thick. Broil 3 inches from heat for 6 minutes. Turn; broil 4 to 6 minutes. Serve corn burgers in 8 hamburger buns, split and toasted. Makes 8 servings.

German Burgers

  1½ pounds ground beef
    1 tablespoon caraway seed
   12 slices rye bread, toasted
    1 cup coleslaw, drained

Combine beef, caraway seed, 1 teaspoon salt, and ⅛ teaspoon pepper; mix well. Shape into 6 patties, ¾ inch thick. Panbroil in hot skillet over medium-high heat for 5 minutes. Turn; cook 4 to 5 minutes more. Place each patty on rye slice. Divide coleslaw and spoon atop; top with remaining bread. Serves 6.

Burgundy Beefburgers

Served atop French bread slices —

In large bowl combine 2 pounds ground chuck,* 1 cup soft bread crumbs, 1 egg, ¼ cup dry red wine, 2 tablespoons sliced green onions, 1 teaspoon salt, and dash pepper; mix well. Shape in 6 doughnut-shaped burgers, about 1 inch thick. For Burgundy sauce, cook 2 tablespoons sliced green onions and tops in ½ cup butter or margarine just till tender; add ¼ cup dry red wine. Brush burgers with sauce.

Broil over coals about 4 inches from heat for 9 minutes, brushing frequently with sauce. Turn burgers and broil till done, about 4 minutes longer, continuing to brush with sauce. Cut 6 thick slices French bread on the diagonal. Brush with melted butter or margarine. Serve burgers on the bread slices. Heat remaining Burgundy sauce to pass with the beefburgers. Makes 6 servings.

*If beef is lean, have 4 ounces suet ground with this amount of meat.

HAND CHEESE—A surface-ripened cheese with a sharp flavor and a pungent aroma. This cheese gets its peculiar name because it was originally molded by hand in Germany. Manufacturers often sell this cheese using a variety of different local names. (See also *Cheese.*)

HANUKKAH, HANUKAH, CHANUKKAH, CHANUKAH *(hä′ nuh kuh′ -noŏ kä′, -kuh′)* —A Jewish holiday which has the welcome combination of serious tradition allied with light-hearted celebration. This traditional holiday begins eight days from the 25th of the Jewish month of Kislew, and is always of eight days' duration. Generally, this is within the first two weeks of December, but occasionally it nearly overlaps the Christmas holiday season.

Hanukkah began in the second century B.C. as the eight day Feast of Dedication or the Feast of the Maccabees, but later it became known as the Feast of Lights.

In 165 B.C., Judas Maccabees, his brothers, and the elders of the congregation of Israel restored the temple in Jerusalem which only three years before had suffered the ignominy of housing a pagan idol in its holy place. The Jews prepared a new altar —hence the Feast of Dedication—puri-fied the temple, and triumphantly brought out some sanctified oil, which had been sealed in a special flask and hidden away, with which to light the great temple lamp —hence, the Feast of Lights.

Spiritual implications: Though the first Hanukkah lamp (or light) glowed within the Temple, its symbolism extended to the outer world. The illumination was intended for the community at large, as well as to offer a special glow for those included within the holy walls. Later, when the celebration of the holidays began to be observed in homes as well as in synagogues or temples, the lamps were set outside the house, one near each door opening onto the street, so that neighbors and passers-by could enjoy the light. Today the Hanukkah *menorah* (or eight-branched candlestick with a ninth holder for the *shamash* or lighting taper) is usually placed in a front window of the house for all the passers-by to notice and to honor.

The lighting of the Hanukkah candles takes place when the first stars (the heavenly candles) appear. The head of the house stands before the *menorah* or individual candles if these are used instead, and holds aloft the small lighted taper (*shamash*) as he says a blessing in which all the family join with a final "amen." Then the night's candle is lighted. This ceremony is repeated throughout the holiday—two candles on the second night, three on the third, and so on. (Some other Jewish communities reverse the order—lighting all eight candles on the first night, and extinguishing one each night.)

Hospitality: Since the holiday is termed a feast, it is natural that food should have an important place in its observance. Usually there are two special dinners—one on the night of the lighting of the fifth candle and another on the eve of the sabbath (a Friday night) that falls within the holiday week. On other evenings, a lighter supper is served. A pleasant custom in some circles is to invite friends in for a social evening when brandy is served accompanied by rich holiday cookies. A late supper follows this, highlighting the traditional Hanukkah specialty, *latkes.* These are really pancakes and are served with a fruit sauce, and perhaps a fruit-cream cheese salad.

Because Middle Europe has been the temporary homeland of many Jews, the *pièce de résistance* at the two important holiday dinners are likely to be goose and duckling—poultry indigenous to Germany, Poland, Hungary, and France. The plump goose is often stuffed with fruit, sauerkraut, or with bread crumbs and chestnuts. Duckling provides variety without too much innovation at the second occasion.

For the more casual evening meals, the obliging *latke* (see *Latke* for recipe) is available in many guises. Most recipes for potato *latkes* are indistinguishable from those for potato pancakes. With them a tart, cinnamon-flavored applesauce is delicious if not *de rigueur*. Pineapple sauce (not too heavily sweetened), blueberry sauce, thick apricot purée lightly touched with mace, or a fixed fruit concoction such as goes into first-course fruit cup, but sweetened with a touch of honey, are all possible go-alongs for *latkes*.

The children's hour: Small fry love all holidays but they have a special reason for liking this mid-December one, when all

This Hanukkah favorite, Sesame-Honey Candy, is an unusual hard candy. Toasted sesame seeds add crunch as well as flavor.

The crisp, airy dough surrounds an apple or pineapple ring in these Fruit Fritters. Sift confectioners' sugar over top.

the air is full of talk of presents, parties, and general festivity. Each child in the household is given, as his natural right, a gift for each of the nights on which a Hanukkah candle is lighted. The gifts may be large or small, but there's one for each evening. Particularly appropriate for both boys and girls is the four-sided top called a *dreidel*, with each side bearing a letter of the Hebrew alphabet. Thus songs, games, and an overall atmosphere of content and warm happiness is the order of the evening on each of these eight special December nights. (See also *Jewish Cookery*.)

Fruit Fritters

Sift together 1 cup sifted all-purpose flour, 2 tablespoons sugar, 2 teaspoons baking powder, and ¼ teaspoon salt. Mix together 1 beaten egg; ⅔ cup milk; and 2 tablespoons butter or margarine, melted. Stir into dry ingredients; blend till smooth, but do not overbeat. (Batter should be heavy enough to coat fruit; if necessary, add more milk or flour.)

Using 3 or 4 apples, peeled, cored, and sliced crosswise into rings *or* 18 thin pineapple slices, dip apple or pineapple rings in batter one at a time. Fry in deep hot fat (375°) for 3 minutes, turning once. Drain on paper toweling. Serve hot with confectioners' sugar or a cinnamon-sugar mixture sprinkled over top of the fritters. Makes 18 fritters.

Sesame-Honey Candy

A brittlelike sweet —

In medium saucepan combine 2 cups sugar, ⅔ cup honey, ½ teaspoon ground ginger, and dash salt. Cook over low heat, stirring constantly, till mixture boils; cook 8 minutes more, stirring occasionally. Remove from heat. Stir in ⅔ cup chopped walnuts and ½ cup toasted sesame seed; pour onto greased platter or into shallow baking pan. Cool slightly.

Butter or oil hands; press and spread candy to very thin sheet. Working quickly, cut into diamond-shaped pieces with kitchen scissors while candy is warm. (Candy will cool quickly.) Makes 72 pieces.

HARD CLAM—An unusual type of clam found most often along the Atlantic coast. *Quahog*, an Indian name for hard clam, is used for these clams in some parts of the country. Small hard clams are often called littlenecks and cherrystones. The larger ones are sometimes referred to as chowder clams. (See also *Clam.*)

HARD SAUCE—A stiff mixture of butter, sugar, usually confectioners', and flavoring such as vanilla, brandy, or rum. This dessert sauce is usually chilled before serving and, if stiff enough, is cut in decorative shapes. Hard sauce is the traditional ac-

A generous mound of Fluffy Hard Sauce tops this Easy Plum Pudding (see *Plum* for recipe). This easy-to-make sauce is also delicious with steamed fruit puddings and fruitcakes.

This hearty Best Oven Hash turns leftover roast beef and potatoes into a delicious casserole. Crushed cornflakes give a crunchy topping. Garnish with poached eggs and parsley.

companiment for steamed plum pudding, but this sweet topping is also delicious served with other desserts such as fruitcakes and spice cakes. (See also *Sauce.*)

Hard Sauce

Thoroughly cream ½ cup butter with 2 cups sifted confectioners' sugar. Add 1 teaspoon vanilla. Spread in 8x8x2-inch pan; chill to harden. Cut in squares.

Fluffy Hard Sauce

Prepare Hard Sauce as above, stirring 1 beaten egg yoke into creamed mixture. Fold in 1 stiffly beaten egg white. Chill the mixture thoroughly.

HARDTACK—Hard bread made of flour and water. In the years before modern methods of food preservation, hardtack, which would keep for long periods of time, was a staple in the diets of soldiers and sailors.

HARD WHEAT—A type of wheat that is high in gluten-forming proteins. Hard wheat flour is especially suited for making bread and pasta. (See also *Wheat.*)

HARE—A long-eared, long-legged relative of the rabbit. The terms hare and rabbit are frequently, yet erroneously, used interchangeably. At birth the hare is covered with fur and has its eyes open; a newborn rabbit is furless and blind. The differences are continued into adult life: an adult hare is usually larger than an adult rabbit. However, both the jack rabbit and snowshoe rabbit that are found in the United States are true types of hares.

Hares, which have dark, flavorful meat, can be cooked like rabbits. Remember to use dry-heat cookery methods (roasting, baking, and broiling) for young animals and moist-heat cookery methods (braising, simmering, and steaming) for the larger and older hares. (See also *Game.*)

HAROSETH, HAROSET, HAROSES *(huh rōs′ uhth, -uht, -uhs)*—A Jewish dish made of chopped apples, nuts, and wine and seasoned with cinnamon. This dish is traditionally served during the Passover celebration. (See also *Jewish Cookery.*)

HARTSHORN—Ammonium carbonate. This compound was once used as a leavening agent, called bakers' ammonia.

HARVARD BEETS—Cooked, diced beets served in a sweet-sour sauce. This dish has been popular in New England for more than a century. (See also *Beet.*)

Harvard Beets

The beets give the sauce a crimson color —

  1 16-ounce can diced beets
          . . .
  2 tablespoons sugar
  1 tablespoon cornstarch
  ¼ teaspoon salt
          . . .
  ¼ cup vinegar
  2 tablespoons butter or margarine

Drain beets, reserving ⅓ cup liquid. In saucepan combine sugar, cornstarch, and salt. Stir in reserved liquid, vinegar, and butter or margarine. Cook, stirring constantly, till mixture is thickened and bubbly. Add beets. Heat through. Serves 4 or 5.

HASENPFEFFER *(hä′ suhn fef′ uhr)*—A hearty stew made of rabbit or hare that has been tenderized by marinating it for several days. This German word literally means "hare in pepper." (See also *Rabbit.*)

Hasenpfeffer

  1 1- to 2-pound ready-to-cook
      rabbit
  3 cups water
  1 cup vinegar
  ½ cup sugar
  1 medium onion, sliced
  1 teaspoon mixed pickling spices
  2 teaspoons salt
  ¼ teaspoon pepper
  2 tablespoons all-purpose flour
  2 tablespoons cooking oil

Cut rabbit into serving pieces. Mix water, vinegar, sugar, onion, pickling spices, salt, and pepper. Add rabbit; refrigerate 2 days. Remove meat, reserving 1 cup marinade; dry meat.

Place flour and meat in plastic bag; shake to coat. Brown meat in hot oil. Gradually add reserved marinade. Cover; simmer till tender, about 45 to 60 minutes (add water, if necessary). Remove meat. Thicken the excess liquid in the skillet for gravy, if desired. Makes 2 or 3 servings.

HASH—A main dish made of diced, chopped, or ground meats and vegetables, particularly potatoes. Hash is a popular way to use leftover roast beef and gravy. Canned corned beef hash and canned or frozen roast beef hash are available.

Yankee Red-Flannel Hash

  ⅓ cup finely chopped onion
  ¼ cup shortening
  3 cups finely chopped cooked
      potatoes
  1 16-ounce can beets, drained
      and finely chopped
  1½ cups finely chopped cooked
      corned beef
  ⅓ cup milk
  1 or 2 drops bottled hot pepper
      sauce

In skillet cook onion in hot shortening till tender but not brown. Lightly toss together potatoes, beets, corned beef, milk, ½ teaspoon salt, and hot pepper sauce. Spread hash evenly in skillet. Cook the corned beef-potato mixture over medium heat till the bottom is brown and crusty. Makes 4 servings.

Best Oven Hash

1 cup coarsely ground cooked beef
1 cup coarsely ground cooked
   potatoes
¼ cup coarsely ground onion
¼ cup snipped parsley
1 teaspoon salt
   Dash pepper
2 teaspoons Worcestershire sauce
1 6-ounce can evaporated milk
   (⅔ cup)
      • • •
¼ cup fine dry bread crumbs
1 tablespoon butter or
   margarine, melted

Lightly mix first 8 ingredients. Turn into 1-quart casserole. Mix bread crumbs and butter; sprinkle over top. Bake at 350° till hot, about 30 minutes. Makes 4 servings.

Skillet Hash

In skillet cook ⅓ cup finely chopped onion in 2 tablespoons butter or margarine till tender but not brown. Add 2 cups diced or ground cooked beef roast; 2 or 3 medium raw potatoes, diced or ground; ½ cup beef broth or leftover gravy; and ½ teaspoon salt. Mix well. Cover; cook over low heat, stirring often till potatoes are tender, about 15 minutes. Makes 4 servings.

Tangiers Hash

½ cup chopped onion
1 pound bulk pork sausage
2 cups ground cooked roast beef
3 medium tomatoes, peeled and
   chopped (1½ cups)
¼ cup snipped parsley
½ cup fine dry bread crumbs
2 tablespoons butter or margarine,
   melted

Slowly cook onion with sausage till sausage is browned, breaking up sausage as it cooks; drain. Stir in roast beef and tomatoes. Divide evenly among 4 or 5 individual casseroles.

Top with parsley. Combine crumbs and butter. Sprinkle over parsley. Bake, uncovered, at 350° for 30 to 35 minutes. Serves 4 or 5.

HASTY PUDDING—A New England dish consisting of cornmeal mush sweetened with maple syrup, brown sugar, or molasses and served with milk. This porridge was most popular during colonial days. Even today, the British use oatmeal for a similar dish.

HAW *(hô)*—The berry of the hawthorn shrub. This berry is often used in jam or jelly.

HAWAIIAN COOKERY—The exotic, varied cuisine of the tropical islands that comprise the state of Hawaii. Hawaii is correctly identified as a melting pot not only in population but also in cuisine. What today is classified as Hawaiian cookery is actually a variety of dishes from various countries.

This Hawaiian cuisine is a mixture of Chinese, Japanese, Filipino, Korean, Portuguese, and American specialties, and, of course, the Pacific islands, making it a delightful surprise to the uninhibited.

The first settlers of Hawaii, believed to have come from other islands in the Pacific, probably Tahiti or the Marquesas Islands, brought with them pigs, chickens, taro, and many tropical fruits such as coconuts and bananas, to add to the staples, fish and seaweed. These foods were eaten raw or were cooked in an underground oven or *imu*.

These first settlers were relatively undisturbed until the nineteenth century when missionaries from the eastern United States arrived, although explorers visited the islands during the eighteenth century. As well as religion and education, the missionaries brought with them foods such as chowders, curries, and puddings which soon became part of the Hawaiian cuisine.

Beginning in the middle 1800s, a scarcity of plantation workers led to the importation of workers from other countries.

The first to arrive were the Chinese. They brought with them foods such as rice, soybeans, and bean sprouts as well as Chinese cooking techniques such as stir-frying.

Hawaiian entrée

The thick, juicy pork chops are glazed with →
a sweet-sour, pineapple-honey sauce in these
Double Fruit-Glazed Pork Chops.

The arrival of workers from Japan meant the introduction of fresh bean curd, soybeans, fermented mashed beans, many pickled foods (especially fruits and vegetables), as well as numerous dishes using fish and a variety of other seafoods.

A third large group of immigrant workers were the Filipinos. For these people, the islands of Hawaii offered tropical fruits and vegetables similar to those growing in the Philippines. The cuisine that these Filipinos imported with them reflected the cuisines of the Chinese, Malayan, and Spanish settlers of the Philippines. Thus, the Filipino cuisine utilized bean sprouts (Chinese) as well as tomatoes and garlic (Spanish).

Other small immigrant groups included the Koreans and Portuguese. Both of these groups brought along the cuisine of their homelands. A great many Korean and Portuguese dishes are now firmly established as part of Hawaiian cookery.

In recent years, the inflow of people from the mainland United States has resulted in the incorporation of typically American dishes, like the hamburger, into the Hawaiian cuisine. As with many of the dishes introduced by other cultures, the people of Hawaii have adapted these dishes to the ingredients that are readily available in the Hawaiian islands.

Well-known foods and recipes: One of the best known and yet most controversial Hawaiian foods is poi. If you ask a native Hawaiian, they are likely to describe this dish as Hawaiian ambrosia. On the other hand, a visitor to the islands will probably tell you that this starchy, gray-colored mixture not only looks like paste but tastes like it as well, for poi is made of the bland, and to some people, flavorless taro roots.

These tuberous, starchy roots have been called the Hawaiian potato. To make poi, the taro root must first be cooked, usually by steaming. Then peeled, cooked taro is pounded into a paste. After allowing this thick paste to partially ferment for a few days, it's ready to eat and enjoy.

Since the fingers are the only utensils needed to eat poi, its thickness is commonly described by calling it one-finger, two-finger, or three-finger poi. One-finger poi is thick enough that a mouthful can be scooped up by swirling one finger in the poi. Two-finger or three-finger poi has been thinned with a small amount of water to the point where the use of two or three fingers are required. However, all these definitions are based on the number of fingers that an experienced poi eater must use. However, bedecked tourists who try poi for the first time usually find that they have to use their three fingers as a scoop in order to eat the one-finger poi.

Like any other cuisine, Hawaiian cookery is characterized by the use of meats, fruits, and vegetables that are indigenous to the area. Naturally, fish and seafood are abundant foods on the islands. One of the most popular food fishes in Hawaii is *mahimahi*. This fish, known on the United States mainland as dolphin, is commonly served broiled or baked.

Although the Hawaiians use fish and seafood in many ways, two favorite dishes deserve special mention—*lomi lomi salmon* and *sashimi*. Shredded smoked salmon, fresh tomatoes, and onion are the basic ingredients in *lomi lomi salmon*. This salad is often served in tomato cups. *Sashimi* was originally a Japanese dish but by now it has become classified as a Hawaiian dish. Many visitors from the mainland enjoy this dish at first but lose enthusiasm when they find out that it is nothing more than raw fish that is dipped in a sauce.

Tropical fruits are one of the delights of Hawaiian cuisine. Pineapples, guavas, coconuts, bananas, passion fruits, and many other fruits grow in abundance on the islands. Given these natural foods, the Hawaiians have learned to use them in all types of dishes as well as to eat them fresh. Very often, the Hawaiians vary dishes of other countries simply by substituting tropical fruits and nuts available on the islands for other types of fruits and nuts.

Probably the two most popular fruits on the islands are pineapple and coconut. The pineapple meat and juice are both used. Pineapple is particularly popular in salads, desserts, and beverages. Even the pineapple shell is often utilized. When hollowed out, this shell serves as a serving bowl for salads or main dishes. Pineapple spears are a popular garnish and sometimes even the stirring sticks for beverages.

The coconut is another fruit with various uses. The white, still-soft meat of underripe coconuts is especially prized by islanders who like to eat this delicately flavored meat right from the shell. Although the coconut meat is frequently used in salads and desserts, usually grated, the coconut flavor of many dishes is provided by coconut milk. The liquid found inside the coconut is sometimes called coconut milk, but this term usually refers to cow's milk flavored with coconut made by steeping grated coconut in warm milk. One of the favorite Hawaiian desserts is *haupia* or coconut pudding made with coconut milk.

Two kinds of leaves—taro and ti leaves—are important in Hawaiian cookery. Taro leaves, sometimes called Hawaiian spinach, are served as a cooked vegetable or used in casserole-type dishes. A popular dish called *laulau* is made of pork, fish, and taro leaves. Ti leaves, which resemble corn husks, are used to wrap foods that are to be baked in an *imu*.

In the mainland United States, a sweet-sour sauce or glaze is one of the characteristics most commonly associated with Hawaiian cookery. Actually, this sweet-sour flavor inherited from the Chinese and Filipinos, is found in only one of the three main sauces that characterize Hawaiian cookery. The others are coconut milk and a marinade made of soy sauce, sugar, wine, oil, and seasonings. All three of these sauces are used on all types of meat as well as in various types of meat dishes.

Hawaiian cookery embraces many dishes that have remained essentially unchanged since they were introduced by the Chinese, Japanese, Portuguese, or other immigrants. Both Japanese *teriyaki* and *sukiyaki* are very popular. In fact, *teriyaki* has become a typical dish for a Hawaiian picnic. Typical Chinese favorites include won ton (similar to ravioli and frequently served in soup) and piquant sweet-sour pork.

An island specialty

An assortment of tropical fruits served with fruit dressings makes a delicious lunch for Hawaiian natives or visitors.

The main Portuguese contributions are a raised doughnut called *malassadas* and a sweet bread called *pao doce*. Many of the pickled foods such as *kim chee* (pickled cabbage) come from Korea. Although these foods originally were limited to the cuisine of the specific immigrant groups, the large extent of intermarrying between these groups led to a mixing of cuisines until now the cuisine of the Hawaiian Islands is actually a blend of dishes from many lands.

The luau: The Hawaiian luau, the ultimate in Hawaiian hospitality, is a blend of fun, and entertainment. These feasts were held by early Hawaiians to celebrate special occasions such as the visits of chiefs, weddings, and births. Everyone helped in the food preparation, decoration, and entertainment for these lively affairs. This spirit of gaiety is still an essential part of any Hawaiian luau that is held.

The setting for a luau is definitely tropical with fruits and flowers decorating the low, leaf-covered, outdoor table. The place setting is simple—a punch cup, fingerbowl, and several leaf dishes that contain condiments—and the guests are asked to sit on the ground. No utensils usually are used.

The food at a luau is hearty and plentiful. The highlight of the meal is usually a suckling pig roasted in an *imu* lined with hot cooking stones. Since it takes many hours to roast the pig, preparation must be started early. Several of the red hot cooking stones are placed in the cavity of the cleaned pig. The pig is then carefully lowered into the hot oven. Other meats, fish,

Bring a touch of Hawaii into your home by serving rich chocolate Mauna Loa Parfaits, Kona Sunset sprinkled with fresh coconut, garnished Passion Fruit Punch, or Bananas in Nectar.

fruits, and vegetables are placed around the pig and the oven is then completely covered with layers of ti and banana leaves, burlap, and finally earth. By the time the guests have arrived, the steamed pig and other foods are ready to be removed from the pit. This uncovering is usually done with great ceremony and dignity as the guests watch with intense interest and anticipation.

An assortment of tropical fruits, punch made from a blend of tropical fruit juices, several salads, other meat dishes such as barbecued spareribs and baked ham, vegetables, and two or three desserts complete the luau menu. Almost any food is appropriate for serving at a luau as long as there is an abundance of food.

After everyone has eaten as much as possible, the luau entertainment begins. This usually consists of Hawaiian music and the hula. But no matter what the setting, menu, and entertainment, the luau is considered successful if it maintains a spirit of pleasurable hospitality and relaxed informality throughout the entire evening.

Po Po

Your guests will enjoy cooking these tiny meatballs over the glowing coals of a hibachi —

½ pound ground beef
½ teaspoon salt
1 teaspoon monosodium glutamate
½ teaspoon Japanese sate spice
  or a mixture of chili powder
  and dry mustard
½ teaspoon chopped fresh or
  dried rosemary leaves
1 egg yolk

. . .

Butter or margarine
Grated Parmesan cheese

Lightly mix together ground beef, ½ teaspoon salt, monosodium glutamate, sate spice *or* chili powder and mustard mixture, rosemary, and egg yolk. Form mixture into balls the size of marbles. Sauté lightly in butter or margarine and roll in Parmesan cheese. Insert a split bamboo stick or long wooden pick in each of the meatballs.

Toast before eating over charcoal in miniature hibachi. Makes about 3 dozen.

Double Fruit-Glazed Pork Chops

6 6- to 8-ounce double rib pork
  chops
1 cup brown sugar
¼ cup pineapple juice
¼ cup honey
1 teaspoon dry mustard
3 whole cloves
6 whole coriander seeds, crushed

. . .

6 slices *each* orange, lemon, and
  lime
6 maraschino cherries
1½ tablespoons cornstarch
¼ teaspoon salt
1 lemon slice

Brown chops in skillet; season with salt and pepper, then place in shallow baking pan. For sauce combine brown sugar, pineapple juice, honey, dry mustard, cloves, and coriander; spoon about 1 tablespoon over each chop. Bake, uncovered, at 350° till done, about 1¼ hours, basting with half of sauce.

With wooden pick, peg one slice of orange, lemon, and lime on each chop; top with maraschino cherry. Baste fruit with the remaining spicy sauce and bake about 10 minutes longer.

Measure pan juices; skim off excess fat. Add liquid to make 1⅓ cups juices. Blend cornstarch with 2 tablespoons water. Stir into juices. Add the ¼ teaspoon salt and lemon slice. Cook, stirring constantly, till sauce is thickened and bubbly. Simmer 2 or 3 minutes, stirring occasionally. Remove lemon slice. Serve sauce with chops. Makes 6 servings.

Hawaiian Shrimp Platter

Includes a pineapple sweet-sour sauce —

Cook one 10-ounce package frozen breaded shrimp according to package directions. Keep warm. Cook ½ cup chopped onion and ¼ cup chopped green pepper in 2 tablespoons butter or margarine. Combine 2 tablespoons sugar, 2 tablespoons cornstarch, 2 tablespoons vinegar, and 1 tablespoon soy sauce. Stir into onion mixture.

Drain one 20½-ounce can pineapple tidbits, reserving syrup. Add syrup to onion mixture. Cook, stirring constantly, till mixture is thickened and bubbly; cook 1 minute more. Stir in pineapple; heat to boiling. Serve over 3 cups hot cooked rice, with shrimp. Makes 4 servings.

Bananas in Nectar

Bananas
Orange, grapefruit, *or* pineapple
juice, chilled
Guava, papaya, *or* apricot nectar
Mandarin oranges
Maraschino cherries
Fresh mint sprigs

To keep bananas pretty and bright, slice them into juice; drain. Fill chilled sherbet dishes with banana. Add enough frosty-cold guava, papaya, *or* apricot nectar to each sherbet to cover the banana slices.

Garnish each serving with mandarin oranges, maraschino cherry, and mint sprig.

Passion Fruit Punch

Passion fruit (lilikoi) juice
Guava *or* peach nectar
Unsweetened pineapple juice
Maraschino cherry syrup *or*
grenadine syrup
. . .
Ice cubes
Maraschino cherries
Orange slices, halved
Pineapple spears
Fresh mint sprigs

Combine equal amounts of passion fruit juice, guava *or* peach nectar, and unsweetened pineapple juice. Add enough maraschino cherry syrup *or* grenadine to tint punch pink.

Pour the punch over ice cubes. Garnish each glass with a maraschino cherry and a halved orange slice slipped on a glass stirrer; also tuck in a pineapple spear and fresh mint sprig.

Kona Sunset

Coconut-ice cream combo —

For each serving roll a large scoop of vanilla ice cream in fresh grated or flaked coconut; coat well. Then place each ice cream ball in a chilled sherbet.

Tint coconut syrup with a few drops of yellow food coloring, then drizzle the syrup over coconut-coated ice cream. Top each serving with a mandarin orange section and maraschino cherry. Trim each serving with two small butter cookies.

Mauna Loa Parfaits

Macadamia nuts add crunch —

Chocolate syrup
Chocolate ice cream
. . .
Whipped cream
Macadamia nuts, toasted

Start each parfait with a large spoonful of chocolate syrup in the bottom of a chilled parfait glass. Add 3 small scoops of chocolate ice cream and then another large spoonful of the chocolate syrup.

To get a pretty marbled effect as in the picture, run a knife down the side of the glass, then lift it up. To serve top parfaits with generous dollop of whipping cream and trim with toasted macadamia nuts.

Island Nut Bananas

Peel and slice all-yellow or fully ripe bananas. Dip slices in mixture of equal parts honey and lime juice, then sprinkle with chopped macadamia nuts.

HAZELNUT—The hard-shelled nut of the hazel tree. Like its relative the filbert, this nut is edible. (See also *Nut.*)

HEAD CHEESE—A jellied meat product, the major ingredient of which is the head of a calf or pig. Other parts of the calf or pig such as the feet, brains, and heart are also commonly used in this product.

Head cheese is made by boiling the head and other meats in liquid to yield a concentrated stock. The chopped meat from the head is added to the clarified stock and the mixture is chilled until it gels.

HEART—The muscular, blood pumping organ of an animal, sometimes used as food. Beef, veal, pork, and lamb hearts are commonly available and are sometimes used as the meat dish of a meal. The smaller hearts of poultry are usually used in the stuffing or giblet gravy for the poultry.

Beef hearts are quite large and average about three pounds each. Veal hearts average about one pound each while the smaller lamb and pork hearts are usually about 1/3 to 1/2 pound each.

Although hearts are high in protein, they have never been a popular American food. Heart is a good buy: the demand is low, and all the meat is edible.

Nutritional value: Like other meats, heart is a source of high quality protein. This meat also contains small amounts of minerals and fair amounts of the B vitamins, thiamine, niacin, and riboflavin. Four ounces of uncooked lean beef heart has about 110 calories while the same amount of pork or lamb heart yields about 130 or 185 calories respectively.

How to select and store: Appearance is the primary basis for selecting a heart. The meat should be red and fresh appearing. Large areas of whitish material are arteries; other vessels, or fat. Since these areas are removed before cooking, their presence cuts down on the edible meat in the heart. Do not purchase hearts that appear discolored or dried out.

Sometimes frozen hearts are available. Avoid frozen hearts that are discolored or show signs of freezer burn.

Since heart is boneless and high in lean meat, figure four to five servings per pound.

The heart is more perishable than meat cuts such as steak. Therefore, purchase only the amount of this meat that can be used at one meal or that you have room to freeze. Enclose the heart loosely in foil or clear plastic wrap and refrigerate. Although it can be stored in the refrigerator for up to three days, use the heart within 24 hours for best quality.

Heart can be frozen satisfactorily. For best quality, freeze it promptly after purchase in meal-size portions. Whether the heart is purchased frozen or is frozen at home, three to four months is the maximum time this type of meat should be kept under frozen storage conditions.

How to prepare and use: To prepare the heart for cooking, wash it, remove the outer membrane, then cut out any hard parts such as arteries. Also trim off any fat.

The heart is a hard working muscle, consequently it is one of the less tender cuts of meat. This means that it requires slow, moist-heat cooking to give a tender product. Heart may be braised, stewed, or simmered either whole or sliced.

Serving a simple gravy or sauce with heart is one way to dress it up. Seasonings

To form the pocket for stuffing, remove the hard parts from the heart. Then close the slit with metal skewers and tie as shown.

Place the heart in a small bowl and gently spoon in the stuffing. Cover the opening with foil and tie to hold in place.

such as marjoram, tarragon, chervil, and thyme give the sauce a distinctive flavor. Another way to subtly season the heart is to add a basil or bay leaf to the cooking liquid so that the meat absorbs some flavor.

There are many uses for heart: a stuffed heart is an interesting and delicious main dish, whether you use a rice or bread stuffing, when a small amount of crushed sage is an appropriate stuffing seasoning; or as ground meat, one use that many homemakers don't associate with heart. Ground heart is very satisfactory in meat loaves or casseroles and is often a more economical buy than other types of ground meat. (See also *Variety Meat*.)

Stuffed Beef Heart

    1 beef heart
    2 tablespoons chopped onion
    2 tablespoons shortening
 1½ cups coarsely crushed saltine
        crackers
    ¼ teaspoon celery salt
    ⅛ teaspoon pepper
    ⅓ cup water

        • • •

    ½ cup water
    1 10½-ounce can condensed beef
        broth
    3 whole black peppercorns
    2 whole cloves
    1 bay leaf

Prepare heart for stuffing (as shown on page 1151). Cook onion in shortening till tender. Add cracker crumbs, celery salt, pepper, and the ⅓ cup water; mix. Stuff into heart. Cover opening with foil; tie securely. Place in Dutch oven. Add ½ cup water, beef broth, peppercorns, cloves, and bay leaf. Cover; simmer 2½ hours. Remove skewers and string from beef heart. Makes 6 servings.

HEARTS OF PALM—The young buds of a palm tree. These delicately flavored buds are used in salads or served as a vegetable.

Although the buds of several varieties of palm trees can be marketed as hearts of palm, buds from the cabbage palm are most commonly used. Whether these vegetables are cooked, after peeling off the tough outer coating, fresh or canned, Brazil and Florida provide the majority of hearts of palm for United States markets. (See also *Vegetable*.)

Hearts of Palm Salad

Unique dressing and salad blend —

    ⅓ cup salad oil
    2 tablespoons lemon juice
    1 teaspoon sugar
    ½ teaspoon salt
    ½ teaspoon aromatic bitters
    ¼ teaspoon paprika
    2 tablespoons finely chopped
        pimiento-stuffed green olives
    1 tablespoon finely chopped onion
    1 tablespoon finely chopped
        celery

        • • •

    1 14-ounce can hearts of palm,
        drained and sliced
    6 cups torn Bibb lettuce

For dressing combine salad oil, lemon juice, sugar, salt, aromatic bitters, paprika, green olives, onion, and celery; beat well. Chill. At serving time, toss together hearts of palm and lettuce in salad bowl. Add dressing; toss. Makes 6 servings.

Bibb lettuce and slices of canned hearts of palm are tossed together with an oil-lemon juice dressing in Hearts of Palm Salad.